Airport Economics in Latin America and the Caribbean

Airport Economics in Latin America and the Caribbean

Benchmarking, Regulation, and Pricing

Tomás Serebrisky

THE WORLD BANK
Washington, D.C.

© 2012 International Bank for Reconstruction and Development / International Development Association or
The World Bank
1818 H Street NW
Washington DC 20433
Telephone: 202-473-1000
Internet: www.worldbank.org

1 2 3 4 14 13 12 11

This volume is a product of the staff of The World Bank with external contributions. The findings, interpretations, and conclusions expressed in this volume do not necessarily reflect the views of The World Bank, its Board of Executive Directors, or the governments they represent.

The World Bank does not guarantee the accuracy of the data included in this work. The boundaries, colors, denominations, and other information shown on any map in this work do not imply any judgment on the part of The World Bank concerning the legal status of any territory or the endorsement or acceptance of such boundaries.

Rights and Permissions
The material in this work is subject to copyright. Because The World Bank encourages dissemination of its knowledge, this work may be reproduced, in whole or in part, for noncommercial purposes as long as full attribution to the work is given.

For permission to reproduce any part of this work for commercial purposes, please send a request with complete information to the Copyright Clearance Center Inc., 222 Rosewood Drive, Danvers, MA 01923, USA; telephone: 978-750-8400; fax: 978-750-4470; Internet: www.copyright.com.

All other queries on rights and licenses, including subsidiary rights, should be addressed to the Office of the Publisher, The World Bank, 1818 H Street NW, Washington, DC 20433, USA; fax: 202-522-2422; e-mail: pubrights@worldbank.org.

ISBN (paper): 978-0-8213-8977-5
ISBN (electronic): 978-0-8213-8933-1
DOI:10.1596/978-0-8213-8977-5

Library of Congress Cataloging-in-Publication Data has been applied for.

Cover photo provided by the author (courtesy of ADC&HAS).

Cover design by Debra Naylor.

Contents

Preface		*xiii*
Acknowledgments		*xvii*
About the Author		*xix*
Abbreviations and Acronyms		*xxi*
	Overview	1
	The Air Transport Sector	2
	Investment in the LAC Airport Sector	4
	Summary of This Report	6
	Conclusions	16
	Note	19
	References	20
Chapter 1	**Recent Evolution of the Air Transport Sector**	**21**
	Latin America and the Caribbean Overview	26
	Notes	34
	References	34
Chapter 2	**Investment in the Airport Sector**	**35**
	Private Project Financing in the Airport Sector Worldwide	42

	Private Investments in the Airport Sector in Developing Countries	44
	Private Investment in the Airport Sector in Latin America and the Caribbean	49
	Conclusions	52
	Notes	53
	References	54
Chapter 3	**Efficiency Estimation**	**55**
	Partial Performance Indicators in LAC Airports: Cross-Comparison for 2005	60
	Partial Performance Indicators: Time Series	84
	Measuring Technical Efficiency of Airports in LAC Countries	111
	Conclusion	130
	Notes	132
	References	135
Chapter 4	**Institutional Design and Governance of Airport Regulators in Latin America**	**137**
	Literature Review	139
	Methodology and Data Sources	141
	Regulatory Governance	143
	Economic Regulation	157
	Conclusions	161
	References	163
Chapter 5	**Benchmarking of Aeronautical Charges at Latin American Airports**	**165**
	Overview	165
	Methodology	167
	Conclusion	195
	Notes	197
	References	198
Appendix A	Survey of Airport Performance for Operators	199
Appendix B	Governance of Airport Regulators Survey	209
Appendix C	Technical Efficiency Calculation	237

Appendix D	Data Sources	**245**
	Air Transport Research Society (ATRS)	245
	Airports Council International (ACI)	246
	Private Participation in Infrastructure Database (PPI)	246
	Dealogic ProjectWare Database	247
	Asociación Latinoamericana de Transporte Aéreo (ALTA)	248
	Airport Charges	249

Figures

1	Air Transport Sector Demand and World GDP, 1980–2008	2
2	Domestic and International Passenger Share, 2008	3
3	Partial Performance Indicator: Passengers per Employee, 2005	8
4	Evolution of Turnaround Costs for an Airbus A320, 1995–2009	15
5	Structure of Turnaround Costs for an Airbus A320	17
1.1	Growth Rates in the Air Transport Sector and Global GDP, 1980–2008	22
1.2	Passenger Traffic Growth, by Region, 2007 and 2008	23
1.3	Domestic and International Passenger Share, 2008	24
1.4	Volume of Cargo Moved, by Region, 2008	25
1.5	Aircraft Movements, by Region, 2008	26
1.6	GDP Growth and Passenger Growth in LAC, 1995–2008	27
2.1	Project Financing in the Airport Sector by Number of Projects, Total Project Amount, and Region, 1996–2008	43
2.2	Share of Project Financing in the Airport Sector, by Region, 1996–2008	44
2.3	Private Investment Commitments to Infrastructure Projects in Developing Countries, by Sector, 1990–2008	47
2.4	Investment Commitments to Transport Projects with Private Participation in Developing Countries, by Subsector, 1990–2008	48
2.5	Total Investment Commitments to Airport Projects with Private Participation in Developing Countries, by Region, 1991–2008	49

2.6	Investment Commitments to Airport Projects with Private Participation in Developing Countries, by Type of Project, 1991–2007	50
2.7	Investment Commitments to Transport Projects with Private Participation in Latin America and the Caribbean, by Subsector, 1990–2008	51
2.8	Investment Commitments to Airport Projects with Private Participation in Latin America and the Caribbean Countries, by Type of Investment, 1993–2008	52
3.1	Passengers per Aircraft Movement, 2005	63
3.2	Cargo per Aircraft Movement, 2005	65
3.3	Passengers per Employee, 2005	67
3.4	Aircraft Movements per Runway, 2005	68
3.5	Labor Costs as a Share of Operating Costs, 2005	70
3.6	Labor Cost per Passenger, 2005	71
3.7	Operating Costs per Passenger, 2005	73
3.8	Operating Costs per Aircraft Movement, 2005	75
3.9	Total Revenue per Passenger, 2005	76
3.10	Aeronautical Revenue Share, 2005	78
3.11	Aeronautical Revenue per Aircraft Movement, 2005	79
3.12	Passengers per Boarding Bridge, 2005	81
3.13	Passengers per Square Meter of Terminal Area, 2005	82
3.14	Evolution of the U.S. Dollar–Euro Exchange Rate, 1999–2009	89
3.15	Passengers per Employee	91
3.16	Labor Costs per Passenger	95
3.17	Operating Costs per Passenger	98
3.18	Total Revenue per Passenger	102
3.19	Total Revenue per Employee	105
3.20	Passengers per Boarding Bridge	108
3.21	DEA-CRS and DEA-VRS Frontiers	113
3.22	Malmquist Index of Total Factor Productivity Change	125
4.1	Decision-Making Autonomy	146
4.2	Appointment Authorities	147
4.3	Budget Composition	149
4.4	Procedure to Remove Decision Makers	150
4.5	Reasons Directors Leave Positions	151
4.6	Bureaucratic Quality	152
4.7	Bureaucratic Quality by Type	153

4.8	Transparency in Airport Regulators	155
4.9	Transparency by Type	156
4.10	Dimensions of Accountability in Airport Regulators	157
4.11	Dimensions of Accountability in IRAs and Non-IRAs	158
5.1	Landing Fees for an Airbus A320, Daylight Operation	170
5.2	Landing Fees for an Airbus A320, Night Operation	171
5.3	Changes in Landing Fees for an Airbus A320, Daylight Operation	172
5.4	Landing Fees Percentage Change for an Airbus A320, Daylight Operation	174
5.5	Parking Charge for an Airbus A320, for 2 Hours	175
5.6	Changes in Parking Charges for an Airbus A320, for 2 Hours	176
5.7	Landing Fees and Parking Charge for an Airbus A320, for 2 Hours, 2009	178
5.8	Landing Fees and Parking Charge for an Airbus A320, for 2 Hours, 1995–2009	179
5.9	Boarding Bridge Charges for an Airbus A320, for 2 Hours, 2009	180
5.10	Boarding Bridge Charges for an Airbus A320, for 2 Hours, 1995–2009	182
5.11	Passenger Charges per Passenger (Charges Levied by the Airport)	183
5.12	Charges and Taxes Levied on Passengers, per Passenger	184
5.13	Changes in Passenger Charges per Passenger (Charges Levied by the Airport)	187
5.14	Turnaround Costs for an Airbus A320 (2 Hours, Daylight Operation)	188
5.15	Changes in Turnaround Costs for an Airbus A320 (2 Hours, Daylight Operation)	190
5.16	Turnaround Costs for a Boeing 767-300 (2 Hours, Daylight Operation)	191
5.17	Changes in Turnaround Costs for a Boeing 767-300 (2 Hours, Daylight Operation)	192
5.18	Turnaround Costs Levied on Airlines for an Airbus A320 (2 Hours, Daylight Operation)	193
5.19	Changes in Turnaround Costs Levied on Airlines for a Boeing 767–300 (2 Hours, Daylight Operation)	194
5.20	Turnaround Costs Levied on Passengers, for an Airbus A320	196

Tables

1	LAC Region's Share of the Air Transport Sector, 2008	4
2	Private Investment Commitments to the Airport Sector in the LAC Region, 1993–2008	5
3	Criteria for Determining Regulatory Agency Governance Ratings	12
1.1	Latin America and the Caribbean Snapshot of the Airport Sector, 2008	29
1.2	Global and LAC Airports Ranking: Passengers, Cargo, and Aircraft Movements, 2008	30
1.3	LAC Airport Ranking (Top 10) by Cargo, 2008	33
1.4	LAC Airport Ranking (Top 10) by Aircraft Movements, 2008	33
2.1	Latin American and Caribbean Airports by Type of PSP Arrangement	36
2.2	Total Project Financing in the Airport Sector by Income Level, Region, and Country, 1996–2008	45
3.1	Partial Performance Indicators Commonly Used in the Airport Sector	57
3.2	Latin American and Caribbean Airports Sampled	61
3.3	Summary of Airport Partial Performance Indicators—Top and Bottom Performers, 2005	85
3.4	Descriptive Statistics by World Region, 2005–06	115
3.5	Average Technical Efficiency Scores and Scale Efficiency by Region, 2005–06	115
3.6	Average Technical Efficiency Scores for LAC Airports, 2005–06	117
3.7	Peer Analysis, DEA VRS, 2005	119
3.8	Potential Explanatory Factors of Technical Inefficiency, 2005–06	121
3.9	Truncated Regression—Marginal Effects	123
3.10	Descriptive Statistics by Period	126
3.11	Average Annual Total Factor Productivity by Airport and Subperiod	127
3.12	Average Total Factor Productivity by Airport Categories	129
3.13	Malmquist Total Factor Productivity Index Decomposition—Averages by Period	130
4.1	Aspects of Governance of Airport Regulators	142
4.2	Mapping of Regulator and Legal Configuration	144

4.3	Answers to Selected Questions on Economic Regulation in the Airport Sector	160
5.1	Airport Sample Used for the Aeronautical Tariff Benchmarking Analysis	166
5.2	Key Parameters of the Aircraft Used in the Analysis	168
5.3	Passenger Charges and Taxes per Departing Passenger	185
C.1	Results for the Technical Efficiency Scores for All Airports Other Than Latin American Airports	237
C.2	LAC Airports Total Factor Productivity Change	241
C.3	Average Technical Efficiency Scores and Scale Efficiency by Region (2005–06 average)	243

Preface

Expanding and enhancing the provision of air transport infrastructure has become an increasingly important policy issue on the development agenda of both high-income and developing countries. The growth of air transport demand, along with the associated need to have efficient airport infrastructure to support it, has prompted the need to evaluate the effects of ownership schemes and regulation on airport performance.

Traditionally, air transport infrastructure was exclusively under government ownership and management in the Latin America and Caribbean (LAC) region. Starting in the late 1990s, private capital flows began to play an increasingly important role through the financing of air transport sector infrastructure and the management of airport operations. The introduction of private sector participation responded to myriad policy objectives, including bringing innovation and efficiency to the management of airports and boosting resources to finance the growing demand for airport infrastructure expansions and maintenance. In this context, governments have undertaken important institutional and regulatory reforms, which in several countries have resulted in the separation of planning and policy formulation functions from the day-to-day operation of airports through the establishment of independent regulatory agencies.

As a global pioneer in the introduction of private sector participation in air transport infrastructure, the LAC region serves as an informative context through which to investigate the evolution of performance in the airport sector and answer a series of pertinent policy questions: Are LAC airports technically efficient? How has efficiency evolved in the past decade? Are privately run airports more efficient than state-operated airports? How do independent regulators compare with government agencies in accountability, transparency, and autonomy? How have the level and structure of airport tariffs changed in recent years?

Purpose of the Report

This report presents the findings of a first-ever, comprehensive study of how LAC region airports have evolved during a notable period of transition in airport ownership. It is an unbiased, positive analysis of what happened, rather than a normative analysis of what should be done to reform and to attract private sector participation to the airport sector. It takes the first step to respond to the need for more conclusive information about the influence of airport ownership on economic performance. The report centers on the study of three dimensions of performance: productive efficiency, institutional setup for the governance of the sector, and financing.

Structure of the Report

This multifaceted report uses a range of advanced quantitative and qualitative methods to assess the relationship between airport ownership and performance in the LAC region. After a comprehensive overview, chapters 1 and 2 provide the necessary background for the air transport sector and the evolution of private sector participation and investment in airport infrastructure. In chapter 3, questionnaires submitted to airport operators and regulators led to the creation of the unique data sets, which were first used to compare performance across 14 partial performance indicators, and next used to develop aggregate measures of efficiency necessary for the benchmarking exercise. In chapter 4, a qualitative study of the relationship between type of regulating agency (independent or government-led) and transparency, accountability, and bureaucracy provides insight into how recent reforms have also affected the quality of regulatory governance. Chapter 5 provides an in-depth analysis of the evolution of tariff structures in the region as compared to a sample of international airports.

Although this report considers Latin America and the Caribbean as its focal region, the questions raised, and the analytical tools employed to respond to those questions, may be applied to other regions. In the future, researchers seeking to evaluate the productive performance of airports can use this study as a guide to anticipate potential challenges as well as to develop successful strategies to overcome them. Several important topics were not included in this report but should be the focus of future research. In particular, the evolution of the quality of services in airports deserves greater attention, as airports are increasingly becoming business centers and key gateways for trade competitiveness. The other main topic that requires detailed practical research is climate change and its relationship with the airport sector.

Acknowledgments

This study was produced by a task team led by Tomás Serebrisky, of the Sustainable Development Department in the Latin America and the Caribbean Region of the World Bank. Members of the core team were Sebastián López Azumendi, Matías Herrera Dappe, Raquel Fernandez, and Juan Matías Ortner. The early preparatory stages of the report benefited from inputs and advice provided by Raúl Medina Caballero (Ministry of Transport, Spain).

The study was conceived by a group that included Tomás Serebrisky, Luis Andrés, and José Luis Irigoyen of the World Bank.

Several individuals contributed to the preparation of the report, including Sebastián López Azumendi (analysis of governance of airport regulators), Sergio Perelman (calculation of aggregate measures of technical efficiency), and Andy Ricover (benchmarking of airport tariffs).

Diana Cubas, Gwyneth Fries, and Sivan Tamir edited the report and provided suggestions on improving its organization.

The report benefited extensively from discussions and feedback provided by Jean François Arvis, Raúl Medina Caballero, Baher El-Hefnawy, Antonio Estache, Shomik Raj Mehndiratta, Aurelio Menéndez, Charles Schlumberger, and Jordan Schwartz.

The author would like to express his gratitude to all individuals responding to the questionnaires. Regulators and airport operators spent valuable time completing the questionnaires and addressing in detail the follow-up clarifications.

Financial support for the preparation of this report was provided by the Public-Private Infrastructure Advisory Facility (PPIAF).

About the Author

Tomás Serebrisky received a Ph.D. in economics from the University of Chicago in 2000. From 2000 to 2002 Mr. Serebrisky worked in Argentina as the Chief Economist of the Antitrust Commission and as a Professor in Universidad Torcuato Di Tella. In 2002 he joined the World Bank and is currently working as Senior Infrastructure Economist in the Latin American Region. His areas of expertise are the economics of infrastructure investments, public-private partnerships, logistics, economic regulation, and antitrust. Mr. Serebrisky has published extensively in refereed journals, including: *Journal of International Economics, Transport Reviews, Journal of Maritime Policy and Management, Telecommunications Policy, Journal of Air Transport Management* and *World Competition*.

Abbreviations and Acronyms

ACI	Airports Council International
AIP	Aeronautical Information Publication
ALTA	Asociación Latinoamericana de Transporte Aéreo (Latin America and the Caribbean Air Transport Association)
ANAC	Agencia Nacional de Aviação Civil (National Civil Aviation Agency of Brazil)
ATI	air transport infrastructure
ATM	air traffic movement
ATRS	Air Transport Research Society
BOT	build, operate, and transfer
BROT	build, rehabilitate, operate, and transfer
CAA	Civil Aviation Authority, Panama
CPI	Consumer Price Index
CRS	constant returns to scale
DEA	data envelopment analysis
DINACIA	Dirección Nacional de Aviación Civil e Infraestructura Aeronaútica (Uruguay)
IATA	International Air Transport Association
ICAO	International Civil Aviation Organization
INFRAERO	Empresa Brasileira de Infra-Estrutura Aeroportuaria (Brazilian Airport Administrator)

IRA	independent regulatory agency
IRR	internal rate of return
LAC	Latin America and the Caribbean
MTOW	maximum takeoff weight
OECD	Organisation for Economic Co-operation and Development
PPI	Private Participation in Infrastructure (World Bank database)
PPIAF	Public-Private Infrastructure Advisory Facility
PSP	private sector participation
RFI	Regulatory Framework Index
RLT	rehabilitate, lease or rent, and transfer
ROT	rehabilitate, operate, and transfer
SFA	Stochastic Frontier Analysis
TC	technical change
TE	technical efficiency
TEC	technical efficiency change
TFP	total factor productivity
TFPC	total factor productivity change
VRS	variable returns to scale
WLU	workload unit

Airport Codes

AEP	Aeroparque Jorge Newbery, Buenos Aires, Argentina
ASU	Silvio Pettirossi International, Asunción, Paraguay
ATL	Hartsfield-Jackson Atlanta International, United States
BAQ	Ernesto Cortissoz International, Barranquilla, Colombia
BOG	El Dorado International, Bogotá, Colombia
BSB	Presidente Juscelino Kubitschek International, Brasilia, Brazil
CCS	Simón Bolivar International, Caracas, República Bolivariana de Venezuela
CDG	Charles de Gaulle International, Paris, France
CGH	Congonhas International, São Paulo, Brazil
CLO	Alfonso Bonilla Aragón International, Cali, Colombia
CUN	Cancún International, Cancún, Mexico
EZE	Ministro Pistarini International, Buenos Aires, Argentina
FRA	Frankfurt am Main International, Frankfurt, Germany
FTE	El Calafate Airport, Argentina
GDL	Miguel Hidalgo y Costilla International, Guadalajara, Mexico
GIG	Antonio Carlos Jobim International (Galeão), Rio de Janeiro, Brazil
GRU	Governador André Franco Montoro International, Guarulhos, São Paulo, Brazil
GUA	La Aurora International, Guatemala City, Guatemala
GYE	José Joaquín de Olmedo International, Guayaquil, Ecuador
ICN	Seoul Incheon International, Republic of Korea
JFK	John F. Kennedy Airport, New York, United States
KIN	Norman Manley International, Kingston, Jamaica
LAX	Los Angeles International, Los Angeles, United States
LHR	Heathrow International, London, United Kingdom
LIM	Jorge Chávez International, Lima, Peru
LPZ	El Alto International, La Paz, Bolivia
MAD	Barajas International, Madrid, Spain
MAO	Brigadeiro Eduardo Gomes International, Manaus, Brazil
MDE	José María Córdova International, Medellín, Colombia
MEM	Memphis International, United States
MEX	Benito Juárez International, Mexico City, Mexico
MIA	Miami International, Miami, United States

MFM	Macau International, Macao SAR, China
MGA	Augusto C. Sandino International, Managua, Nicaragua
MTY	General Mariano Escobedo International, Monterrey, Mexico
MVD	General Cesareo Berisso International, Carrasco, Montevideo, Uruguay
NAS	Lynden Pindling International, Nassau, The Bahamas
POS	Piarco International, Port of Spain, Trinidad and Tobago
PTY	Tocumen International, Panama City, Panama
SAL	Comalapa International, San Salvador, El Salvador
SCL	Comodoro Arturo Merino Benítez International, Santiago de Chile, Chile
SDF	Louisville International, United States
SDQ	Las Américas International, Santo Domingo, Dominican Republic
SJO	Juan Santamaría International, San José, Costa Rica
SNA	John Wayne Airport, Santa Ana, United States
TGU	Toncontín International, Tegucigalpa, Honduras
UIO	Mariscal Sucre International, Quito, Ecuador
VCP	Viracopos-Campinas International, São Paulo, Brazil
VVI	Viru Viru International, Santa Cruz, Bolivia
XMN	Xiamen Gaoqi International, China

Overview

As core components of the air transport sector, airports play a key role in catalyzing social and economic development at the regional, national, and global levels. As a dynamic service industry with multiple inputs and outputs, the airport sector facilitates domestic and international trade (by providing access to markets); creates employment opportunities related to both aeronautical and nonaeronautical activities; and enhances communication and integration between people, countries, and cultures through tourism, business activities, and merchandise trade. Airports operate in different environments (large cities, remote areas) and have users with varying needs (business and leisure travelers), thus making efficiency assessments very challenging. Multiple stakeholders, including airlines, regulatory agencies, ground-handling companies, and many others, have varied interests and objectives that further complicate an evaluation of airport performance.

This overview includes developed countries, such as Japan and Australia, in the World Bank regional designation of East Asia and Pacific.

The Air Transport Sector

The air transport sector is uniquely volatile (figure 1). Over time, its fluctuations have followed those of the global economy, though they have been more intense. Heavily dependent on business activity, trade flows, and tourism, the sector has experienced long periods of continued growth alternated with brief crisis periods of negative growth.

This amplifying effect has meant that global crises, such as the 1979 oil crisis; the Gulf War in 1990; the terrorist attacks of September 11, 2001; and the 2008 global financial crisis had a profoundly negative impact on the air transport sector as compared to other sectors of the economy. Among relevant stakeholders in the air transport sector, airlines are particularly sensitive to severe global downturns. The progressive liberalization of different aviation markets, notably in the European Union and the United States in the late 1990s and 1970s, respectively, led to an overall increase in competition and to narrower operating margins, which further increased the particular vulnerability of airlines. Airports themselves, with facilities that can often be classified as natural monopolies, are less sensitive to these effects.

The air transport sector (in terms of passenger and cargo demand) is dominated by Europe and North America (Canada and the United States),

Figure 1 Air Transport Sector Demand and World GDP, 1980–2008

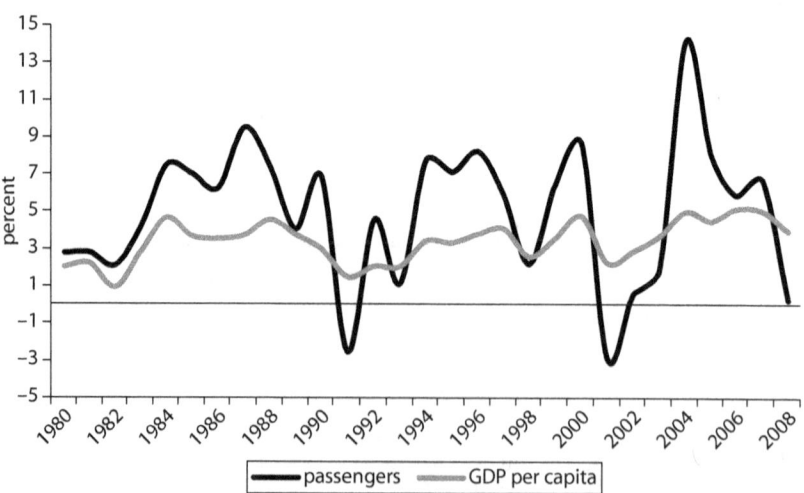

Source: World Bank estimation based on data from Airports Council International (ACI), International Air Transport Association (IATA), and International Monetary Fund (IMF) data.

which together account for more than 60 percent of the market (figure 2). Airports handled 4.874 billion arriving and departing passengers in 2008, of which approximately 2 billion were international and 2.8 billion were domestic. Of these, North America (Canada and the United States) represented 48 percent of domestic traffic, while Europe represented more than half of global international traffic. The share of passengers, and especially

Figure 2   Domestic and International Passenger Share, 2008

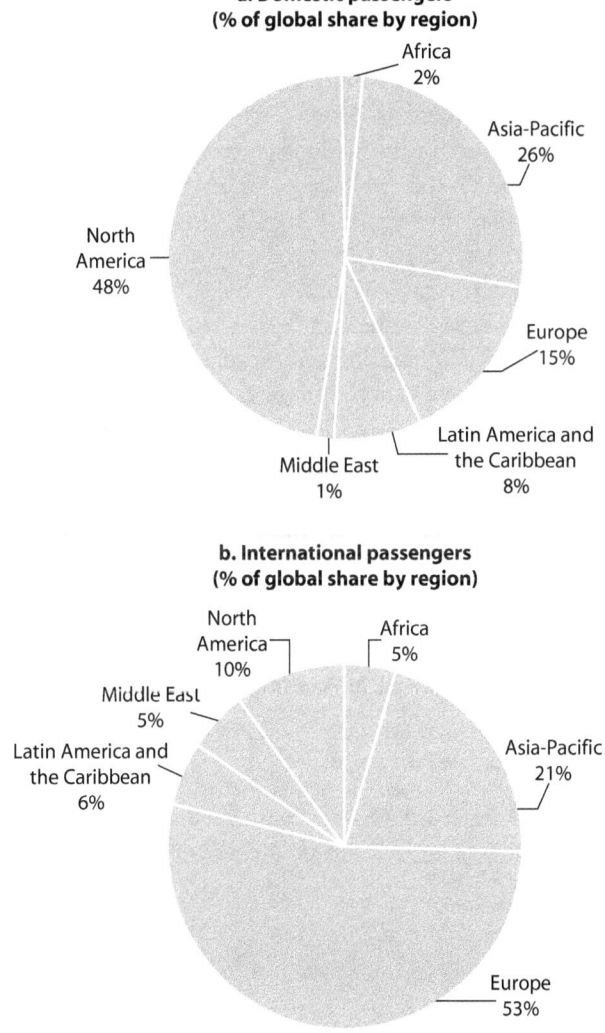

a. Domestic passengers (% of global share by region)
- Africa 2%
- Asia-Pacific 26%
- North America 48%
- Europe 15%
- Latin America and the Caribbean 8%
- Middle East 1%

b. International passengers (% of global share by region)
- North America 10%
- Africa 5%
- Middle East 5%
- Latin America and the Caribbean 6%
- Asia-Pacific 21%
- Europe 53%

Source: Author's estimation based on ACI data.

of cargo in North America and Europe, has fallen slightly (5 percent) since 2000, with the East Asia and Pacific region picking up most of the gains, primarily because of the significant increase of air traffic demand in China. In 2008, the East Asia and Pacific region accounted for 38 percent of the cargo market (measured in volume), while North America was second with 33 percent.

Latin America and the Caribbean (LAC) accounts for a small share of the air transport sector worldwide. Based on 2008 figures, the region only accounted for 7 percent of total passengers, 5 percent of cargo, and 8 percent of aircraft movements (table 1). Airports are relatively small when ranked on a global scale. LAC has a total of just 4 airports among the top 100 airports worldwide and 14 airports among the top 200. Aeropuerto Internacional Benito Juárez in Mexico City, ranked 43rd globally, is the most important airport in the region in terms of passenger traffic, handling a total of about 26.2 million passengers in 2008 (approximately three times less than the number handled by first-ranked Hartsfield-Jackson Airport in Atlanta). As for cargo, the entire LAC region handled a total of 4.6 million metric tons in 2008, only 1 million metric tons more than the amount of cargo traffic handled by the global leader, Hong Kong International Airport (3.6 million metric tons) and three times as much as Miami, North America's cargo hub (1.5 million metric tons).

Investment in the LAC Airport Sector

For much of the 20th century, commercial and business pressures were weak within the airport sector since airports around the world were not only owned and managed by governments, but also seen solely as public

Table 1   LAC Region's Share of the Air Transport Sector, 2008

Domestic passengers	224,531,098
Share of global domestic passengers	8%
International passengers	113,850,200
Share of global international passengers	6%
Total passengers	338,381,298
Share of global total passengers	7%
Growth rate of total passengers (2007–08)	8%
Cargo (metric tons)	4,589,092
Share of global cargo	5%
Growth rate of cargo (2007–08)	4%
Share of global aircraft movements	8%
Growth rate of aircraft movements (2007–08)	0%

Source: Author's estimation based on Airports Council International data.

utilities and strategic assets for national defense purposes. During the late 1980s and early 1990s, however, there was a slow shift toward a view of airports as more commercially oriented enterprises. Consequently, several countries introduced private sector participation (PSP) into the operation of airports.

According to the ProjectWare database, US$64 billion in private investment went to a total of 110 air transport infrastructure projects between 1996 and 2008. Australia; Hong Kong SAR, China; and Turkey led the globe over the studied time period, representing 57 percent of total project financing. Australia has clearly been leading, with total project financing of US$19,326 million, followed by Hong Kong SAR, China, with US$11,050 million and Turkey with US$6,188 million. From 1993 to 2008, the private sector invested more than US$9.5 billion in the LAC region's airports. Argentina, Colombia, and Mexico together represented almost 80 percent of total investments in the LAC region (table 2).

Compared to other regions, LAC was a pioneer in introducing PSP in the airport sector, though the intensity of the process has decreased dramatically in recent years. According to the World Bank's Private Participation in Infrastructure (PPI) Database, which is perhaps the most complete public source of information on private investment in infrastructure, within just the developing world, the LAC region accounted for 30 percent of total investment commitments in the airport sector between 1991 and 2008. However, the relative share of total private investment in

Table 2 Private Investment Commitments to the Airport Sector in the LAC Region, 1993–2008

Country	Investments (US$ millions)	Share of total (%)
Mexico	3,223.9	33.9
Argentina	2,375.4	25.0
Colombia	1,224.3	12.9
Ecuador	665.0	7.0
Peru	430.0	4.5
Dominican Republic	350.0	3.7
Chile	345.0	3.6
Uruguay	195.0	2.0
Jamaica	175.0	1.8
Costa Rica	161.0	1.7
Venezuela, RB	134.0	1.4
Honduras	120.0	1.3
Bolivia	116.6	1.2

Source: Private Participation in Infrastructure (PPI) Database.

LAC fell from 70 percent of commitments in the late 1990s to only 12 percent between 2000 and 2008. The PPI database reports that investments in the airport sector in LAC peaked in 2006 with a total of US$2,346 million, but fell to US$746 million in 2007 and US$231 million in 2008. This reduction could be the result of the successful upgrade of airport infrastructure, or it could also be that the region lost its attractiveness or that individual country governments have decided not to open the sector for new or more private investment. For example, as this report was being written, Brazil had yet to decide whether to open its airport sector to PSP.

Summary of This Report

This report presents the findings of a first-ever, comprehensive study of how LAC region airports have evolved during a notable period of transition in airport ownership. It is an unbiased, positive analysis of what happened, rather than a normative analysis of what should be done to reform the airport sector or to attract and structure PSP. It takes the first step to respond to the need for more conclusive information about the influence of airport ownership on economic performance and the measurable side of operational performance. The report is centered on the study of three dimensions of performance: productive efficiency, institutional set up for the governance of the sector, and financing.

The analytical weight is divided into three chapters. In chapter 3, a benchmarking exercise provides a thorough analysis of the technical performance of LAC region airports. Chapter 4 compares the performance of independent regulatory agencies and government regulatory agencies as it relates to transparency, accountability, and the quality of their bureaucracies. Chapter 5 investigates the growth and change of airport tariff levels within the LAC region.

Efficiency Performance: A Benchmarking Approach

The use of benchmarking to measure performance in the transport sector and airport subsector, more specifically, is relatively new. Increased PSP in the 1990s led to a call for a more thorough evaluation of airport performance, both (a) to negotiate the terms and conditions of private involvement and (b) to track the improvements or lack thereof resulting from such involvement. As a result of this process, in the late 1990s, benchmarking began to be accepted as an important management tool within the airport industry. However, current papers using advanced efficiency techniques neglect Latin American airports, focusing instead on those of Asia, Europe, and North America. This report is a first attempt to bring this kind of advanced analysis to the LAC region, and includes four separate but complementary sections: (a) an investigation of technical efficiency using partial performance indicators, (b) the positioning of LAC airports on a global efficiency frontier, (c) an analysis of the relationship between airport performance and selected socioeconomic factors and unique airport characteristics, and (d) an assessment of the evolution of the airports' productivity in the LAC region from 1995 to 2007.

The first part of chapter 3 investigates airport efficiency through partial performance indicators, which are widely used not only in the airport sector but also in other infrastructure sectors, such as water and electricity and telecommunications.[1] First, 14 partial performance indicators from 2005 put the LAC region in a global perspective through a comparison of mean levels for the East Asia and Pacific region, Europe, and North America. Second, an analysis of how these indicators changed over the period from 1997 to 2005 provides some insight into how the advent of PSP affected the technical efficiency of the region's airports. Responses to an original questionnaire from a representative sample of LAC airports that covers more than 80 percent of passengers and aircraft movements and 70 percent of air cargo allowed for a global comparison with partial performance data collected by the Air Transports Research Society for its periodic reports calculating airport technical efficiency in Asia, Europe, and North America. Figure 3 shows results for one partial performance indicator, passengers per employee, which is taken as an example for this overview. For this particular indicator, Comodoro Arturo Merino Benítez International in Santiago, Chile, and Congonhas International Airport in São Paulo, Brazil, are the top performers. Partial performance indicators in the airport sector should be interpreted with extreme care. In a multi-input and multi-output service industry, like airports, they do not allow for a conclusive identification of performance. For example, a high number of passengers per employee could represent either high efficiency or low quality of service.

This particular stage in the analysis revealed a great deal of variation in the performance of LAC region airports. However, Congonhas International Airport (CGH) in São Paulo, Brazil; Cancún International Airport (CUN) in Mexico; and Comodoro Arturo Merino Benítez International (SCL) in Santiago, Chile, were the airports that most frequently appeared among the top three performers in the 14 partial performance indicators calculated.

Figure 3 Partial Performance Indicator: Passengers per Employee, 2005

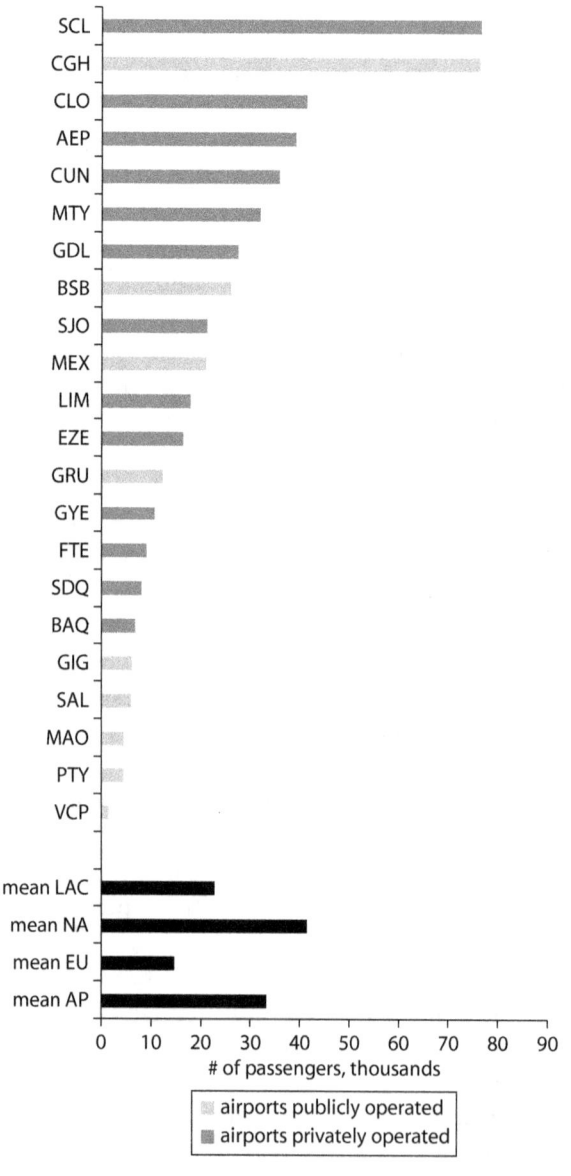

Source: Author's calculation.
Note: LAC = Latin America and the Caribbean; NA = North America; EU = European Union; AP = Asia-Pacific. For a list of airport codes and the airports they represent, see page xxiii.

The second section of chapter 3 conducts an analysis of efficiency using aggregate measures and econometric techniques to compute a global efficiency frontier for the airport sector and to identify the position of Latin American airports relative to the best practice worldwide. The Data Envelope Analysis (DEA) method used for this stage positions LAC region airports around the frontier relative to best-performing peers of the same scale. Results relating to technical efficiency in global perspective reinforced the findings of the initial analysis of partial performance indicators. Privately operated airports were positioned closer to the frontier than were their publicly operated counterparts, though this effect was not significant across all the different specifications tested.

Two final tests round out the benchmarking exercise in chapter 3. First, a truncated regression was performed to investigate the relationship between socioeconomic factors and airport performance, using the aggregate technical efficiency measures from the previous section. Results suggest that variation in technical efficiency is largely the result of factors exogenous to airport management. The models identified hub airports and population size as the main drivers of technical efficiency in the airport sector. Hub airports are, on average, 10 to 15 percent more efficient than other airports. Airports located in areas with more than 5 million inhabitants are 17 to 20 percent more efficient than airports that serve less populated areas. The only variable within the control of airport management that appeared to drive technical efficiency was the proportion of revenue acquired through sources other than aeronautical tariffs. Those airports that rely on sources other than aeronautical tariffs tend to be more efficient. This relationship could not be used to make further conclusions on the relationship between type of ownership and airport efficiency, because both public and private airports surveyed varied considerably in terms of the proportion of total revenue acquired from aeronautical tariffs.

Finally, a Malmquist quantity index of total factor productivity change shows how airport productivity has changed across three sequences: 1995 to 1999, 2000 to 2003, and 2003 to 2007. From 2003 to 2007, strong average annual productivity growth (3.9 percent) of the airport sector reflected the strong economic growth of the region as a whole. Larger airports tend to register faster productivity growth. Both publicly and privately operated airports performed similarly over the three time periods, with publicly operated airports performing slightly better over the whole period. The Malmquist index requires panel data for each unit sampled. Because this panel data was largely unavailable for the region's airports, the first and second time series have very small sample sizes and consequently produce results that are largely skewed by outliers. For example, Argentina's financial crisis precipitated the airport sector's average annual productivity change of −18.1 percent over the 2000 to 2003 period, which pulled down the index's reported regional average of −1.2 percent over the same period.

Overall, thorough data collection and extensive quantitative analysis in chapter 3 suggests that, when multiple factors are considered, LAC airports are not radically better or worse performers than those of Asia, Europe, or North America. Within the LAC region, results were not significant enough to declare a definitive relationship between ownership (public or private) and technical efficiency. Technical efficiency appears to be driven largely by factors outside of the control of airport management, though high levels of nonaeronautical revenues (that is, revenues accruing from commercial sources rather than airport tariffs) appear to have a positive relationship with technical efficiency.

With this study being an initial attempt to perform benchmarking analysis on LAC region airports, inconclusive results are to be expected. Data limitations hampered the scope of the analysis of chapter 3 and influenced decisions on the types of models used and analysis performed, which, in some cases, led to less forceful results (these limitations are diligently described within chapter 3). More frequent data collection, combined with a common methodology, will considerably improve the usefulness of the LAC experience as a resource for the study of PSP and technical efficiency in the airport sector. A regional body of airport regulators or an air transport specialized institution, such as Airports Council International (ACI) or the International Civil Aviation Organization (ICAO), would be best poised to design this methodology. Given the wide variety of private participation schemes used by Latin American countries, further research should consider individual airports on a case-by-case basis. In addition, future research should also assess financial efficiency as well as the impact of PSP on the quality of services delivered.

Institutional Design and the Governance of Airport Regulators

Changes to the structure of economic regulation of LAC region airports accompanied the increased role of private investment in airport infrastructure. Chapter 4 addresses the realities and challenges of airport regulators from a public sector governance perspective and analyzes institutional design, comparing both independent regulatory agencies (IRAs) and government agencies (non-IRAs). It focuses on only those aspects of governance that are directly related to economic regulation. The ultimate objective of this governance analysis is to identify under which arrangement regulatory governance can be enhanced.

In Latin America, the introduction of PSP in the airport sector was often accompanied by the creation of IRAs to enforce concession contracts and quality of service. In cases where the bulk of airport services remained state owned, the role of regulator was placed in the hands of government departments, with limited independence from sector authorities. Brazil represents an interesting case, in which an independent regulator was created but only regulates one state-owned enterprise.

In chapter 4, qualitative comparative analysis is used to describe the design and practices of airport regulatory agencies. Survey responses from 13 LAC region airport regulators (4 independent and 9 government agencies) provided information on four main aspects of the governance of airport regulators: (a) the autonomy of the decision-making process, (b) the transparency of policies implemented by airport regulators, (c) their accountability to stakeholders, and (d) the quality of bureaucracy (table 3). Regulatory agencies were assigned values between 0 and 1 for each of the four main aspects of governance according to predetermined criteria.

Regardless of the existence of private sector provision of airport services, an institutional design associated with an IRA appears to provide a better channel for good regulatory governance than a government department. Both regional and international experiences show the importance of a government body that is highly specialized and has consumers as the focus of its policies. At the same time, a regulatory agency is not capable on its own to introduce institutional quality into an airport system where policies are ill designed. However, even in an adverse context, chapter 4 shows that regulatory agencies enable an adequate representation of stakeholders and act as a filter against discretional decisions.

A clear advantage of making regulations in regulatory agencies rather than in government departments is related to measures aimed at enhancing the transparency of regulation. The division of transparency into different dimensions within the report allowed for the identification of several advantages in IRAs versus government departments. Consultations are the most notable of these advantages. The consumer orientation of regulatory agencies versus government departments, whether in the context of state-owned companies or private providers, is a powerful factor in bringing stakeholders' opinions into the decision-making process.

Table 3 Criteria for Determining Regulatory Agency Governance Ratings

	Autonomy of decision making	Transparency	Accountability	Quality of bureaucracy
Characteristics	• Regulatory powers (tariffs, quality of service, and so forth) • Status of agency • Procedures to appoint or remove board members • Budget sources	• Civic engagement in rule making • Consultations • Publication of agency's decisions • E-government • Registry of board meetings and decisions	• Appeals of agency's decisions • Effects of consultations • Evaluation of agency's performance • Accountability instrument • Performance instrument	• Structure of staff positions within the agency • Educational levels of agency's staff • Publication of vacancies

Source: Authors' elaboration.

Technical expertise is another aspect where IRAs show advantages. The measure of bureaucratic quality found higher bureaucratic quality levels in independent commissions than in government departments, on average. These results are reflected not only in the educational levels of the staff but also in the way vacancies are posted and filled. The most controversial aspect of the governance of IRAs is autonomy. The measure of autonomy found, on average, more guarantees of autonomy in IRAs than in non-IRAs.

A worrisome outcome of the surveys' analysis was the serious deficiency of economic regulation in the airport sector in the LAC region. On the one hand, very few of the agencies in charge of enforcing regulations have in place the necessary information systems (regulatory accounting manuals, economic and financial models) necessary to perform their tasks correctly. On the other hand, even when agencies claim to have the adequate information systems in place, the vast majority are not using them to estimate the weighted average cost of capital, which is an essential variable for a regulator. In addition, the regulatory frameworks do not seem to provide appropriate incentives for regulators to properly carry out a frequent oversight of the quality of services provided by operators.

Despite the overall advantage of the IRA as a model for good regulatory governance, conclusions should not be interpreted as a "one model fits all" approach. Rather, they should be used to identify those mechanisms that better guarantee open and sound decision making in the regulation of airport services. The comparison between IRAs and non-IRAs as alternative institutional arrangements to regulate airports allowed the disaggregation of governance into different dimensions and the identification of advantages and disadvantages in both models. It is up to policy makers to prioritize those aspects that better fit their institutional and policy frameworks.

Financing Performance: Evolution and Benchmarking of Aeronautical Charges at Latin American Airports

Given the size of the demand for air transport services and the significant minimum investments necessary to have adequate airport services, most airports in LAC can be considered natural monopolies. Accordingly, the economic theory indicates that tariffs should be carefully regulated. Aeronautical tariffs are, indeed, heavily regulated in Latin America and the Caribbean. However, survey responses illustrate the poor record of the LAC region's airport regulators and ministerial departments when it comes to the use of regional tariff benchmarking tools, indicating that decisions about tariff levels and structure are often poorly informed. In some cases, either airport regulators lack the technical capacity to perform this kind of analysis, or structural inefficiencies prevent or deter qualified individuals from doing so.

The tariff benchmarking analysis presented in this report constitutes an important first step in fostering dialogue on these issues and in setting the basis for a more robust tariff benchmarking exercise at the regional level, a task that should be led by sector regulators. Survey responses from 26 airports in 20 LAC countries provide the basis for the identification of changes in tariff structures and levels in three different years: 1995, 2003, and 2009. The selection of years responds to the objective of identifying whether changes in tariff structures and levels were the direct outcome of the introduction of private sector participation in the management of airports. Since most airport concessions in the region took place before 2002, 2003 was selected to discern whether changes in tariff levels and structure corresponded with the introduction of PSP in the airport sector. The year 2009 was included to present the most recent tariffs available at the time this report was written, while 1995 was chosen because PSP had not yet come to occupy a prominent role in the LAC region.

Within this overview, regulated tariffs are understood as the total turnaround costs faced by an aircraft, including landing fees (and night surcharges for lighting), aircraft parking, use of boarding bridges, and passenger charges (passenger facility charges, security). The aircrafts selected for comparison, the Airbus A320 and the Boeing 767 are consistent with the type of fleets most commonly found in the LAC region in 2009. To provide an international reference to the benchmarking analysis, the following airports were included in the sample: New York (JFK), Los Angeles (LAX), Miami (MIA), Madrid (MAD), Paris (CDG), London (LHR), and Frankfurt (FRA). These European and North American airports concentrate most of the Latin America and Caribbean–based airlines' international flights outside of the LAC region.

The following preview of results from chapter 5 shows how, in most cases, total turnaround costs for most LAC region airports have increased in recent years (see figure 4). Turnaround costs, as defined in this report, for an Airbus A320 increased by 34 percent in real terms at most LAC airports between 1995 and 2009. Very similar increases apply to a Boeing 767. For both types of aircraft used in this report, current total turnaround costs in LAC region airports are, on average, at a comparable or higher level than those in European and U.S. airports that are most frequently served by Latin American and Caribbean airlines.

Figure 4 Evolution of Turnaround Costs for an Airbus A320, 1995–2009

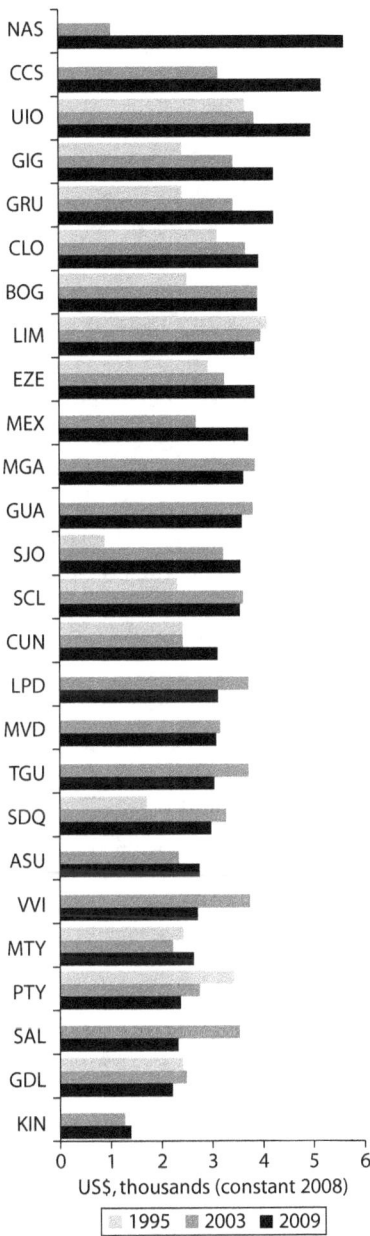

Source: World Bank elaboration based on information from IATA (1995, 2003, and 2009), Aeronautical Information Publication (AIP) Colombia, AIP Costa Rica, El Salvador Airport, AIP Nicaragua, Panama Civil Aviation Authority (CAA), Dirección Nacional de Aviación Civil e Infraestructura Aeronaútica (DINACIA—National Authority of Civil Aviation and Aeronautical Infrastructure), Uruguay.
Note: Calculated turnaround costs assume a load factor of 71 percent; a daylight operation includes landing, parking (initial 2 hours), boarding bridge, passenger facility charge, and security. Figure assumes a 71 percent load factor. For a list of airport codes and the airports they represent, see page xxiii.

The increase in turnaround costs in real terms between 1995 and 2009 for the Airbus A320 and Boeing 767 has been accompanied by changes in the tariff structure. Fees paid by airlines decreased between 1995 and 2009, while those levied on passengers increased. In fact, charges applied to passengers, which currently account for over 85 percent of total aeronautical charges, increased in real terms by 44 percent between 1995 and 2009. The current tariff structure in LAC airports is similar to that prevailing in the sample of European and U.S. airports, with a slightly higher percentage of the share devoted to passenger charges as opposed to airline charges in the LAC region (figure 5).

The tariff benchmarking analysis carried out in this report does not allow for definitive conclusions on the relationship between changes in aeronautical charges and the introduction of private sector participation. The increase in aeronautical charges observed between 1995 and 2009 was shared by both publicly and privately operated airports. Further research through a case-specific approach should be conducted (a) to assess whether the introduction of private sector participation has led to an increase in aeronautical charges and (b) to link changes in aeronautical charges to the changes in the level and quality of airport services.

The study of airport tariffs is followed by a bibliography of sources used in the creation of this report, as well as appendixes that include the surveys submitted to airport operators to measure performance and to airport regulators to gather information on their governance.

Conclusions

The air transport sector in the LAC region faces the same basic problem as the other transport subsectors (roads, ports, rail, and urban transport): the lack of objective data to construct a reasonable baseline to assess its economic performance. Using that well-known initial diagnostic, this report presents a comprehensive assessment of the evolution of airport performance, investments, tariffs, and governance institutions. The assessment is the result of extensive research to compile the very limited public information available, complemented with questionnaires developed exclusively for this report.

In summary, the main findings of the report are as follows:

- In the LAC region, pioneering the introduction of PSP in the operation and expansion of airport infrastructure has led to total investments in

Overview   17

Figure 5   Structure of Turnaround Costs for an Airbus A320

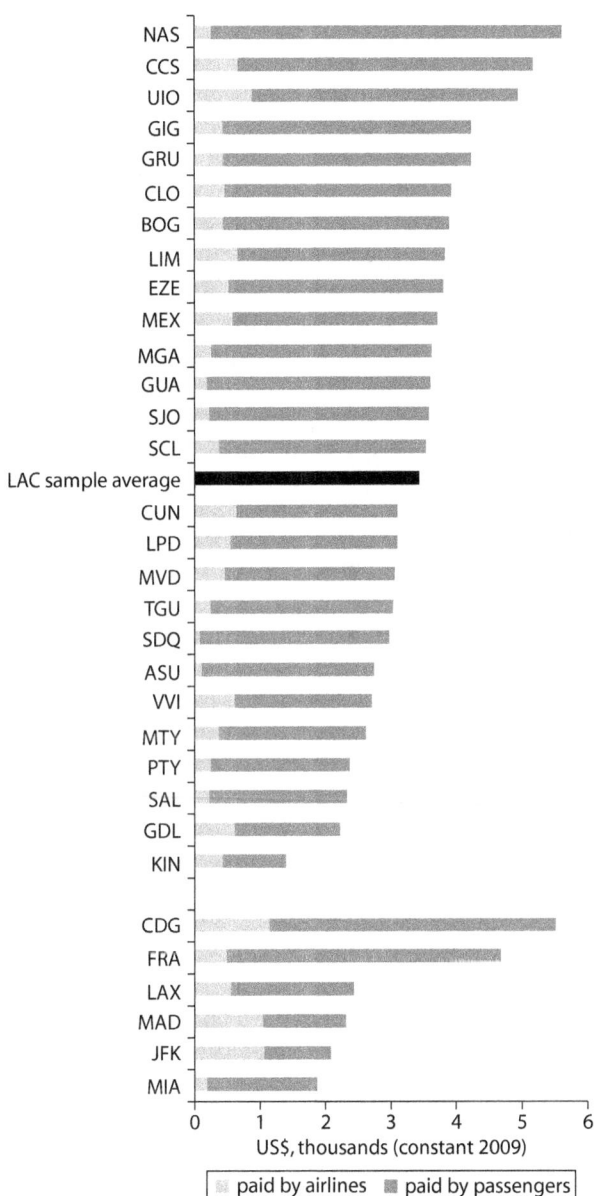

Source: World Bank elaboration based on information from IATA 2009, AIP Colombia, AIP Costa Rica, El Salvador Airport, AIP Nicaragua, Panama CAA, DINACIA Uruguay.
Note: Calculated turnaround costs assume a load factor of 71 percent; a daylight operation includes landing, parking (initial 2 hours), boarding bridge, passenger facility charge, and security. Figure assumes a 71 percent load factor. For a list of airport codes and the airports they represent, see page xxiii.

excess of US$10 billion since 1995. Increased investment has not been confined solely to large, privately operated airports. Demonstration effects may have led publicly operated airports to emulate the successful example of private counterparts through the pursuit of increased investment.

- From 1995 to 2007, LAC region airports have become increasingly productive, though they remain on average consistently less efficient than those of Asia, Europe, and the United States. Even though the smaller size of LAC airports prohibits them from exploiting economies of scale, the alignment of management to international best practices improved their productive performance in global comparisons.

- From 1995 to 2009, both publicly and privately operated airports saw an increase in aeronautical charges of more than 30 percent in real terms. The structure of aeronautical tariffs also changed toward higher tariffs for passengers and lower tariffs for airlines. Among possible explanations are a decision to set tariffs following a cost-recovery principle; less reliance on public sector subsidies; a need to cover higher costs associated with better quality of services; and the need to compensate private operators and more commercially oriented, corporatized public airport operators.

- Airport economic regulation in the LAC region is weak. Independent agencies and government departments do not meet the international best practice criteria for transparency and accountability. Lack of technical capacity, inadequate funding, and the incorrect or insufficient use of regulatory instruments are all likely causes.

Several key questions regarding the quality of airport services remain unanswered. Did an increase in PSP affect the evolution and improvement of airport service quality? How much? Were improvements cost-effective? Who paid? Some anecdotal evidence indicates that quality improved mainly owing to the expansion of related air and land infrastructure. A proper impact evaluation of airport investments, including micro- and macroeconomic effects, is overdue but requires data on quality that are currently unavailable.

To improve the productive performance of LAC region airports, this report recommends, first and foremost, the enhancement of the capacity of airport regulators to measure the impact of public policies. Higher-quality regulation will call for consistent data collection and analysis, allowing for the generation of a robust and well-grounded benchmark of airport performance that highlights best performers. Better analysis will make it possible to determine whether policies (introduction of PSP, expansion of capacity, changes in the level of tariffs) achieve the desired objectives. A strong foundation of information will increase the quality of decision making, thereby reducing the unpredictability of regulatory decisions and consequently the cost of capital. Ultimately, stronger airport regulation will further enhance the positive image of PSP in the LAC region's airports and encourage sustained investment. National efforts to strengthen airport regulation will be most effective if supported by the knowledge and experience of established institutions, such as Airports Council International (ACI) and the International Civil Aviation Organization (ICAO).

Each of the analytical chapters (chapters 3, 4, and 5) suggests additional next steps to enrich future studies. In addition to the analysis performed in chapter 3, further research into technical efficiency should collect and explore information on the quality of service provided, as this is a major determinant of airports' costs and a key input for strengthening programs aimed at increasing competitiveness and growth (through tourism, industry, and clusters of development or high-value-added air cargo trade). Chapter 4 emphasizes continued investigation into regulatory governance on a case-by-case basis. Chapter 5 recommends the systematic incorporation of regional tariff benchmarking exercises into the regular operations of regulatory agencies, in addition to further research into the due diligence performed, the actual process for setting aeronautical tariffs in Latin America, and the incentives they provide for infrastructure investments.

The overall purpose of this report is to enhance the understanding of airport performance in the LAC region. It is expected that the findings of the report will motivate further analytical work to provide a menu of policy options aimed at increasing the contribution of the airport sector to economic growth.

Note

1. See Andrés et al. (2008) for a survey of the recent literature and an application of partial performance indicators in the electricity, water distribution, and fixed telecommunications sectors.

References

ACI (Airports Council International). 2009. "World Airport Traffic Report 2009." ACI, Geneva, Switzerland.

Andrés, L. A., J. L. Guasch, T. Haven, and V. Foster. 2008. *The Impact of Private Sector Participation in Infrastructure: Lights, Shadows, and the Road Ahead.* Washington, DC: World Bank.

IATA (International Air Transport Association). 1995. *Airport and Air Navigation Charges Manual.* Montreal: IATA.

———. 2003. *Airport and Air Navigation Charges Manual.* Montreal: IATA.

———. 2009. *Airport and Air Navigation Charges Manual.* Montreal: IATA.

Private Participation in Infrastructure (PPI) Database. World Bank, Washington, DC. http://ppi.worldbank.org/.

CHAPTER 1

Recent Evolution of the Air Transport Sector

The evolution of the air transport sector has been closely linked with the fluctuations of the global economy. Air transport demand, which is heavily dependent on business activity, trade flows, and tourism, has experienced long periods of continued growth alternated with brief crisis periods of negative growth (figure 1.1).

Air traffic fluctuations are more intense than changes in the gross domestic product (GDP). In fact, air transport traffic, measured as passenger-kilometers (km), has a high income elasticity of demand of about 2.[1] This amplifying effect has meant that, in times of crisis (such as those associated with the second oil crisis in 1979, the Gulf War in 1990, the terrorist attacks of September 11, 2001, or the global financial crisis of 2008), the impact on the sector has been much more negative than on other segments of the economy. This feature has especially affected the airlines because the progressive liberalization of the most important aviation markets (most notably the liberalization process initiated by the United States and the European Union in the late 1970s and 1990s, respectively) resulted in an overall increase in competition and in the

---

This chapter includes developed countries, such as Japan and Australia, in the World Bank regional designation of East Asia and Pacific.

Figure 1.1 Growth Rates in the Air Transport Sector and Global GDP, 1980–2008

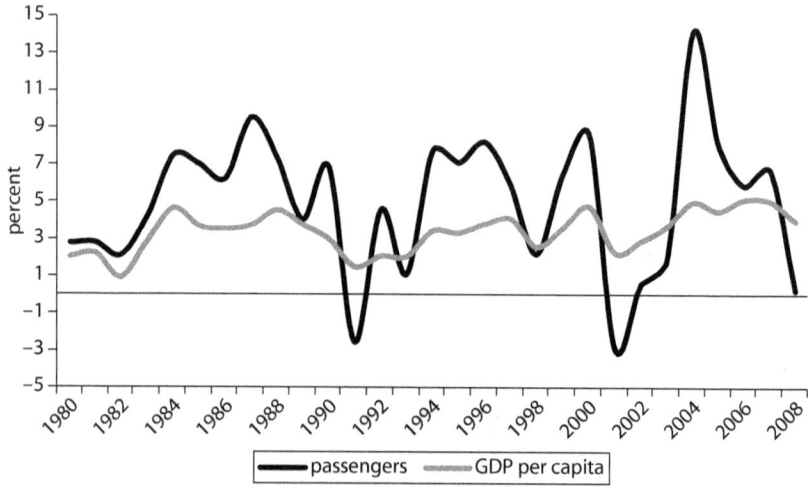

Source: World Bank estimation based on Airports Council International (ACI), International Air Transport Association (IATA), and International Monetary Fund (IMF) data.

narrowing of their operating margins, which increased their vulnerability in periods of crisis. In the airport sector, where many of its facilities are natural monopolies and consequently are regulated, these effects have not been so evident.

Evidence of the impact of the economic slowdown that began in late 2008 confirms the strong relationship between the level of economic activity and air transport passenger demand. According to traffic statistics released by the International Air Transport Association (IATA), international passenger traffic fell by 3.5 percent in 2009 relative to 2008 (IATA 2009).

The significant passenger traffic growth observed between 2007 and 2008 has been heterogeneous across regions. Figure 1.2 demonstrates that all regions experienced high rates of growth in passenger demand in 2007 but the rate of growth has since decreased sharply across regions. In 2008, the last year for which annual data across regions were available (at the time this report was written), the Middle East experienced the greatest increase in passenger traffic (5.8 percent), followed by Africa (4.9 percent), and Latin America and the Caribbean (2.1 percent). Europe and the East Asia and Pacific region both grew by 1.2 percent. North America, on the other hand, was the only region with a negative growth rate, at −3.1 percent.

Figure 1.2 Passenger Traffic Growth, by Region, 2007 and 2008

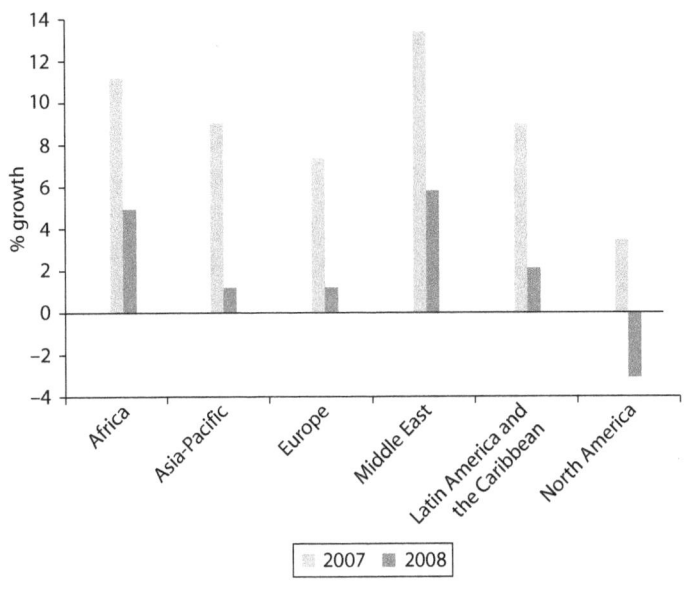

Source: World Bank estimation based on ACI data.

In absolute numbers, the airport sector handled 4.874 billion arriving and departing passengers in 2008, as compared to 4.869 billion in 2007 and 4.5 billion in 2006, of which approximately 2.0 billion were international and 2.8 billion were domestic. As shown in figure 1.3, North America (the United States and Canada) by itself represented 48 percent of domestic traffic, with 1.3 billion domestic passengers, and Europe represented more than half of global international traffic, with approximately 1.1 billion international passengers.

The results for global air cargo traffic for 2008 show that traffic slowed down from the previous year by 3.7 percent, with domestic freight declining more severely than international freight, at −5.4 percent versus 2.4 percent. Such a deceleration could be attributed in part to increases in fuel prices, which diverted traffic to other transport alternatives such as maritime, road, and rail. More recently, passenger and cargo traffic have been considerably affected by the global economic crisis that caused a major drop in international trade volumes; worldwide demand for air cargo capacity began to dwindle in December 2008. The latest data from IATA indicate that compared to 2008, air freight fell by 10.1 percent in 2009, representing the largest decline the

Figure 1.3 Domestic and International Passenger Share, 2008

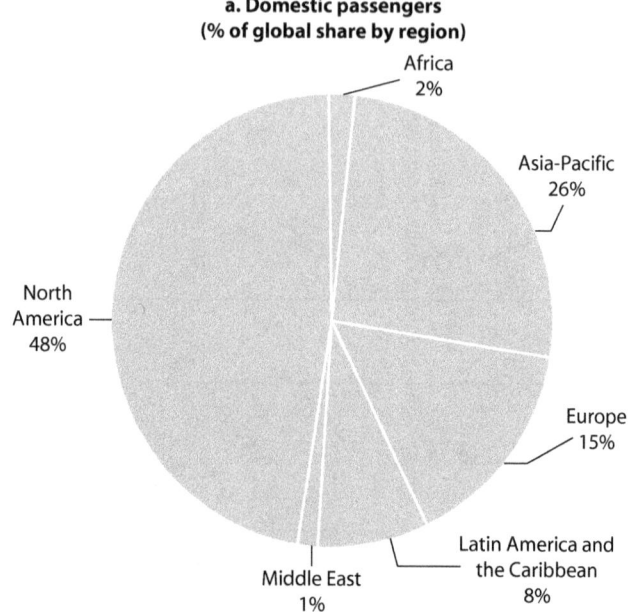

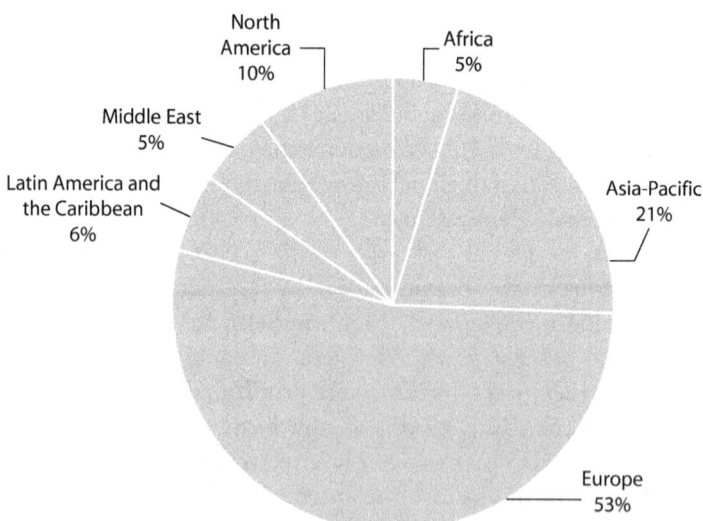

Source: World Bank estimation based on ACI data.

industry has seen in the postwar period. This fall has been driven primarily by reductions experienced in Africa, Europe, and North America. These regions experienced year-on-year output declines of significant proportions: 11.2 percent, 16.1 percent, and 10.6 percent, respectively (IATA 2009).

Disaggregating total cargo by region, figure 1.4 shows that North America and the East Asia and Pacific region contributed the greatest share (33 percent and 34 percent, respectively) to the industry's 86 million cargo tons handled in 2008, followed by Europe (20 percent), the Middle East (5 percent), Latin America and the Caribbean (5 percent), and Africa (3 percent).

The total aircraft movements handled by airports in 2008 was 77 million, a decrease of 2.1 percent compared to 2007. This figure includes cargo, military, general aviation, and passenger aircraft movements and translates into 87.3 passengers per movement. Ranking of airports by number of aircraft movements shows that 9 out of the top 10 airports are located in the United States, with the exception of

Figure 1.4 Volume of Cargo Moved, by Region, 2008
percent

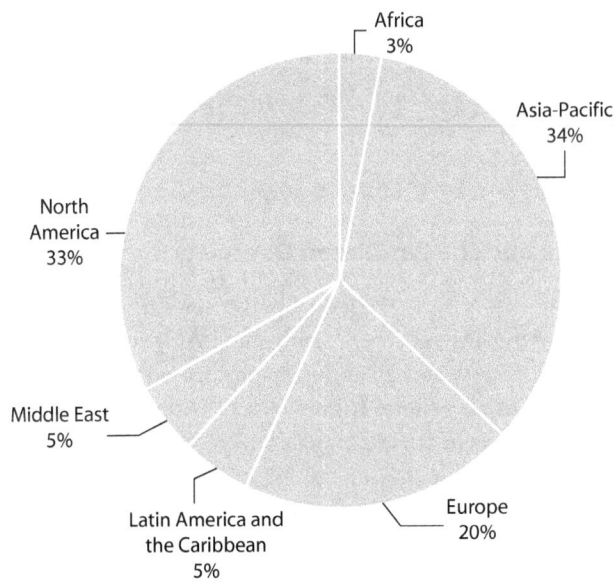

Source: World Bank estimation based on ACI data.

Figure 1.5   Aircraft Movements, by Region, 2008
percent

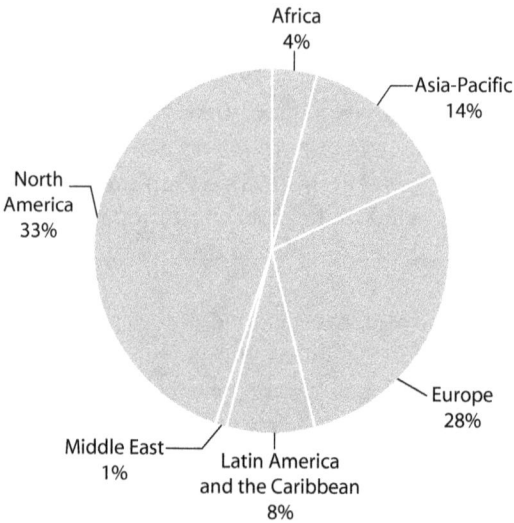

Source: World Bank estimation based on ACI data.

Charles de Gaulle airport in Paris, France. On the other hand, as indicated by figure 1.5, the regions with the lowest share of aircraft movements are Latin America and the Caribbean, along with the Middle East and Africa. Together, they comprise only 13 percent of global aircraft movements.

Latin America and the Caribbean Overview

The objective of this report is to gain a better understanding of the airport sector in Latin America and the Caribbean (LAC) through an analysis of the evolution of airport and air industry performance. Consequently, it is important to present a general framework of recent regional trends, thus expanding on the previous global analysis.

The LAC region has experienced great fluctuations in GDP growth, with particularly sharp declines from 1997 to 1999 and 2000 to 2001 (figure 1.6). Periods of high growth rates, on the other hand, took place between 1996 and 1997 and between 2004 and 2008. Specifically, in 2007, GDP grew at 5.6 percent, as commodity exporters benefited from

Figure 1.6 GDP Growth and Passenger Growth in LAC, 1995–2008

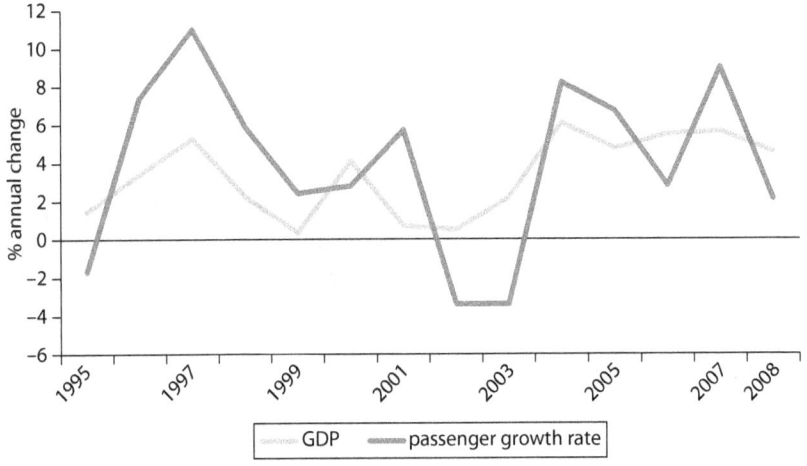

Source: GDP data obtained from World Bank Open Data; available at http://data.worldbank.org. Passenger data obtained from ACI.
Note: GDP in constant U.S. dollars. GDP growth rates calculated as the weighted average of the following countries: Antigua and Barbuda, Argentina, The Bahamas, Barbados, Belize, Bolivia, Brazil, Chile, Colombia, Costa Rica, Dominica, Dominican Republic, Ecuador, El Salvador, Grenada, Guatemala, Guyana, Haiti, Honduras, Jamaica, Mexico, Nicaragua, Panama, Paraguay, Peru, St. Kitts and Nevis, St. Lucia, St. Vincent and the Grenadines, Suriname, Trinidad and Tobago, Uruguay, and República Bolivariana de Venezuela.

record prices and rapid growth in global demand. In 2008, however, growth eased by 1 percent, due mainly to spillovers from the slowdown in worldwide activity and to decreased demand for commodity exports arising from the global economic crisis.

Overall, the region's airport sector, measured by changes in passenger traffic, has followed the economic cycle, and given the high elasticity of demand with respect to GDP, changes in passenger growth rates fluctuated more than GDP growth rates.

The LAC region accounts for a small share of the air transport sector worldwide. Even though its total GDP is approximately 30 percent of the U.S. GDP, the size of the air transport sector is one-fifth that of the U. S. sector. Clearly, it has significant room for growth, which will depend primarily on economic growth, but also on a wide combination of variables, including availability and quality of infrastructure (airports, access to airports), an efficient air traffic control system, adequate investment climate, and tourism development, among others.

In 2008, the LAC region handled approximately 338 million passengers, 4.6 million metric tons of cargo, and 6.4 million aircraft movements. Globally, this translates into 7 percent of passenger traffic, 5 percent of cargo traffic, and 8 percent of aircraft movements (table 1.1).

Table 1.2 provides a ranking of airports in the LAC region in a global context, as measured by passenger numbers and organized according to the 10 largest airports worldwide, followed by all LAC airports included in the sample used for this report. Mexico City Airport, ranked 43rd globally, is the most important airport in the region in terms of passenger traffic, handling a total of about 26.2 million passengers in 2008, approximately one-third the number handled in Atlanta, which ranked first worldwide. Furthermore, it should be noted that LAC countries have only four airports among the top 100 airports worldwide and 14 airports in the top 200.[2]

As for cargo, the entire LAC region handled a total of 4.6 million metric tons in 2008, only 1 million metric tons more than the amount of cargo traffic handled by the Hong Kong International Airport, the global leader with 3.6 million cargo metric tons, and three times as much as Miami, the North American cargo hub that handled 1.5 million metric tons. Within the region, the top 10 cargo airports account for approximately 59 percent of the region's cargo volume (see table 1.3). Among those, Brazil boasts four airports (Guarulhos, Manaus, Viracopos, and Galeão); Mexico two (Mexico City and Guadalajara); Chile one (Santiago de Chile); Colombia one (Bogotá); Peru one (Lima); and Argentina one (Ezeiza, Buenos Aires).

On the aircraft movements level, table 1.4 outlines the 10 top-performing LAC airports, out of which six (Bogotá, São Paulo GRU, Brasilia, Rio de Janeiro, Cancún, and Santiago de Chile) experienced positive growth between 2007 and 2008, with the Brasilia airport taking the lead.

Several stylized facts can be drawn from the available data: (a) considering passengers as the unit of measurement, airports in LAC, on average, are smaller than those in North America, Europe, and the East Asia and Pacific region; (b) airports in LAC, on average, have fewer aircraft movements than airports in North America, Europe, and the East Asia and Pacific region; (c) the most significant difference in output size between the average airport in LAC and that of the other regions is cargo; and (d) airports in LAC tend to rely heavily on international passengers relative to airports in North America and the East Asia and Pacific region. Also, it is important to note that there is great heterogeneity among LAC airports with respect to how they rank in terms of passengers, aircraft

Table 1.1 Latin America and the Caribbean Snapshot of the Airport Sector, 2008

Domestic passengers	Share of global domestic passengers	International passengers	Share of global international passengers	Total passengers	Share of global total passengers	Growth rate of total passengers (2007–08)	Cargo (metric tons)	Share of global cargo	Growth rate of cargo (2007–08)	Aircraft movements	Share of global aircraft movements	Growth rate of aircraft movements (2007–08)
224,531,098	8%	113,850,200	6%	338,381,298	7%	8%	4,589,092	5%	4%	6,403,629	8%	0%

Source: Airports Council International (ACI) 2009.

Table 1.2 Global and LAC Airports Ranking: Passengers, Cargo, and Aircraft Movements, 2008

Global rank	Airport	Passengers	% change 2007–08	Cargo (metric tons)	% change 2007–08	Aircraft movements	% change 2007–08
World							
1	Atlanta, United States (ATL)	90,039,280	0.7	655,277	–9.0	978,824	–1.6
2	Chicago, United States (ORD)	69,353,876	–9.0	1,332,123	–13.1	881,566	–4.9
3	London, United Kingdom (LHR)	67,056,379	–1.5	1,486,260	6.5	478,518	–0.6
4	Tokyo, Japan (HND)	66,754,829	–0.2	852,444	–0.1	339,614	2.4
5	Paris, France (CDG)	60,874,681	1.6	2,280,050	–0.8	559,806	1.3
6	Los Angeles, United States (LAX)	59,497,539	–4.7	1,629,525	–11.9	622,506	–8.6
7	Dallas, United States (DFW)	57,093,187	–4.5	660,036	–8.7	656,310	–2.0
8	Beijing, China (PEK)	55,937,289	4.4	1,365,768	14.5	431,670	8.0
9	Frankfurt, Germany (FRA)	53,467,450	–1.3	2,111,031	–2.7	485,783	–1.4
10	Denver, United States (DEN)	51,245,334	2.8	250,994	–6.1	619,503	0.9
Latin America and the Caribbean							
43	Mexico City, Mexico (MEX)	26,210,217	1.3	382,417	–7.0	366,561	–3.1
62	São Paulo, Brazil (GRU)	20,990,662	7.3	470,404	–3.7	194,186	3.3
96	São Paulo, Brazil (CGH)	13,661,227	10.4	32,521	–6.8	186,356	–9.3

99	Bogotá, Colombia (BOG)	13,456,330	4.9	547,928	−1.8	248,642	7.0
105	Cancún, Mexico (CUN)	12,786,423	11.3	16,496	−6.2	121,397	6.4
120	Brasilia, Brazil (BSB)	10,892,330	−6.2	56,619	−18.2	141,477	11.5
122	Rio de Janeiro, Brazil (GIG)	10,695,992	−0.8	114,581	−1.2	130,595	8.9
144	Santiago de Chile, Chile (SCL)	9,017,718	7.4	298,457	−1.1	101,103	7.0
156	Lima, Peru (LIM)	8,285,688	10.4	239,112	6.1	98,734	6.3
165	Buenos Aires, Argentina (EZE)	8,012,794	7.0	205,506	0.3	71,037	0.7
172	Guadalajara, Mexico (GDL)	7,393,500	−5.0	113,340	−8.8	152,353	−7.2
182	Monterrey, Mexico (MTY)	6,749,240	−1.7	40,979	−1.0	110,150	−5.7
207	Buenos Aires, Argentina (AEP)	5,687,221	0.4	14,690	4.3	85,793	5.5
242	Panama City, Panama (PTY)	4,549,170	19.6	86,588	5.0	80,694	8.4
306	San José, Costa Rica (SJO)	3,238,602	6.8	78,850	−1.0	77,114	2.6
307	Guayaquil, Ecuador (GYE)	3,236,768	8.0	66,936	−8.9	74,205	4.1
334	Santo Domingo, Dominican Republic (SDQ)	2,719,899	−2.0	54,500	−5.4	41,454	6.0

(continued next page)

Table 1.2 (continued)

Global rank	Airport	Passengers	% change 2007–08	Cargo (metric tons)	% change 2007–08	Aircraft movements	% change 2007–08
339	Nassau, Bahamas, The (NAS)	2,665,000	0.8	NA	–1.2	NA	NA
344	Piarco, Trinidad and Tobago (POS)	2,566,200	7.0	31,535	–3.9	65,401	–1.4
356	Cali, Colombia (CLO)	2,418,644	–0.7	41,354	–1.2	55,502	0.7
360	Medellín, Colombia (MDE)	2,367,555	1.4	99,078	–20.4	46,470	1.1
365	Guatemala City, Guatemala (GUA)	2,109,086	5.7	58,834	–15.3	102,519	11.2
384	Manaus, Brazil (MAO)	1,957,050	–13.1	130,723	–23.2	44,925	1.4
430	San Salvador, El Salvador (SAL)	1,570,012	–1.7	28,162	–4.3	33,922	–4.7
483	Campinas, Brazil (VCP)	1,260,112	4.5	223,023	–2.8	32,399	10.9
493	Barranquilla, Colombia (BAQ)	1,207,084	4.3	33,023	6.1	37,168	7.7
708	El Calafate, Argentina (FTE)	494,722	14.1	120	7.3	6,355	20.9

Source: Author's estimation based on ACI 2009 and the World Bank Benchmarking LAC Airports Database.
Note: Global rank is determined by total number of passengers. Rankings for Nassau (NAS), Guatemala City (GUA), and Santo Domingo (SDQ) correspond to 2007 data. Accordingly, the percentage change corresponds to the change between 2006 and 2007.

Table 1.3 LAC Airport Ranking (Top 10) by Cargo, 2008

Rank LAC	Airport	Cargo (metric tons)	Percentage change (2007–08)
1	Bogotá, Colombia (BOG)	547,928	−1.8
2	São Paulo, Brazil (GRU)	470,404	−3.7
3	Mexico City, Mexico (MEX)	382,417	−7.0
4	Santiago de Chile, Chile (SCL)	298,457	−1.1
5	Lima, Peru (LIM)	239,112	6.1
6	Campinas, Brazil (VCP)	223,023	−2.8
7	Buenos Aires, Argentina (EZE)	205,506	0.3
8	Manaus, Brazil (MAO)	130,723	−23.2
9	Rio de Janeiro, Brazil (GIG)	114,581	−1.2
10	Guadalajara, Mexico (GDL)	113,340	−8.8

Source: Author's estimation based on ACI 2009 and the World Bank Benchmarking LAC Airports Database.

Table 1.4 LAC Airport Ranking (Top 10) by Aircraft Movements, 2008

Rank LAC	Airport	Aircraft movements	Percentage change (2007–08)
1	Mexico City, Mexico (MEX)	366,561	−3.1
2	Bogotá, Colombia (BOG)	248,642	7.0
3	São Paulo, Brazil (GRU)	194,186	3.3
4	São Paulo, Brazil (CGH)	186,356	−9.3
5	Guadalajara, Mexico (GDL)	152,353	−7.2
6	Brasilia, Brazil (BSB)	141,477	11.5
7	Rio de Janeiro, Brazil (GIG)	130,595	8.9
8	Cancún, Mexico (CUN)	121,397	6.4
9	Monterrey, Mexico (MTY)	110,150	−5.7
10	Santiago de Chile, Chile (SCL)	101,103	7.0

Source: Author's estimation based on ACI 2009 and World Bank Benchmarking LAC Airports Database.

movements, and cargo. For example, airports such as Guarulhos International in São Paulo (GRU) and Mexico City's Benito Juárez International Airport (MEX) exhibit a similar scale of rankings across the three outputs (passengers, aircraft movements, and cargo). However, other airports rank differently for different outputs. Cancún International Airport (CUN), for instance, ranks high in terms of passengers, average in terms of aircraft movements, and low in terms of cargo. Another example is Viracopos-Campinas International (VCP), which ranks low in terms of passengers and aircraft movements but is the sixth highest in terms of cargo, with about 223,000 metric tons in 2008.

In summary, the LAC region accounts for a small share of the air transport sector worldwide. It accounts for only 7 percent of total passengers,

5 percent of cargo, and 8 percent of aircraft movements. Airports are relatively small when ranked on a global scale.[3] The LAC region has four airports among the top 100 airports worldwide and only 14 among the top 200.

Notes

1. Doganis 2006. An income elasticity of demand of 2 implies that when income (GDP) grows by 1 percent, demand for air travel grows by 2 percent.
2. The airport that serves the city of Caracas in the República Bolivariana de Venezuela occupies position 148 and handled 8.9 million passengers in 2008. This airport was not included in the table because it was not possible to obtain a response to the questionnaire submitted to the operator. Similarly, the Luis E. Magalhaes Airport, serving the city of Salvador in Bahía, Brazil, occupies position 186, but it was not included in this report.
3. The average airport in LAC served almost 5.8 million passengers in 2005, whereas the average airports in North America, Europe, and the East Asia and Pacific regions served 21.2, 17.8, and 16.5 million passengers, respectively.

References

ACI (Airports Council International). 2009. "World Airport Traffic Report 2009." ACI, Geneva, Switzerland.

Doganis, R. 2006. *The Airline Business*. London: Routledge.

IATA (International Air Transport Association). 2009. "Air Transport Market Analysis." IATA, Montreal, Quebec.

World Bank Benchmarking LAC Airports Database.

World Bank Open Data (database). World Bank, Washington, DC. http://data.worldbank.org/.

CHAPTER 2

Investment in the Airport Sector

Several Latin American and Caribbean (LAC) countries embarked upon a structural reform process in the 1990s. This process included, as a major component, the deregulation and privatization of several infrastructure services. In this context, the airport sector experienced a transformation that resulted in the introduction of private sector participation (PSP) in most LAC countries. A wide variation of PSP schemes was adopted. While Argentina opted to concession its airport network to a single operator, Chile adopted a case-by-case strategy and Mexico concessioned its airports by groups. Peru used a mix of single and group concessions, while Colombia and Costa Rica opted for the single concession scheme. The most important economy in the region, Brazil, continues to operate the largest airports through a state-owned corporatized enterprise. However, in 2008 the federal government launched a consultation process to introduce private participation in the airport sector. Table 2.1 shows the countries that, as of 2008, have introduced PSP in the management of airports and details the type of contractual arrangement chosen to incorporate the private sector.

This chapter includes developed countries, such as Japan and Australia, in the World Bank regional designation of East Asia and Pacific.

Table 2.1 Latin American and Caribbean Airports by Type of PSP Arrangement

Country	Project name	Financial closure year	Type of PSP arrangement	Subtype of PSP arrangement	Contract period (years)	Total investment (US$ millions)
Argentina	Islas Malvinas International Airport	1996	Concession	Rehabilitate, operate, and transfer	30	1996: 8; 2007: 6
	Argentina Airport System	1998	Concession	Rehabilitate, lease or rent, and transfer	30	1998: 1,581; 2007: 698
	El Calafate Airport Terminal	2000	Concession	Build, rehabilitate, operate, and transfer	25	2000: 25 2007: 15
	Neuquen Airport	2001	Concession	Build, rehabilitate, operate, and transfer	20	42
Bolivia	Bolivia Airports Concession	1996	Concession	Rehabilitate, lease or rent, and transfer	25	100
	Bolivian Airports Fuel Terminals	2000	Divestiture	Full	n.a.	17
Chile	Diego Aracena Airport	1995	Concession	Build, rehabilitate, operate, and transfer	12	8
	El Tepual Airport	1996	Concession	Build, rehabilitate, operate, and transfer	12	6

Country	Airport	Year	Type	Subtype		
	El Loa Airport	1997	Concession	Build, rehabilitate, operate, and transfer	12	4
	La Florida Airport	1997	Concession	Build, rehabilitate, operate, and transfer	15	4
	Santiago International Airport	1997	Concession	Build, rehabilitate, operate, and transfer	15	*1997: 220; 2004: 22*
	Carriel Sur Airport	1999	Concession	Build, rehabilitate, operate, and transfer	16	32
	Cerro Moreno Airport	1999	Concession	Rehabilitate, operate, and transfer	10	10
	Carlos Ibanez Del Campo Airport	2000	Concession	Build, rehabilitate, operate, and transfer	9	10
Colombia	El Dorado International Airport Runway	1995	Greenfield project	Build, operate, and transfer	20	145
	El Dorado International Airport	2006	Concession	Build, rehabilitate, operate, and transfer	20	650
	Rafael Nunez International Airport	1996	Management and lease contract	Lease contract	15	22

(continued next page)

Table 2.1 (continued)

Country	Project name	Financial closure year	Type of PSP arrangement	Subtype of PSP arrangement	Contract period (years)	Total investment (US$ millions)
	Ernesto Cortissoz International Airport	1997	Management and lease contract	Lease contract	15	9
	Cali Alfonso Bonilla Airport	2000	Concession	Build, rehabilitate, operate, and transfer	20	178
	San Andres and Providencia Airports	2007	Concession	Rehabilitate, operate, and transfer	20	20
Costa Rica	San Jose International Airport	2000	Concession	Build, rehabilitate, operate, and transfer	20	161
Dominican Republic	Dominican Republic Airport Network	2000	Concession	Build, rehabilitate, operate, and transfer	20	265
	La Romana International Airport	2000	Greenfield project	Merchant	n.a.	55
	Licey al Medio Airport	2000	Greenfield project	Merchant	n.a.	30
Ecuador	Mariscal Sucre Airport	2002	Management and lease contract	Management contract	n.a.	0
	New Quito Airport	2005	Greenfield project	Build, operate, and transfer	35	585

	Guayaquil International Airport	2004	Concession	Build, rehabilitate, operate, and transfer	15	80
Honduras	Honduras Airport Network	2000	Concession	Build, rehabilitate, operate, and transfer	20	120
Jamaica	Sangster International Airport	2003	Concession	Build, rehabilitate, operate, and transfer	30	175
Mexico	Southeast Airports Group	1998	Concession	Build, rehabilitate, operate, and transfer	50	*1998: 120; 2000: 394; 2001: 28; 2002: 19; 2003: 7; 2004: 32; 2005: 61*
	Pacific Airports Group	1999	Concession	Build, rehabilitate, operate, and transfer	50	*1999: 264; 2000: 57; 2001: 26; 2002: 52; 2003: 29; 2004: 64; 2005: 73; 2006: 1,000*
	Northern Central Airports Group	2000	Concession	Build, rehabilitate, operate, and transfer	50	*2000: 230; 2005: 203; 2006: 376*
	Puebla Airport	2000	Concession	Rehabilitate, operate, and transfer	n.a	80
	Toluca Airport	2006	Concession	Build, rehabilitate, operate, and transfer	50	100

(continued next page)

Table 2.1 (continued)

Country	Project name	Financial closure year	Type of PSP arrangement	Subtype of PSP arrangement	Contract period (years)	Total investment (US$ millions)
	Nuevo Laredo Cargo Terminal	2007	Greenfield project	Build, operate, and transfer	20	7
Peru	Jorge Chavez Airport Cargo Terminal	1998	Greenfield project	Build, operate, and transfer	30	8
	Jorge Chavez Airport	2001	Concession	Build, rehabilitate, operate, and transfer	30	*2001*: 110; *2005*: 92
	Regional Airport Network Group I	2006	Concession	Rehabilitate, operate, and transfer	25	220
Uruguay	Laguna del Sauce Airport	1993	Concession	Build, rehabilitate, operate, and transfer	26	31
	Punta del Este Airport	1996	Concession	Build, operate, own	20	30
	Carrasco International Airport	2003	Concession	Build, rehabilitate, operate, and transfer	20	164
Venezuela, RB	Margarita General Santiago Marino International Airport	1994	Concession	Rehabilitate, lease or rent, and transfer	20	*1994*: 100; *2004*: 34

Source: Authors' compilation based on the World Bank's Private Participation in Infrastructure (PPI) Database and ProjectWare.

Note: The projects listed for each country correspond to those listed in the PPI database. The column for total investment reports investment commitments. When new investment commitments are reported, the year (in italics) and amount are included. Otherwise, the amount reported corresponds to the financial closure year. n.a. = not available.

It is important to highlight that the need to attract new investment financing sources to improve the quality of services has been the statement most commonly used by governments in the LAC region to justify introducing PSP in airport infrastructure. The LAC region, with its diversity in PSP schemes and more than 10 years of experience with the private management of airports, is able to provide valuable insights into the nature of investments in the sector. An analysis of the evolution of investments in the airport sector in the LAC region, therefore, is useful in answering questions such as the following: Did the investment commitments that were announced when the contractual agreement was signed with the private airport operators eventually materialize? Were investments allocated to address the most urgent infrastructure needs? Were there savings in construction costs brought about by the private concessionaires? Did airport regulators satisfactorily supervise the compliance of investment commitments made by airport operators? Questions along these lines should also be answered by state-owned airport operator companies to allow a comparison between the performance of public and private airport operators.

Data requests on investment were a central part of the surveys distributed to airport operators and regulators in LAC during the preparation phase of this report. Approximately half of the airports provided detailed responses regarding airport investment commitments, but only a few regulators reported on the compliance of investment commitments by airport operators. In addition to the incomplete nature of the investment data, comparability is difficult whenever investment information is gathered from different operators and countries. Investment reporting is not homogeneous because (a) tax laws allow for different depreciation methodologies, (b) regulatory accounting methods differ with respect to the types of investments that can be considered operation and maintenance or capital costs, and (c) investments in airports can be made in aeronautical activities and nonaeronautical activities, with each definition being different among airports.

Given the lack of a complete set of responses and the difficulties in producing homogeneous estimates, this report does not answer several of the questions raised in previous paragraphs. The only possible way to answer them is through an in-depth case-specific analysis of each airport and airport operator, a task that is pending for the LAC region.

Given the aforementioned limitations on the data gathered through this study's survey methodology, this report relies on specialized databases to track the evolution of private investment in LAC airports, comparing it to private investment in airports in other regions as well as to that in other infrastructure sectors. Two data sources are considered: the Private Participation in Infrastructure (PPI) Database, a joint initiative of the World Bank and the Public-Private Infrastructure Advisory Facility (PPIAF), and ProjectWare, a database produced by a private firm, Dealogic. Both databases collect airport investment information, but whereas the PPI database tracks private investment commitments exclusively for developing countries as classified by the World Bank, ProjectWare tracks project financing for both developing and developed nations. It should be noted, however, that ProjectWare is not as complete as the PPI database, since some cases of private financing are not recorded.[1]

Overall, the PPI and ProjectWare databases present partial investment information. Their major limitation when analyzing investments in the airport sector is that none of them report public investment, and thus they underestimate total investments. For instance, neither database registers airport investments in Brazil, the largest economy in LAC, where Infraero, the country's state-owned airport operator, channels investments through operating resources or through transfers made by the federal government. A similar problem is found for the biggest air transport market in the world, the United States, where investments in airports are done through federal funds, by issuance of bonds with municipal or state guarantees, and by airlines.

Private Project Financing in the Airport Sector Worldwide

The ProjectWare database, which covers financing in the airport sector from 1996 to 2008, reported a total of 110 projects worldwide amounting to US$64 billion during this period. Figure 2.1 details the historical investment in airports worldwide: 2003 experienced the largest volume and largest annual increase for airport financing, measured by the number of projects across all regions. More recently, however, the number of airport projects receiving financing as reported by the database has decreased, from 14 in 2007 to 9 in 2008. With respect to project financing in value terms, the greatest financing amount took place in 1996, with 77 percent of the total amount attributed to the East Asia and Pacific region alone as a result of significant investment commitments of approximately US$10 billion for the Hong Kong SAR, China, airport.

Figure 2.1 Project Financing in the Airport Sector by Number of Projects, Total Project Amount, and Region, 1996–2008

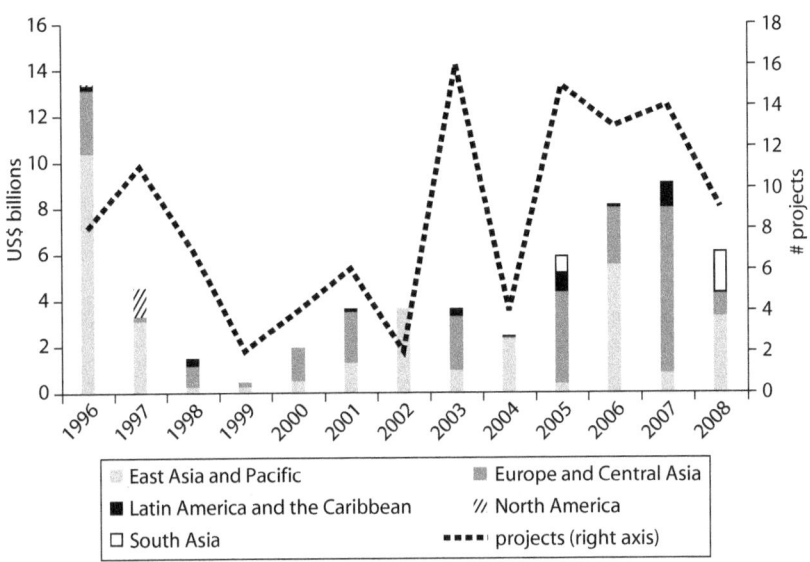

Source: Author's estimation based on ProjectWare data.

When analyzing regional contributions to private airport project financing, it becomes evident that, historically, the two regions receiving the largest financing share are East Asia and Pacific, and Europe and Central Asia. Traditionally, both regions accounted for approximately 90 percent of total project financing in the airport sector. These have been followed by Latin America and the Caribbean, South Asia, and finally North America (see figure 2.2).

If countries with project financing are divided into income-level categories, it would be reasonable to assume that countries with higher levels of economic development would have higher levels of financing, as those are the countries that handle greater amounts of passenger and cargo traffic and therefore require greater investments to maintain or expand their airport capacity. Moreover, these countries tend to provide better conditions to attract large quantities of private financing. The evidence supports this hypothesis, as high-income countries received most of the private financing, accounting for 81 percent of the total, while middle-income countries accounted for 19 percent for the period 1996–2008.

Figure 2.2 Share of Project Financing in the Airport Sector, by Region, 1996–2008

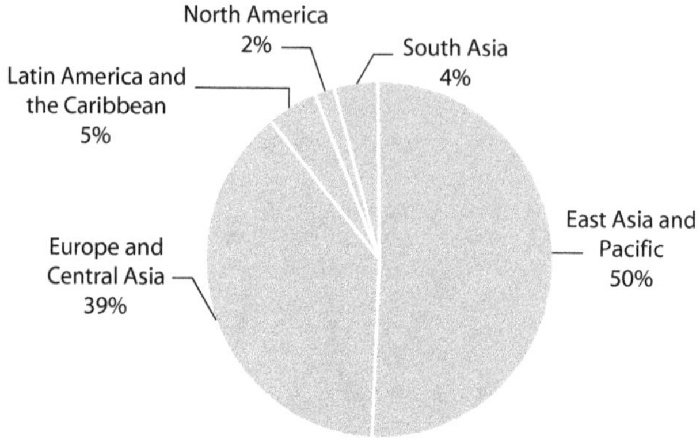

- North America 2%
- South Asia 4%
- Latin America and the Caribbean 5%
- Europe and Central Asia 39%
- East Asia and Pacific 50%

Source: Author's estimation based on ProjectWare data.

These results are reason for concern, as developing nations within the middle-income category have received fewer resources for investing in their airport sectors. Given that, in recent years, airports in developing countries have experienced very high rates of growth of passengers and cargo volumes, it is important to realize that they also require significant investments to upgrade their facilities and broaden their operations in response to such growth in demand. The economic crises that began in 2008 has reduced the pressure on the available infrastructure as demand fell, but if the relative growth rates return to the levels observed prior to the crisis, the remark made about investment needs in fast-growing developing regions will hold true.

Table 2.2 disaggregates project financing to the income level, region, and country between 1996 and 2008. Across countries, Australia has clearly been leading, with total project financing of US$19,326 million, followed by Hong Kong SAR, China, with US$11,050 million, and Turkey with US$6,188 million. Combined, these three countries represented 57 percent of total financing for airport projects worldwide.

Private Investments in the Airport Sector in Developing Countries

Investment commitments to infrastructure projects across sectors (energy, telecommunications, transport, and water and sewerage) in developing countries with private participation have been increasing on

Table 2.2 Total Project Financing in the Airport Sector by Income Level, Region, and Country, 1996–2008

Income level, region, and country	US$ millions
High Income: OECD	
East Asia and Pacific	
Australia	19,326
Japan	1,302
Korea, Rep.	127
New Zealand	115
Europe and Central Asia	
Belgium	1,544
Denmark	1,369
Germany	924
Greece	2,700
Hungary	2,660
Italy	4,220
Spain	155
United Kingdom	4,068
North America	
United States	1,275
High Income: Non-OECD	
East Asia and Pacific	
Hong Kong SAR, China	11,050
Europe and Central Asia	
Cyprus	783
Netherlands Antilles	55
Latin America and the Caribbean	
Bahamas, The	170
Upper Middle Income	
Europe and Central Asia	
Turkey	6,188
Latin America and the Caribbean	
Chile	463
Costa Rica	161
Jamaica	145
Mexico	509
Panama	70
Uruguay	31
Lower Middle Income	
East Asia and Pacific	
Philippines	629
Europe and Central Asia	
Albania	65
Armenia	30

(continued next page)

Table 2.2 *(continued)*

Income level, region, and country	US$ millions
South Asia	
India	2,678
Latin America and the Caribbean	
Colombia	795
Dominican Republic	265
Peru	378

Source: Author's estimation based on the ProjectWare database.
Note: OECD = Organisation for Economic Co-operation and Development.

average over the years (figure 2.3). However, there was a reduction in private investment between 1999 and 2004 and in 2008 due to the financial crises.[2] More specifically for the transport sector, roads have been at the forefront of private investment in developing countries every year since 1990, except for 1999 when they were led by railways (figure 2.4).

Regional contributions to investment commitments in airport projects were heterogeneous between 1991 and 2008. Overall, the LAC region accounts for 30 percent of total commitments (figure 2.5). If this time period is divided in two: from 1991 to 2000 and 2001 to 2008, the LAC region would account for 70 percent of commitments between 1991 and 2000 and only 12 percent between 2001 and 2008. This fact shows that LAC was a pioneer in introducing PSP in the airport sector compared to other regions and that the intensity of the process has recently decreased dramatically, either because most airports have already received the necessary private investment to upgrade airport infrastructure, the region lost its attractiveness, or governments decided not to open the sector for new or more private investment.

An important dimension to consider when analyzing private sector participation in infrastructure is the extent of participation of the private sector. Generally this is summarized by the type of contractual agreement and type of project. The PPI database divides investment commitments into four subtypes of private participation in infrastructure: management and lease contracts, concessions, greenfield projects, and divestitures. Concessions, in turn, include three categories: (a) rehabilitate, operate, and transfer (ROT); (b) rehabilitate, lease or rent, and transfer (RLT); and (c) build, rehabilitate, operate, and transfer (BROT). Greenfield projects, on the other hand, include a variety of different types of categories,

Figure 2.3 Private Investment Commitments to Infrastructure Projects in Developing Countries, by Sector, 1990–2008

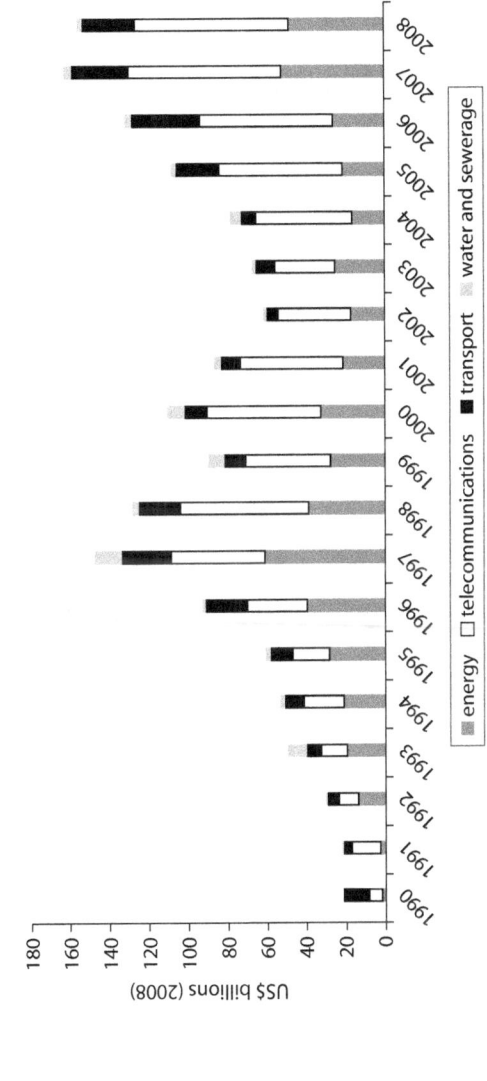

Source: Private Participation in Infrastructure (PPI) Database.

Figure 2.4 Investment Commitments to Transport Projects with Private Participation in Developing Countries, by Subsector, 1990–2008

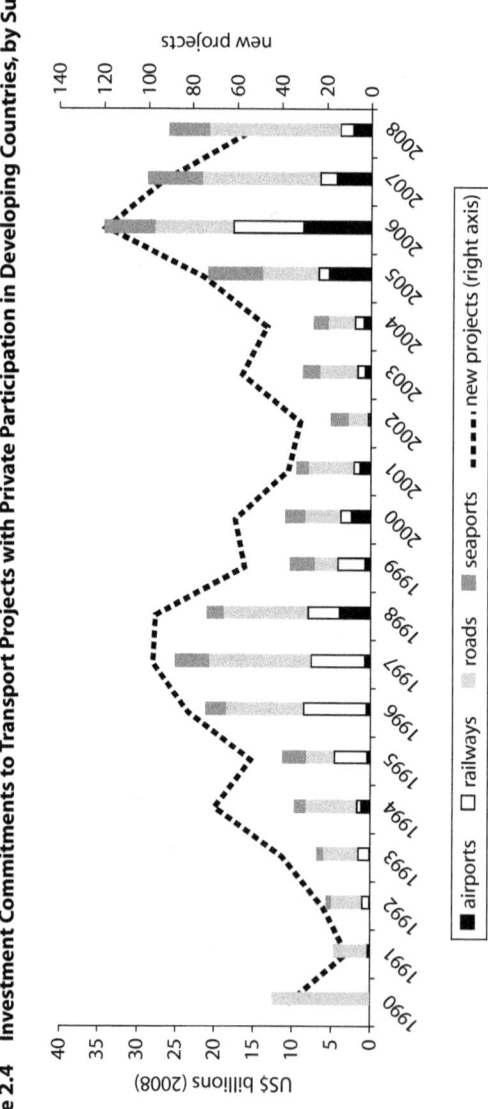

Source: PPI database.

Figure 2.5 Total Investment Commitments to Airport Projects with Private Participation in Developing Countries, by Region, 1991–2008

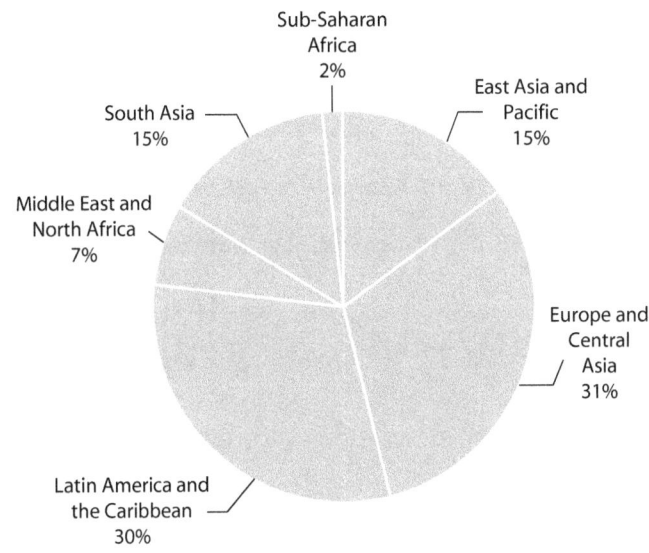

Source: PPI database.

among which the most prevalent in the airport sector is build, operate, and transfer (BOT). As can be seen in figure 2.6, from 1993 to 2008, the predominant type of private participation in the airport sector in terms of investment has been BROTs, followed by management and lease contracts, BOTs, and ROTs.

Private Investment in the Airport Sector in Latin America and the Caribbean

Focusing on LAC, the two databases under consideration present significant differences. According to the PPI database, consistent with global trends, the airport sector in LAC represents a small fraction of projects and investment amounts in infrastructure in the region compared to roads (figures 2.7 and 2.8). Investments in the airport sector in LAC peaked in 2006 with a total of US$2,346 million but fell to US$746 million in 2007 and US$231 million in 2008. The observed fall in the investment commitments does not imply a significant reduction in the actual investments directed to the airport sector because, as figure 2.8

Figure 2.6 Investment Commitments to Airport Projects with Private Participation in Developing Countries, by Type of Project, 1991–2007

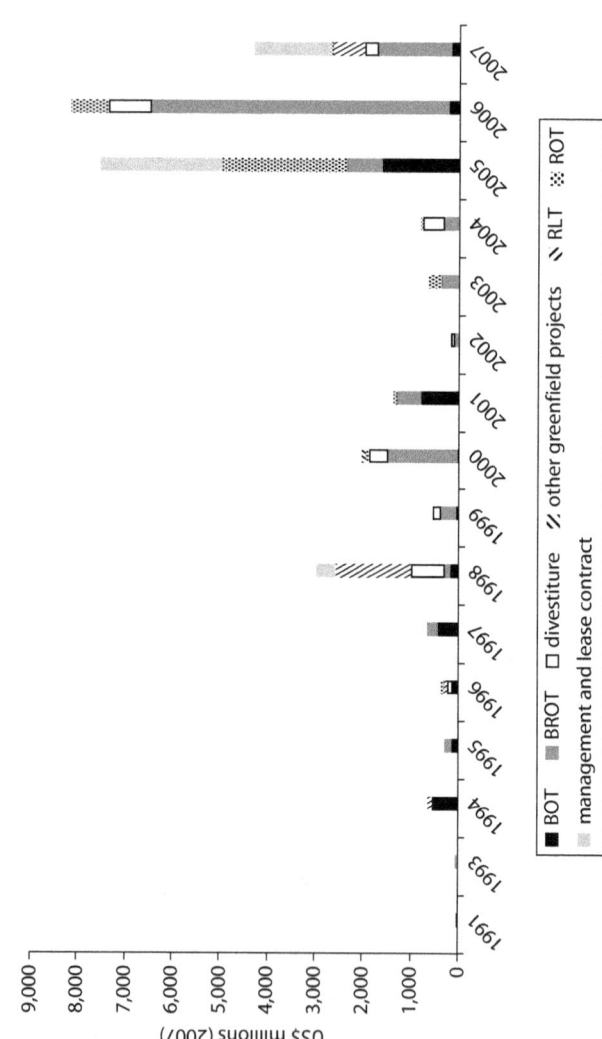

Source: PPI database.

Figure 2.7 Investment Commitments to Transport Projects with Private Participation in Latin America and the Caribbean, by Subsector, 1990–2008

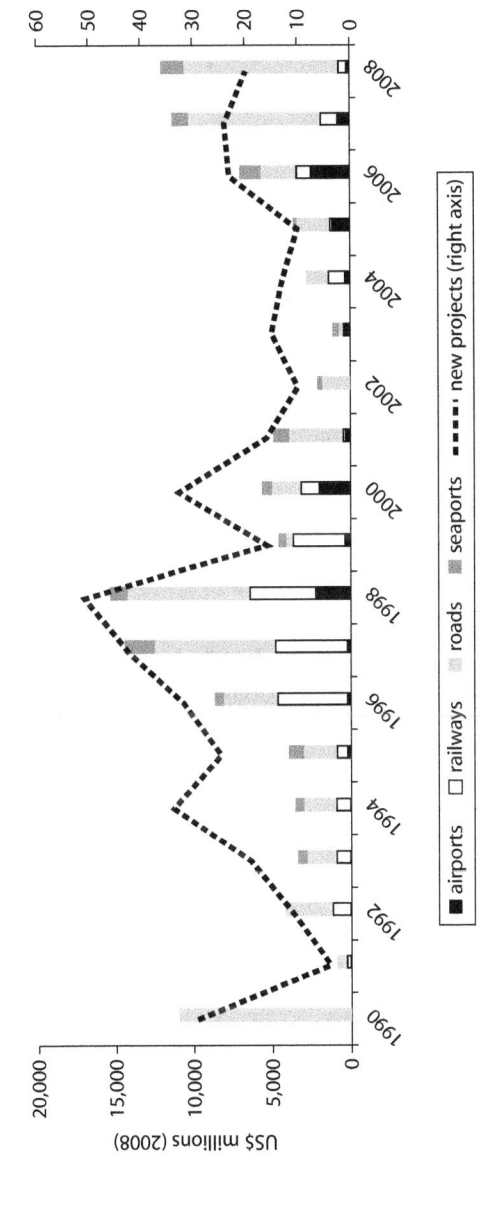

Source: PPI database.

Figure 2.8 Investment Commitments to Airport Projects with Private Participation in Latin America and the Caribbean Countries, by Type of Investment, 1993–2008

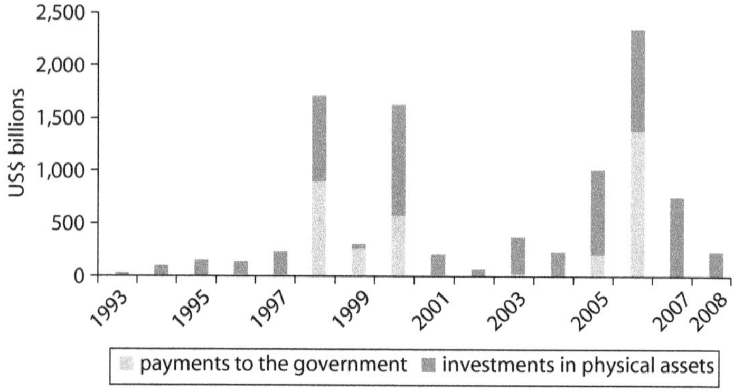

[Bar chart: US$ billions (0 to 2,500) by year 1993–2008, showing payments to the government and investments in physical assets]

Source: PPI database.

shows, almost US$1,500 million reported in 2006 were payments made to governments in the form of concession rights.

As shown in the PPI database, from 1993 to 2007, private participation in the airport sector in the region has been led by Mexico, followed by Argentina and Colombia (see table 2 in the overview). Together, these countries account for 71 percent of total investments in the region. In Mexico, all projects have been concessions, except for the most recent greenfield project of the Nuevo Laredo Cargo Terminal. In Argentina, on the other hand, most of the investments have been allocated to the rehabilitation of 33 airports under the AA2000 concession, while Colombia shows a mixture of greenfield projects, management and lease contracts, and concessions.

Conclusions

Among all developing regions, LAC pioneered the introduction of PSP in the airport sector. Until 2001, according to the PPI database, LAC accounted for 70 percent of private sector investment in airports among developing regions. This region has also implemented the widest variety of types of public-private partnerships in the airport sector. In order to gain a deeper understanding of the role and impact of such private participation in the sector, one must be able to effectively track investments in a standardized and reliable manner. Despite the availability of comprehensive databases that aim at tracking private investments in infrastructure sectors, the information is insufficient. The major problem is that these databases do not track investments in airports operated by public companies. Moreover, there are significant differences in the investment information reported by the databases. The ProjectWare database shows very different total amounts and sequencing (the date the investment is registered) of investment projects: signed airport projects for LAC amounted to US$2,986 million from 1996 to 2007, which represents 27 percent of the investment amount reported by the PPI database.

There is a clear need for further analysis, which should be made on a case-by-case basis and implemented with a common methodology to measure investments to be able to aggregate and make cross-country comparisons. Such analysis would be important if the endeavor to complete the information vacuum described is carried out by a regional body of airport regulators or by institutions specializing in air transport, such as the Airports Council International (ACI) or the International Civil Aviation Organization (ICAO).

Notes

1. The PPI data set represents the more comprehensive and detailed attempt to quantify investments in LAC countries. For instance ProjectWare does not include private financing in the Argentine airport sector, which accounted for 25 percent of total private sector investment in the LAC airport sector from 1993 to 2007, according to the PPI database. These databases differ in the types of data collected. PPI records total investment commitments entered into by the project entity at the beginning of the project (at contract signature or financial closure). ProjectWare, in contrast, presents total project amounts and their breakdown by financing sources, including shares in loans, bonds, and equity, from which investment then is identified. In the ProjectWare database, project amounts reflect investments in infrastructure in the form of construction, expansion, and refurbishment of physical assets as well as in the financing of acquisitions and the refinancing of existing debt. Any given project can consist of one or a combination of any of the above. ProjectWare presents details on projects in five categories: preapproval, in tender, in finance, signed, and cancelled projects, with the purpose of making the PPI and the ProjectWare comparable; therefore, in this report, investment data included in the category "signed" in ProjectWare were considered as investment.
2. This section relies exclusively on information from the PPI database. Information contained in this database is based on contractual arrangements with and without investments in which private parties have assumed operating risks. Projects included in the database are not limited to those that are entirely

privately owned, financed, or operated, but rather some of them have some degree of public participation. To be included in the database, projects are required to have at least 25 percent participation from the private sector except for divestitures, which are required to have at least 5 percent of equity owned by private parties. Investment amounts reflect investments that were committed to at the time of contract signature or financial closure, *not* the investments that have actually been executed. They represent the total of private and public investments for a particular project. The database does not provide information about the difference between investment commitments and actual investment. Accordingly, the PPI database provides an upper bound of total private investment in infrastructure (in other words, actual investment is at most equal to the one reported by the database).

References

Private Participation in Infrastructure (PPI) Database. Public-Private Infrastructure Advisory Facility (PPIAF) and World Bank, Washington, DC. http://ppi.worldbank.org/.

ProjectWare (database). Dealogic. http://www.dealogic.com.

CHAPTER 3

Efficiency Estimation

Commercial firms constantly search for ways to improve their operational performance. In identifying potential areas for improvement, the first step a company should take is to assess its performance. There are two general approaches to achieve this. At the firm level, an analysis can be conducted based on the evolution of the firm's performance through time. Alternatively, the same firm's performance can be evaluated through a comparison with that of other firms in the same industry, namely, through a benchmarking exercise. This section of the report intends to appraise the performance of airports in the Latin America and Caribbean (LAC) region using this second approach.

The use of benchmarking in the infrastructure sector is a relatively recent practice. Having gained significant ground with the creation of economic regulators, the first attempt to use benchmarking for regulatory purposes dates back to the late 1990s, when an initial methodology was developed by the Office of Water Services (OFWAT) in the United Kingdom.

This chapter includes developed countries, such as Japan and Australia, in the World Bank regional designation of East Asia and Pacific.

In the transport sector, and airport subsector more specifically, benchmarking has made limited strides. This can be partly attributed to the fact that for a long period of time, commercial and business pressures were weak within the airport sector since airports around the world were not only owned and managed by governments, but also seen solely as public utilities and strategic assets for national defense purposes. During the late 1980s and early 1990s, however, there was a slow shift toward a view of airports as more commercially oriented enterprises. Consequently, this led several countries to introduce private sector participation in the operation of airports, which in turn called for a more thorough evaluation of airport performance, both to be able to initially negotiate the terms and conditions of private involvement and to track the improvements or lack thereof resulting from such involvement. As a result of this process, in the late 1990s, benchmarking began to be accepted as an important management tool within the airport industry. It was not until this time that the academic literature embarked upon the study of airport benchmarking through advanced efficiency estimation techniques, when the first papers were published in academic journals.[1] Most of the academic literature focuses on developed countries, with the exception of several papers written by University of British Columbia researchers, which use data from several Asian countries, most of them in China. For Latin American countries, a very limited quantity of papers using advanced efficiency estimation techniques were written.[2]

As highlighted by the specialized literature, benchmarking, as a tool to assess performance, is a multifaceted task that must be viewed within the context of a firm's complexity. A firm can be seen as a collection of different processes needed to bring its products or services to the market. Therefore, even though it would be ideal to evaluate a firm based on a single measure of performance, this is not feasible, since a firm's performance depends on the performance of each one of these processes and their interaction. Thus, a firm's performance needs to be measured from several angles, with the three main ones being economic, financial, and operational (see table 3.1 for several examples of performance indicators). First, the economic angle takes into account factors such as the mix of inputs used, technology to transform inputs into outputs, and the firm's productive scale. Second, the financial perspective addresses the mix of financial resources and profitability indicators. Finally, the operational perspective refers to the quality of the products or services provided and can be divided into two categories: the unobserved perception of quality, which looks at clients' satisfaction, and the measured quality,

Table 3.1 Partial Performance Indicators Commonly Used in the Airport Sector

Perspective	Key performance indicators	Metric
Financial	Revenue diversification	Aeronautical revenue as a percentage of total revenue
	Depreciation impact	Depreciation costs as a percentage of total revenue
	ROCE	Return on capital employed
	Operating profits	Operating margin as a percentage of total revenue
Economic: Productivity	ATM staff productivity	Aircraft movements per employee
	Pax staff productivity	Passenger throughput per employee
	ATM capital productivity	Aircraft movements per capital employed
	Pax capital productivity	Passenger throughput per capital employed
Economic: Cost-effectiveness	Unit ATM service cost	Total revenue per air traffic movement
	Unit pax service cost	Total revenue per passenger
	Unit staff employment cost	Total staff costs per passenger
	Unit operating cost	Total operating costs per passenger
Quality of service	Stand availability	Stand availability per landing
	Runway capacity availability	Average throughput capacity vs. maximum capacity
	Passenger satisfaction	Aggregated output of passenger satisfaction surveys
	Baggage system availability	Aggregated serviceable hours of system vs. desired hours

Source: Author's compilation based on IATA.

which is based on the firm's measurement of the product or service quality. The focus of this report is on economic performance and the measurable side of operational performance.[3]

In some cases, infrastructure utilities have a single output, such as an electricity generator, which solely produces energy. In others, firms have several outputs, but the main production technologies and inputs are clearly different for each output. For example, a water utility provides drinkable water and sewage treatment, but the production technologies and inputs to provide each service are different. In the airport sector, on the other hand, there are three different outputs (passengers, aircraft movements, and cargo), but the production technologies and inputs are shared among all of them. The multi-input characteristic of airports' production function might explain why benchmarking performance has developed faster in the energy and water sectors.

This chapter introduces the benchmarking of airports' performance through partial performance indicators. The calculation of partial performance indicators is the simplest and most intuitive way to compare airports' performance. Most of the airport regulatory agencies, airport operators, and industry organizations rely on the information obtained from partial performance indicators to adopt sector-specific policies, including airport tariffs, taxes, and investments. Due to data availability, the first section of this chapter presents several partial performance indicators for 2005. With the intention of conducting a more in-depth analysis, the second section of this chapter develops time series of some partial indicators for selected airports for the period 1995–2006. Finally, following the latest developments in the literature, the third section of the chapter conducts an analysis of efficiency using aggregate measures and econometric techniques to compute a globally efficient frontier for the airport sector and identify the position of the LAC countries' airports relative to the best practice worldwide.

As mentioned earlier, partial performance measures are widely used not only in the airport sector but also in other infrastructure sectors such as water and electricity and telecommunications.[4] The main advantage of these measures is that they are simple to calculate and easy to understand, a feature shared by the traditional accounting ratios widely used for financial performance.

At the same time, partial performance measures have severe limitations. As partial performance indicators ignore the interaction between inputs and outputs produced, they can provide a distorted picture of performance. For example, good performance translated into a high number of passengers per check-in desk may reflect underperformance in another partial measure, such as waiting time per passenger spent in line to check in. In addition, partial measures do not reflect differences in factor prices nor take into account possible substitution of inputs. For instance, if labor relative to capital is cheaper in city A than in city B, partial performance measures can signal that the city A airport is using too much labor even though the airports in cities A and B are both using an efficient mix of labor and capital given the input prices in their respective markets.

Another problem with partial indicators is that they do not account for differences in economic frameworks. For example, indicators such as aircraft movements per employee could be misleading if some countries have more rigid labor markets than others. This is most likely to be relevant when analyzing the time series of this type of indicator, since labor market rigidities in some countries might make it impossible for airports to cut their workforce during a recession.

Furthermore, partial indicators can be problematic because they do not take into account airports' differences with respect to scales and demands (infrastructure and personnel endowment are different for international and domestic passenger airports). Finally, partial measures do not take into account differences in operating environments between firms and are unable to handle multiple outputs, thus ignoring the multi-output characteristics of airports.

As previously stated, there are many reasons behind why the use of benchmarking for airports is harder than for other industries. First, appropriate outputs have to be defined, and also have to reflect the quality dimension of the services airports provide. Second, even if outputs are relatively homogeneous, data adjustments have to be made to take into account differences in the operational environment and the legal framework under which each airport operates. Finally, airports are faced with lump-sum investments, and different airport investment cycles may distort efficiency comparisons if those investments are not properly taken into account.

To overcome the shortcomings of partial performance indicators, aggregate measures and estimation techniques were developed by the academic literature in the last few years, and their use is becoming increasingly popular. The problem of sophisticated productivity measurement methods is their inherent complexity, which poses a problem for their use by airport regulators, especially in some developing countries where regulators lack the technical expertise and where the quality of data is inadequate. Aggregate measures include stochastic and nonstochastic methods, as well as parametric and nonparametric ones. A nonstochastic and nonparametric method is that of price index numbers such as the Tornqvist total factor productivity (TFP). This method requires the aggregation of all outputs into a weighted output index and all inputs into a weighted input index. It is a price index number because the prices of inputs and outputs are used as weights. Another nonstochastic technique is Data Envelopment Analysis (DEA), which compares a weighted output index relative to a weighted input index. The key difference between DEA and price index number TFP is that the weights in DEA are not predetermined but instead the result of linear programming. Hence, the data requirements in DEA are less demanding than in price index numbers. On the other hand, an example of a stochastic method is Stochastic Frontier Analysis (SFA), which is also a parametric method. It estimates a production frontier by allowing decomposition of the model residuals into a random component and an error component that represents the actual level of inefficiency. The third section of this chapter explains and uses DEA techniques to benchmark the performance of LAC airports.[5]

Partial Performance Indicators in LAC Airports: Cross-Comparison for 2005

The information used to compute partial performance indicators was obtained from the responses to the questionnaire developed for this report, a copy of which is included in appendix A. Table 3.2 lists all LAC airports that submitted a response to the questionnaire. To calculate the cross-comparison of partial performance indicators, this report used data for 2005. Two reasons can be cited for the selection of 2005 as the comparison year: (a) it is the year for which the dataset is the most complete; and (b) 2005 is the year used in the latest available version of the Airport Benchmarking Report by the Air Transport Research Society (ATRS 2008) at the time this report was written. The ATRS report, which covers airports from North America (Canada and the United States), Europe, and the East Asia and Pacific region, along with the Airport Performance Indicators report by Jacobs Consultancy (2007),[6] are the only two periodic reports that calculate partial performance indicators for airports. The ATRS report provides the regional mean for a series of partial performance indicators, thus providing the opportunity for comparison with the means for North America, Europe, and East Asia and Pacific. The two reports are the most widely known sources for benchmarking analysis in the airport sector. However, neither of them have data for Latin American airports. No source was found that systematically collects data and estimates partial performance indicators for Latin America and the Caribbean. Thus, the partial performance indicators presented in this chapter and the subsequent calculation of technical efficiency are the first attempts to conduct an overall assessment of airport efficiency for the main airports of the LAC region.

The sample assembled for this chapter is representative of the air transport sector in the LAC region. It accounts for more than 80 percent of passengers and aircraft movements and for 70 percent of air cargo. As such, the database has a similar representativeness compared to the sample constructed by the ATRS and Jacobs Consultancy.

Table 3.2 Latin American and Caribbean Airports Sampled

Location	Airport name	IATA code
Buenos Aires, Argentina	Aeroparque Jorge Newbery	AEP
Buenos Aires, Argentina	Aeropuerto Internacional Ministro Pistarini	EZE
El Calafate, Argentina	Aeropuerto Internacional El Calafate	FTE
Nassau, The Bahamas	Lynden Pindling International Airport	NAS
São Paulo, Brazil	Aeroporto Congonhas	CGH
São Paulo, Brazil	Aeroporto Internacional de Viracopos-Campinas	VCP
São Paulo, Brazil	Aeroporto Internacional de Guarulhos Governador Andre Franco Montoro	GRU
Brasilia, Brazil	Aeroporto Internacional Presidente Juscelino Kubitschek	BSB
Manaus, Brazil	Aeroporto Internacional Eduardo Gomes	MAO
Rio de Janeiro, Brazil	Aeroporto Internacional Antonio Carlos Jobim/Galeao	GIG
Santiago de Chile, Chile	Aeropuerto Internacional Comodoro Arturo Merino Benítez	SCL
Bogotá, Colombia	Aeropuerto Internacional El Dorado	BOG
Cali, Colombia	Aeropuerto Alfonso Bonilla Aragón	CLO
Barranquilla, Colombia	Aeropuerto Internacional Ernesto Cortissoz	BAQ
Medellín, Colombia	Aeropuerto Internacional José María Córdova	MDE
San José, Costa Rica	Aeropuerto Internacional Juan Santamaría	SJO
Guayaquil, Ecuador	Aeropuerto Internacional José Joaquín de Olmedo	GYE
San Salvador, El Salvador	Aeropuerto Internacional Comalapa	SAL
Guatemala City, Guatemala	Aeropuerto Internacional La Aurora	GUA
Guadalajara, Mexico	Aeropuerto Internacional Miguel Hidalgo y Costilla	GDL
Monterrey, Mexico	Aeropuerto Internacional General Mariano Escobedo	MTY
Mexico City, Mexico	Aeropuerto Internacional Benito Juárez	MEX
Cancún, Mexico	Aeropuerto Internacional de Cancún	CUN
Panama City, Panama	Aeropuerto Internacional de Tocumen	PTY
Lima, Peru	Aeropuerto Internacional Jorge Chávez	LIM
Santo Domingo, Dominican Republic	Aeropuerto Internacional de Las Américas	SDQ
Port of Spain, Trinidad and Tobago	Piarco International Airport	POS

Source: Author's compilation.

The rest of this section presents several partial performance indicators. The indicators are those most commonly found in assessments of the air transport industry. The results of the calculations of all partial performance indicators are illustrated in the figures and described through examples from airports in the sample. An assessment of practical limitations and caveats to consider when analyzing partial performance indicators is also included for most of the indicators presented. In all figures, those airports that were operated by the government or by a government-owned enterprise in 2005 are in light gray, while those that were operated by a private enterprise are in dark gray. Regional means appear in black. Each airport is identified by its code (three letters).

Passengers per Aircraft Movement

The average number of passengers per aircraft movement in 2005 for LAC was approximately 59, which is quite similar to the average for North America, but smaller than for Europe and the East Asia and Pacific region (figure 3.1). There are airports such as Buenos Aires (EZE), Cancún (CUN), or Santiago de Chile (SCL) where the average flight in 2005 carried about 100 passengers. At the other end of the scale are airports such as Nassau, The Bahamas (NAS), or Guatemala City (GUA), where the average flight in 2005 carried only 20 passengers.

Ideally, this indicator should be calculated differentiating passengers and air traffic movements (ATMs) by destination (domestic and international). Due to data limitations, it was not possible to disaggregate this indicator. However, it is safe to argue that differences in the number of passengers per aircraft movement cannot be fully explained by the percentage of international passengers served by the airports. For example, the airports in Buenos Aires (EZE), Cancún (CUN), Nassau (NAS), and San Salvador (SAL) are four of the five airports with the largest percentage of international passengers, but they show very different values for the ratio of passengers per aircraft movement. The mix of airplane sizes may explain such differences, and that mix in turn depends on the geographical location of the airport that determines the distance from the most popular origin and destination markets served. As a general rule, the closer the distance is between the airport and the markets it serves, the smaller the aircraft the airport will handle. However, this hypothesis cannot be tested, since several of the airports in the sample did not provide information about the size of the airplanes they handle.

It can be concluded, therefore, that the indicator of passengers per aircraft movement is not necessarily an accurate indicator of an airport's performance, as it is influenced by the airport's geographical location; the type of passengers served; the structure of the network designed and served by airlines—for instance, SCL, GRU (São Paulo, Brazil), and EZE

Figure 3.1   Passengers per Aircraft Movement, 2005

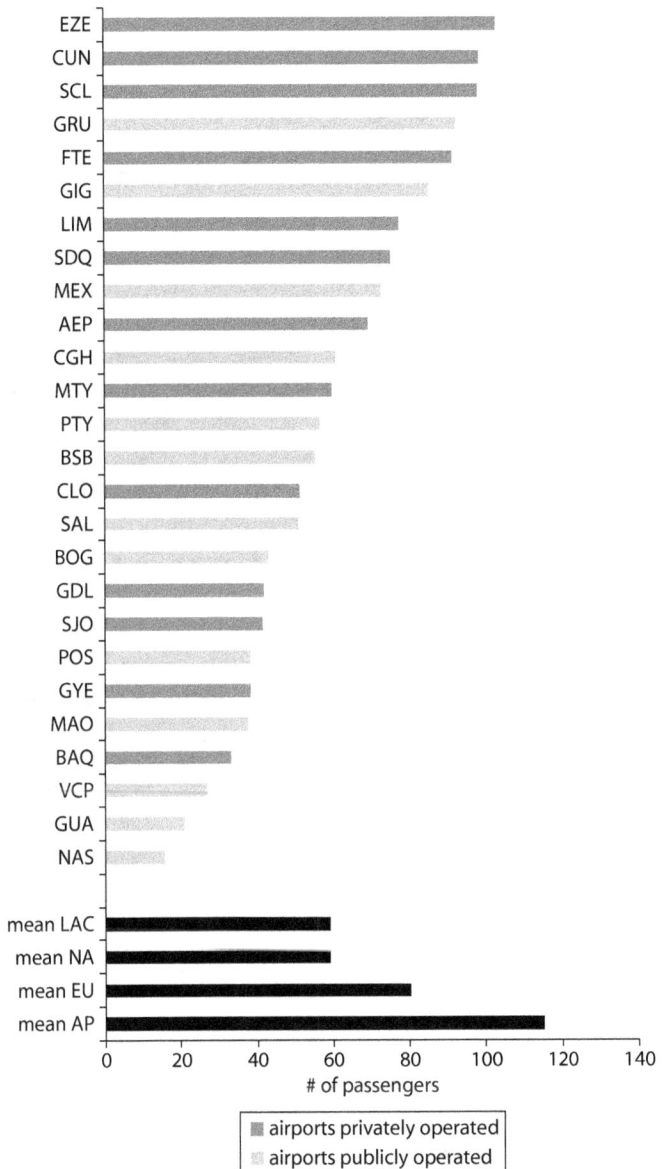

Source: Author's calculation.
Note: LAC = Latin America and the Caribbean; NA = North America; EU = European Union; AP = Asia-Pacific. For a list of airport codes and the airports they represent, see page xxiii.

are terminal airports with a high percentage of long-haul flights served by large aircrafts; and runway and apron characteristics.

Cargo per Aircraft Movement

The airport in Santiago de Chile (SCL) not only ranks in third place in terms of passengers per aircraft movement in 2005, but also ranks high regarding cargo per aircraft movement, with almost 4 tons per aircraft movement (figure 3.2). Santiago de Chile's airport is surpassed only by Viracopos-Campinas International (VCP) in São Paulo, with the average flight in 2005 carrying almost 6 tons of cargo and only 27 passengers. VCP is the only major airport dedicated to cargo in the LAC region—although the share of passengers is increasing due to the expansion of the catchment area of São Paulo and to the capacity constraints faced by the two other São Paulo airports, GRU and Congonhas (CGH)—with an important presence of industry consolidators (FEDEX, among others). An average flight in LAC in 2005 carried only 1.5 tons of cargo, which is more than what an average flight in Europe and North America carried for that same year (1.3 tons), but it is 3 tons less than the cargo in an average flight in East Asia and Pacific. Those airports included within the sample that are located in tourist areas within LAC, such as in Cancún (CUN) and El Calafate (FTE), handle the lowest cargo per aircraft.

In a good example of the limitations of partial performance indicators, figure 3.2 seems to suggest that the LAC air cargo market is larger than that of North America or Europe. The ratio of cargo-to-aircraft movements appears smaller for North American and European markets, not because there is less cargo, but because there are more aircraft movements. In order to handle large volumes of cargo, North America, Europe, and the East Asia and Pacific region rely more on dedicated freight flights than on using space in regular passenger commercial flights to carry cargo. Whereas cargo per aircraft movement might be a fitting measurement for Latin America, tons of cargo per cargo-dedicated aircraft movement would provide a better idea of the size of North American and European air cargo markets relative to Latin America.[7]

Passengers per Employee

Probably the most popular partial performance indicator in airports is the ratio of passengers per employee.[8] If we assume that the number of passengers is the only output of an airport and labor is its only input, then we could conclude that in 2005 the average airports in North America and East Asia and Pacific were more efficient than the average airport in

Figure 3.2 Cargo per Aircraft Movement, 2005

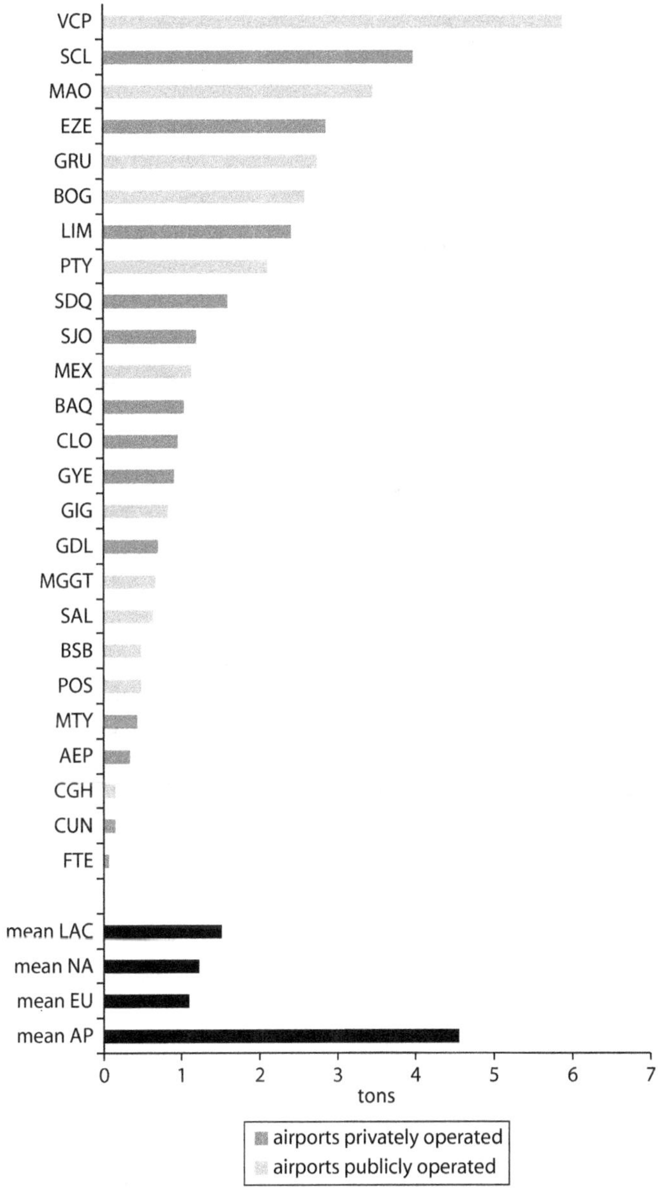

Source: Author's calculation.
Note: LAC = Latin America and the Caribbean; NA = North America; EU = European Union; AP = Asia-Pacific. For a list of airport codes and the airports they represent, see page xxiii.

Latin America, which, with a little over 22,500 passengers per employee, was more efficient than the average airport in Europe (figure 3.3). This is certainly a surprising result. Given the relatively lower cost of labor in Latin America and the smaller scale of airports compared to Europe, one would have expected a lower ratio of passengers per employee in Latin America. As figure 3.3 shows, the airport in Santiago de Chile (SCL) and Congonhas International (CGH) in São Paulo are the most efficient in terms of number of passengers per employee. Also, the airports in Santiago de Chile (SCL) and Buenos Aires (EZE) served almost the same number of passengers in 2005, but the number of employees in EZE is over four times the number of employees in SCL. However, since this is a partial measure, which is strongly influenced by the degree of outsourcing in each airport, one should be careful when drawing conclusions regarding economic and operational efficiency.[9]

Aircraft Movements per Runway

In 2005, the average airport in the LAC region had the lowest number of aircraft movements per runway when compared with North America, Europe, and the East Asia and Pacific region. If we consider aircraft movements as the only output and available runways as the only input, then the average airport in LAC is less efficient than the average airports in North America, Europe, and East Asia and Pacific. This finding indicates that in the average airport in LAC there was more excess capacity or less congestion than in airports in the other regions. The results of figure 3.4, as with all partial performance indicators, should be interpreted with caution. A simple look at figure 3.4 indicates that some airports in LAC are underutilized. Although this may be true for airports at the lower end of the scale, at least one caveat should be mentioned. The case may be that a given airport constructed a new runway in 2005 or in recent years to accommodate future demand growth. Since airport runways are a typical example of lump-sum investments, this partial performance indicator may not be providing accurate information. On the other hand, it is possible that despite available capacity, an airport is not allowed to accommodate additional aircraft movements due to restrictions imposed by air traffic control agencies that have low endowment of technological equipment and human capital resources. As a matter of fact, this is very common in the LAC region.

The airport in Mexico City (MEX) and Congonhas International (CGH) in São Paulo have the most congested runways in Latin America,

Figure 3.3 Passengers per Employee, 2005

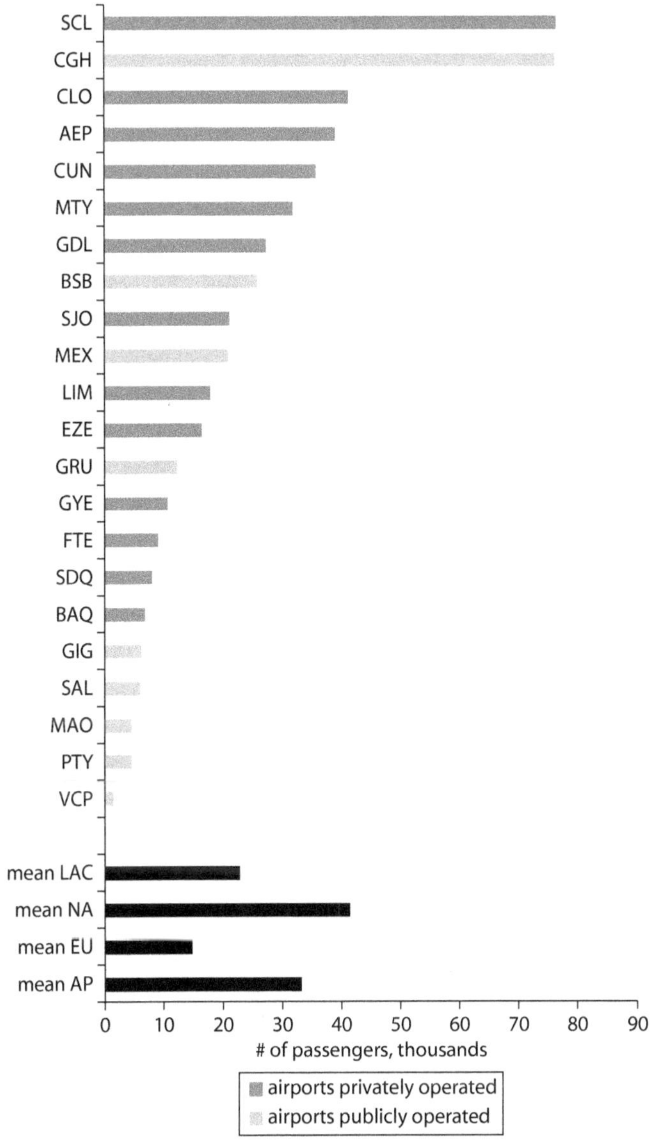

Source: Author's calculation.
Note: LAC = Latin America and the Caribbean; NA = North America; EU = European Union; AP = Asia-Pacific. For a list of airport codes and the airports they represent, see page xxiii.

Figure 3.4 Aircraft Movements per Runway, 2005

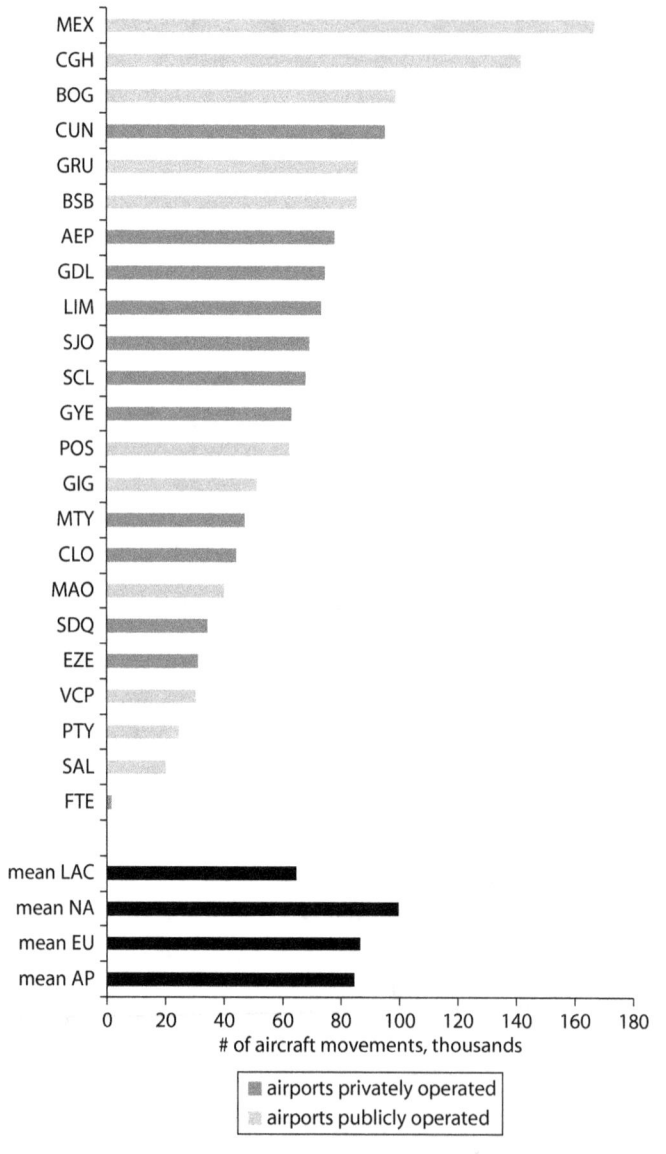

Source: Author's calculation.
Note: LAC = Latin America and the Caribbean; NA = North America; EU = European Union; AP = Asia-Pacific. For a list of airport codes and the airports they represent, see page xxiii.

with 166,500 and 141,314 aircraft movements per runway, respectively. According to the sample assembled for this report, the airport with the least congested runway is El Calafate (FTE) in Argentina, with almost 2,000 aircraft movements in 2005.

Labor Costs as a Share of Operating Costs

As expected, labor costs represent a smaller share of operating costs in LAC than in North America, Europe, or East Asia and Pacific (figure 3.5). According to the data reported by the airport operators and further calculations of total labor costs produced for this report, labor costs represent, on average, only 16 percent of the costs incurred in the operation of an airport in Latin America in 2005. A striking finding is the large difference between the Colombian airports in Barranquilla (BAQ) and Cali (CLO), with labor costs representing almost 40 percent of operating costs in BAQ and only 5 percent in CLO. One possible explanation could be that the outsourcing of labor-intensive jobs is more prevalent in CLO than in BAQ. However, this is just speculation, since we do not have information on the degree of outsourcing in each airport. The airport comparison of this indicator can suffer from an important accounting bias. It is common that concessioned airports include as operating costs their annual payments to the government for the right to operate the airport. This would tend to increase operating costs of privately operated airports when compared to public airports that do not have this expense, thus reducing the ratio of labor costs over operating costs. Given that the two effects, outsourcing and the reporting of annual payments as operating costs, move in the same direction, we should expect privately operated airports to show a lower value for this indicator, providing a bias that cannot identify whether privately managed airports have lower labor costs due to higher average labor productivity.

Labor Cost per Passenger

The smallest average labor cost per passenger in 2005 was found in LAC, where the average airport spent US$1 per passenger in labor-related costs. In Europe, the average airport spent almost US$6 per passenger in labor-related costs. As figure 3.6 shows, the two extremes in LAC were represented by the Tocumen International Airport (PTY) in Panama, which spent US$3.20 per passenger in labor-related costs, while Congonhas International (CGH) in São Paulo, Brazil, spent only US$0.14 per passenger.

Figure 3.5 Labor Costs as a Share of Operating Costs, 2005

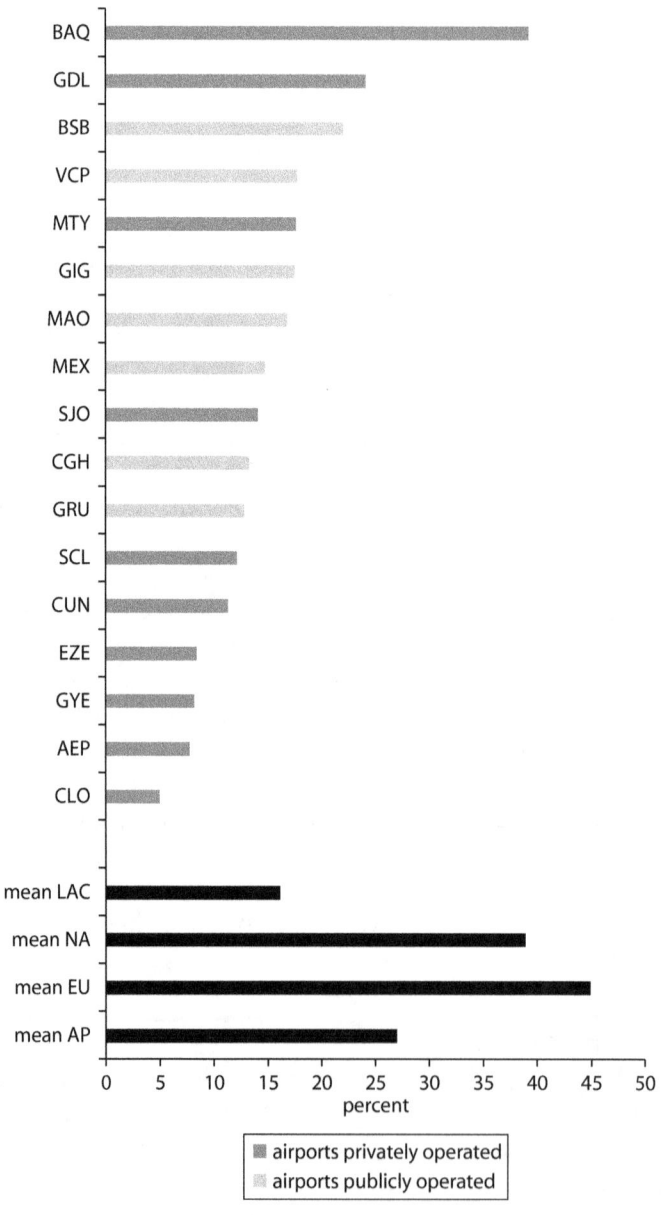

Source: Author's calculation.
Note: LAC = Latin America and the Caribbean; NA = North America; EU = European Union; AP = Asia-Pacific. For a list of airport codes and the airports they represent, see page xxiii.

Figure 3.6 Labor Cost per Passenger, 2005

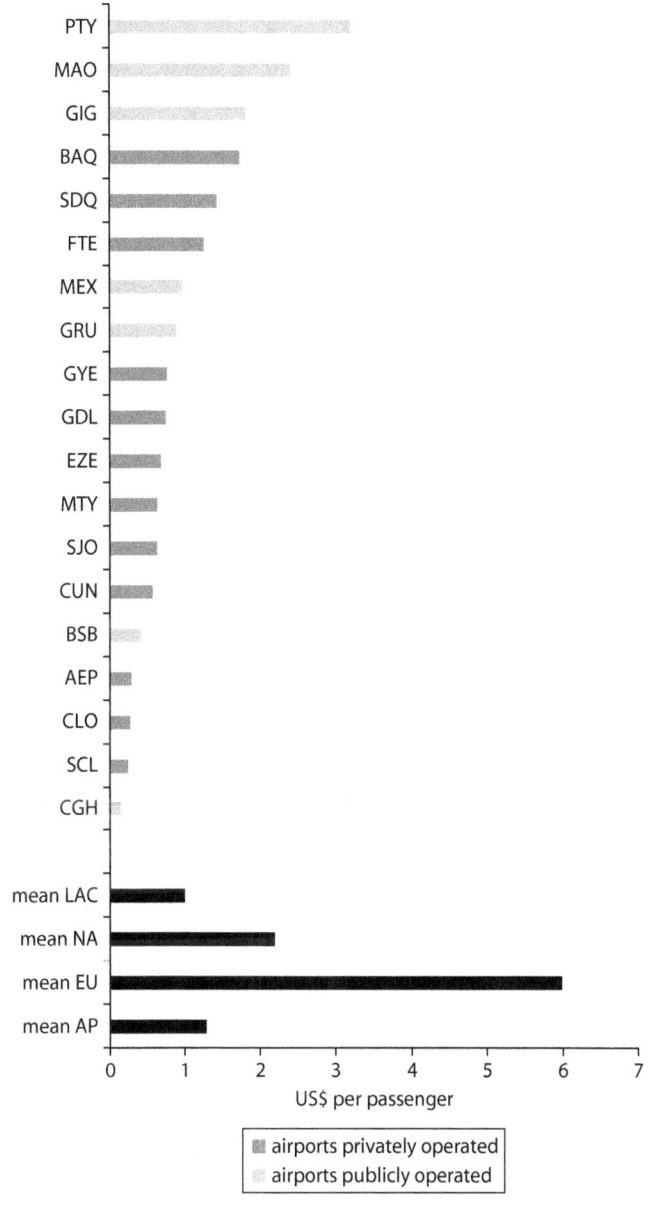

Source: Author's calculation.
Note: LAC = Latin America and the Caribbean; NA = North America; EU = European Union; AP = Asia-Pacific. For a list of airport codes and the airports they represent, see page xxiii.

Obtaining definitive conclusions from this indicator is a difficult task as its construction suffers from the same problems as the indicator of labor costs as a share of operating costs. The labor practices adopted by each airport, reflected in how much labor is outsourced, can make the calculation of this indicator meaningless for performance benchmarking.

Operating Costs per Passenger

When analyzing operating costs per passenger for 2005, we observe that even though the average airport in LAC is the least costly to operate, with US$5.56 per passenger, it is quite similar to those in North America and East Asia and Pacific (figure 3.7). On the other end of the scale is Europe, with an average of US$14.23 of operating costs per passenger in 2005. The available data do not allow us to conduct a cross-regional comparison of the determinants of airports' operating costs in each region. The fact that the average airport in LAC shows a similar value of this indicator to that in North America and East Asia and Pacific is somewhat worrisome, given that labor costs as a share of operating costs are much lower in LAC (see figure 3.5). This would indicate that airport operators might be including cost items as operating costs that operators in other regions do not include (possible candidates are payments to the government and higher rates of depreciation). More research consisting of in-depth case studies should be carried out to understand the differences in input costs across regions.

The Brazilian airports are an interesting case regarding operating costs per passenger. The top two airports in this category are Eduardo Gomes International (MAO) in Manaus and Galeão International in Rio de Janeiro (GIG), while the lowest and third-lowest airports are Congonhas International in São Paulo (CGH) and Juscelino Kubitschek in Brasilia (BSB). MAO is one of the smallest airports in terms of number of passengers in the sample, while CGH, BSB, and GIG are the second-, fourth-, and sixth-largest airports in that same category, respectively. The most striking difference is between BSB and GIG. The airport in Brasilia (BSB) had approximately US$19 million in operating costs and served 9.4 million passengers, while the airport in Rio de Janeiro (GIG) had approximately US$91 million in operating costs and served 8.6 million passengers.

With the exception of Guayaquil (GYE), in Ecuador, and Buenos Aires (EZE), in Argentina, privately operated airports seem to have lower operating costs per passenger than those operated by public companies.

Figure 3.7 Operating Costs per Passenger, 2005

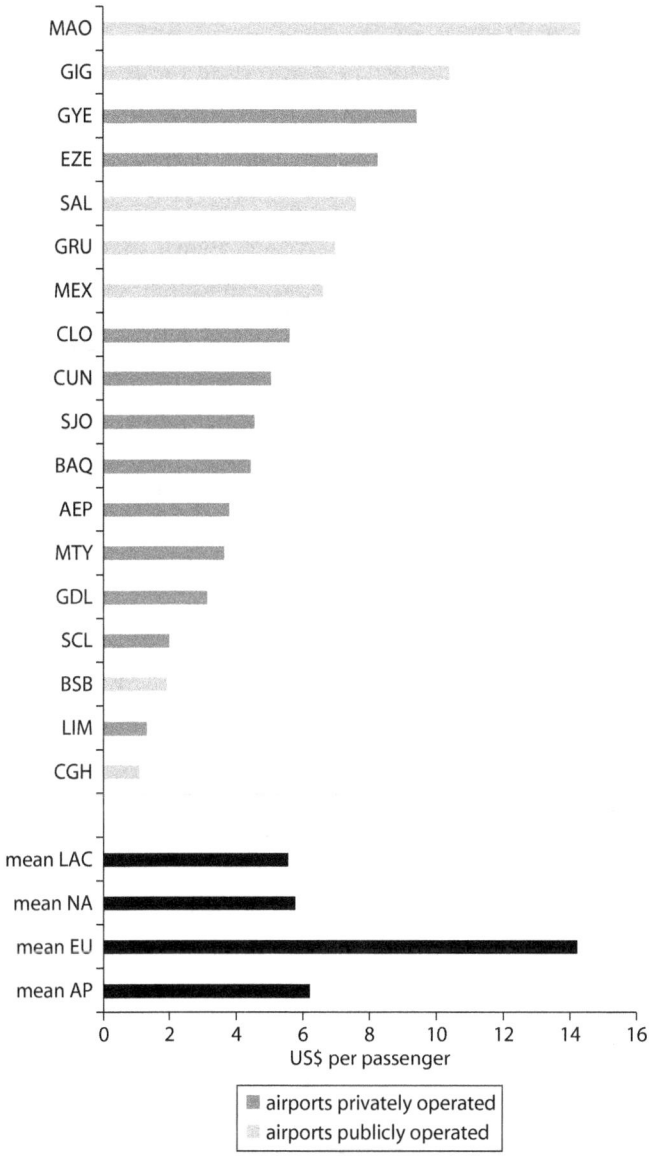

Source: Author's calculation.
Note: LAC = Latin America and the Caribbean; NA = North America; EU = European Union; AP = Asia-Pacific. For a list of airport codes and the airports they represent, see page xxiii.

Operating Costs per Aircraft Movement

The average airports in Europe and East Asia and Pacific spent significantly more U.S. dollars per aircraft movement than those in North America and LAC (figure 3.8). An interesting finding is that the average airport in North America has a lower operating cost per aircraft movement than the average airport in LAC. The most likely explanation for this result is the difference in scale, as airports in North America have, on average, three times as many aircraft movements per year than LAC airports. Moreover, the network structure of the air transport market in North America, which is based on the hub-and-spoke system, generates a more intensive use of aircraft than the LAC system, leading to increased numbers of aircraft movements. The ratio of operating costs to aircraft movements for all the LAC airports, with the exception of Viracopos-Campinas (VCP), was less than US$1,000 in 2005.

As in the case of operating costs per passenger, Congonhas (CGH) in São Paulo and Juscelino Kubitschek (BSB) in Brasilia are the lowest and third-lowest airports, in terms of U.S. dollars spent on operating costs per aircraft movement in 2005. Viracopos-Campinas (VCP), with US$1,174 of operating costs per aircraft movement, was the costliest airport to run per aircraft movement, while Galeão International (GIG) with US$881, ranked second in this category.

Total Revenue per Passenger

The average airport in LAC had almost US$10 of revenue per passenger in 2005, which is similar to the revenue per passenger in the average North American airport (figure 3.9). However, this number is small compared to the revenue per passenger generated in the average European airport, which was US$23 in 2005.

Airports generate revenues from two distinct categories: (a) aeronautical services and (b) nonaeronautical services. Aeronautical revenue refers to the income directly related to the aviation activities at an airport, including landing fees, passenger and terminal charges, and in some cases ground-handling charges. Traditionally, aeronautical revenues are the primary source of income for airports. However, increasingly, more airports are actively seeking other sources of nonaeronautical revenues, including car parking, retail shops and concessions, and real estate leasing, among others. Airport regulators tend to look closely at the aeronautical services, as these are services considered, for most airports in the world, a natural monopoly. Accordingly, from a policy perspective, aeronautical revenue

Figure 3.8 Operating Costs per Aircraft Movement, 2005

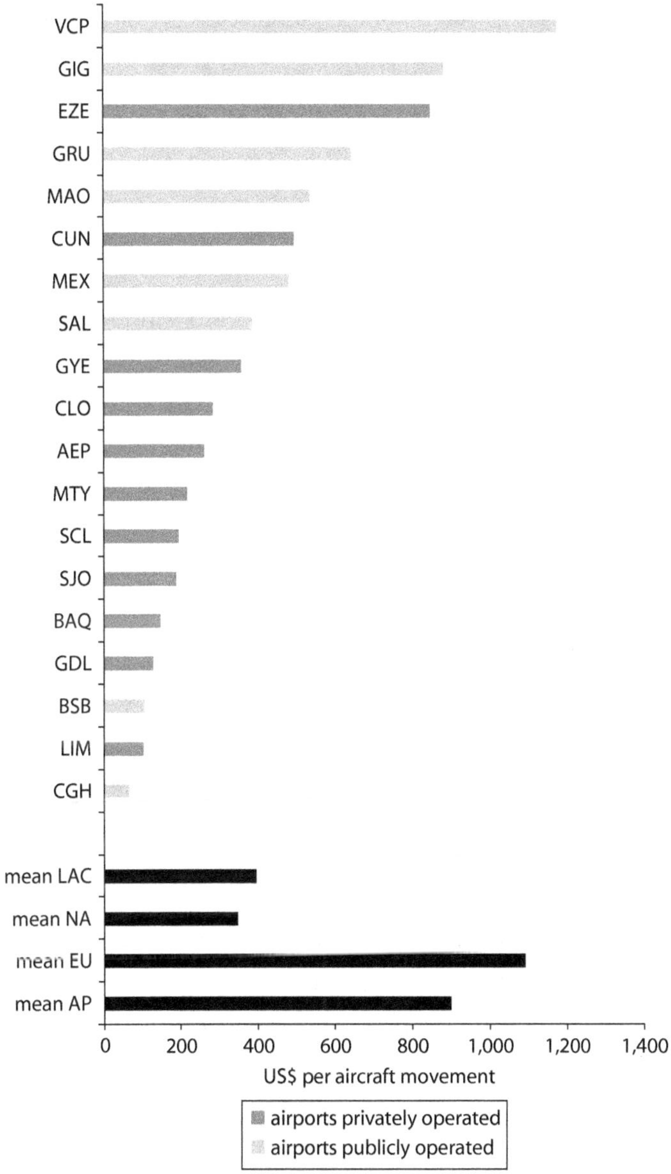

Source: Author's calculation.
Note: LAC = Latin America and the Caribbean; NA = North America; EU = European Union; AP = Asia-Pacific. For a list of airport codes and the airports they represent, see page xxiii.

Figure 3.9 Total Revenue per Passenger, 2005

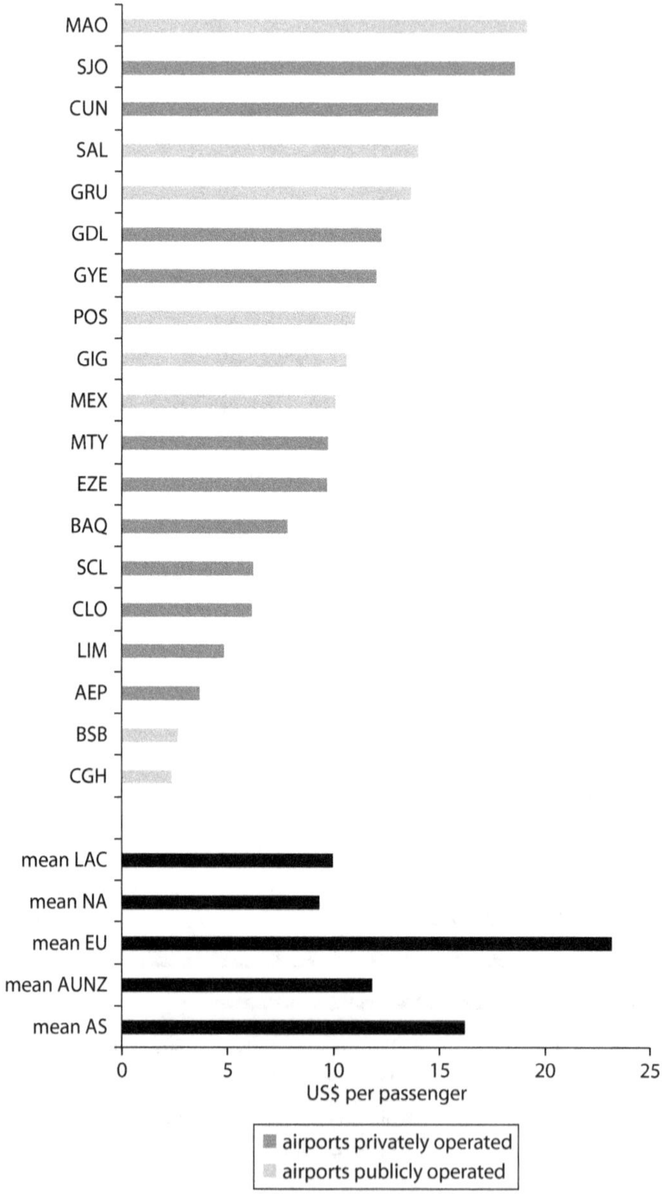

Source: Author's calculation.
Note: LAC = Latin America and the Caribbean; NA = North America; EU = European Union; AP = Asia-Pacific. For a list of airport codes and the airports they represent, see page xxiii.

and its determinants (that is, tariff structures and levels) tend to be studied in more detail by regulators and airlines.

The worldwide trend in commercial airports has been an increase in nonaeronautical revenues. Most regulatory regimes generate incentives for airport operators to increase revenues from commercial activities.

Aeronautical Revenue Share

In the average airports in North America and East Asia and Pacific, aeronautical revenue amounts to 50 percent of total revenue. In LAC, the average airport draws 56 percent of its revenue from aeronautical sources, which is 4 percent more than the average airport in Europe (figure 3.10).

The Colombian airports in Cali (CLO) and Barranquilla (BAQ), as well as the airports in Lima (LIM) and Santo Domingo (SDQ), drew more than 80 percent of their total revenue from aeronautical sources. Santiago de Chile's airport (SCL) and Viracopos-Campinas (VCP) are on the other end of the ranking for LAC, with only around 15 percent of their revenue in 2005 coming from aeronautical fees and charges. The low value for Santiago de Chile (SCL) is explained by the type of concession, which exclusively covers the terminals, and consequently the operator does not receive landing fees, a major aeronautical revenue factor. Chapter 5 provides a comparison of airport tariffs and their evolution.

Aeronautical Revenue per Aircraft Movement

The average airport in LAC trailed those in Europe, Asia, and Australia and New Zealand[10] in terms of aeronautical revenue per aircraft movement in 2005 (figure 3.11). The average airport in LAC generated US$339 in aeronautical revenue per aircraft movement, while those in the other three regions generated US$972, US$1,168, and US$687, respectively. An unexpected finding is that the average airport in LAC earned US$41 more than the average airport in North America during 2005. The top four LAC airports earned more than US$500 per average flight in 2005, with the airport in Cancún (CUN) earning more than US$1,000, while the six lowest-earning airports received no more than US$200 from similar sources. The Mexican airports tend to earn more aeronautical revenues per aircraft movement than the Brazilian airports.

Ideally, according to the International Civil Aviation Organization (ICAO) guidelines, aeronautical revenues should cover the cost of providing aeronautical services. Aeronautical revenues include several tariffs, some charged to aircraft and others to passengers. The most common tariffs are landing, parking, gate use, and passenger. There are different

Figure 3.10 Aeronautical Revenue Share, 2005

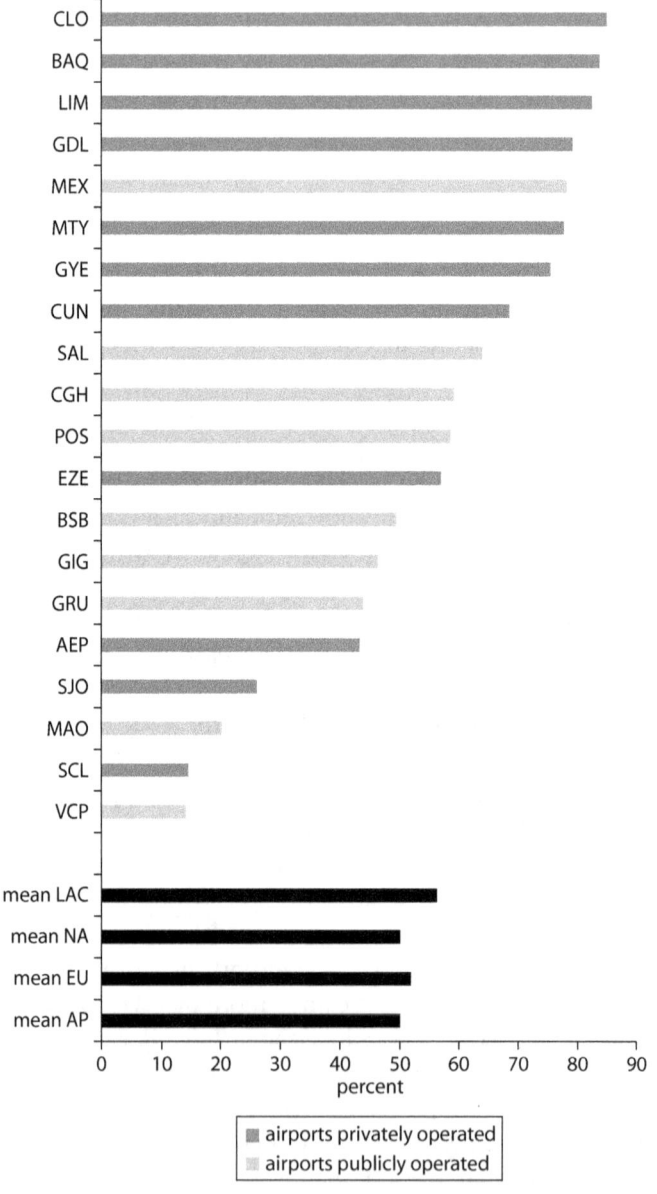

Source: Author's calculation.
Note: LAC = Latin America and the Caribbean; NA = North America; EU = European Union; AP = Asia-Pacific. For a list of airport codes and the airports they represent, see page xxiii.

Figure 3.11 Aeronautical Revenue per Aircraft Movement, 2005

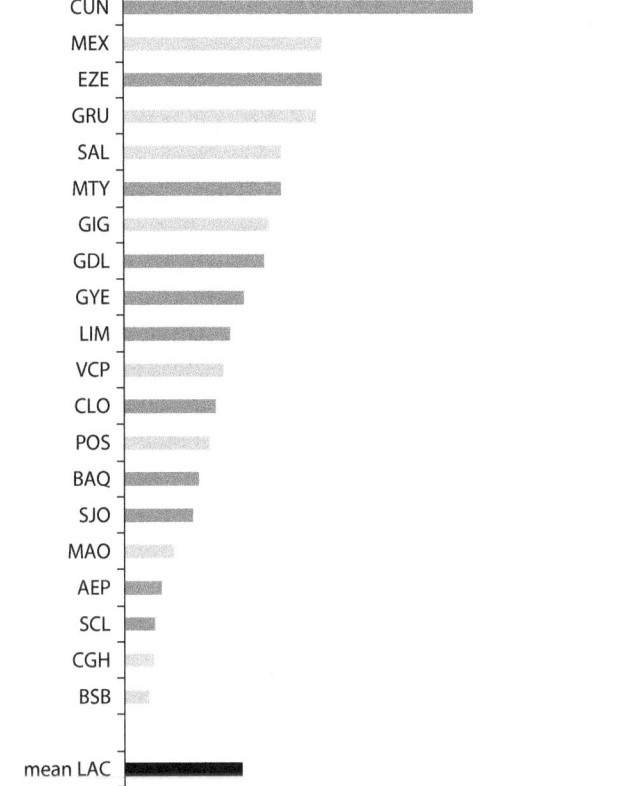

Source: Author's calculation.
Note: LAC = Latin America and the Caribbean; NA = North America; EU: European Union; AUNZ = Australia and New Zealand; AP = Asia-Pacific. For a list of airport codes and the airports they represent, see page xxiii.

tariff regimes that are used to finance airports' costs, with the most common being single till, dual till, compensatory, and residual schemes. It is seldom the case that aeronautical tariffs are set to cover the cost of providing aeronautical services. Instead, tariff structure and levels are set to accomplish other objectives, including providing enough revenue to cross-subsidize loss-making airports, subsidizing domestic passengers, and generating revenue for the government (taxes included in tariffs).

Chapter 5 presents a detailed benchmarking of aeronautical tariffs for 26 airports in Latin America. This comparison provides more detailed information than figure 3.11 about the costs airlines and passengers incur when using a specific airport. The benchmarking shows that there is a significant heterogeneity in the tariff structure across airports in the LAC region, indicating that when setting tariffs, regulatory authorities have very different objectives (the observed dispersion in aeronautical tariffs among airports cannot be explained exclusively by different cost functions).

Passengers per Boarding Bridge and Passengers per Square Meter of Terminal Area

Two interesting partial measures of efficiency are passengers per boarding bridge (figure 3.12) and passengers per square meter of terminal area (figure 3.13). The number of boarding bridges and the area of the terminal are both proxies for capital inputs, while the number of passengers that fly through an airport is one of the outputs of an airport. Hence, these two measures can be read as output per capital input. At the same time, these measures give an idea of the quality of the service provided by the airport, as a large number of passengers per boarding bridge or per square meter of terminal area tell us whether the service provided by the airport could be improved. In the first indicator, if we observe a large number of passengers per boarding bridge, we could infer that the airport relies heavily on remote aircraft parking and bus transportation, which generates discomfort, since passengers need to walk to and from planes unprotected from weather conditions.[11] In the second indicator, a large number of passengers per square meter of terminal area could indicate that the terminal is too crowded, meaning passengers cannot move around at ease. On the other hand, if these ratios are very small, we could conclude that the physical facilities are underused or even infer that the capacity was inadequately planned or, in the other extreme, that the airport is a "white elephant."

The problem when assessing these types of quality variables is that in the case of a low ratio of number of passengers per boarding bridge or per

Figure 3.12 Passengers per Boarding Bridge, 2005

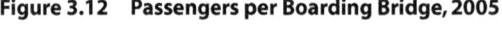

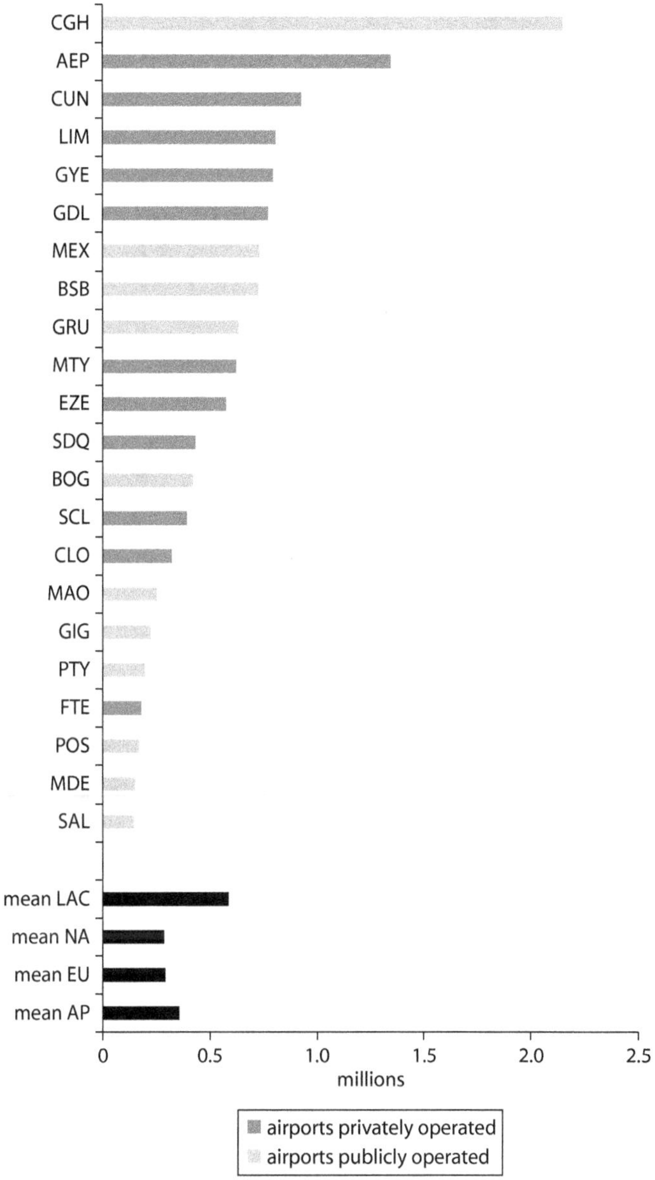

Source: Author's calculation.
Note: LAC = Latin America and the Caribbean; NA = North America; EU = European Union; AP = Asia-Pacific. For a list of airport codes and the airports they represent, see page xxiii.

Figure 3.13 Passengers per Square Meter of Terminal Area, 2005

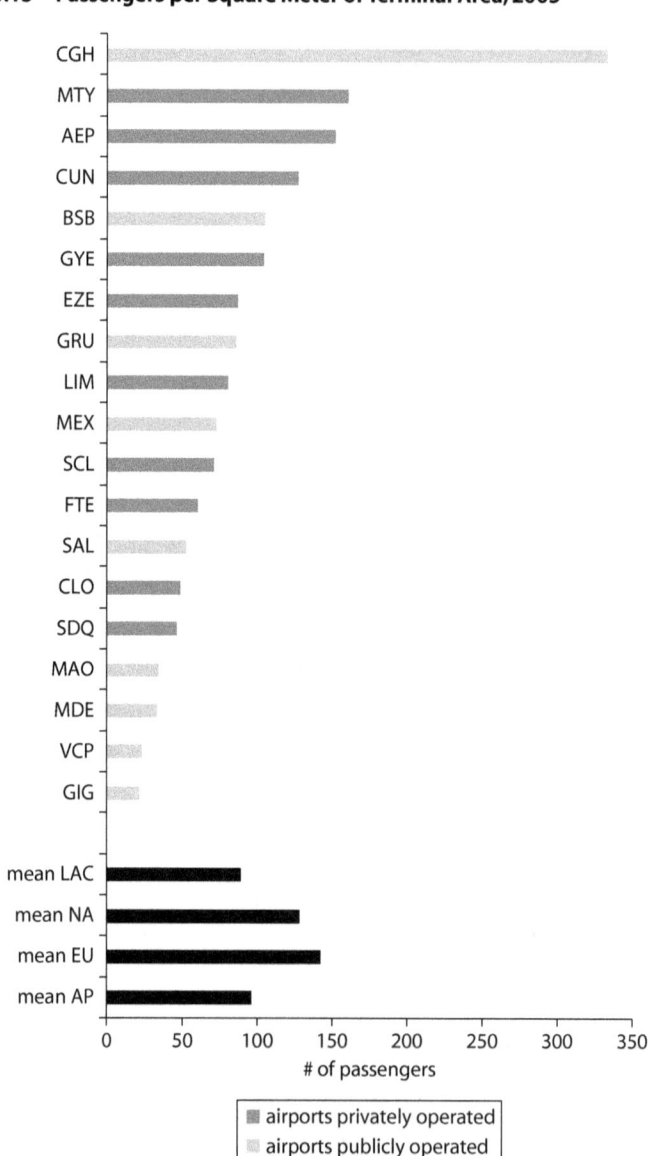

Source: Author's calculation.
Note: LAC = Latin America and the Caribbean; NA = North America; EU = European Union; AP = Asia-Pacific. For a list of airport codes and the airports they represent, see page xxiii.

square meter of terminal area, for example, a growth of the indicator would reflect a more efficient use of the installed capacity (available capital). Once a certain threshold is reached, however, the high intensity of use of the installed capacity would translate into congestion, possible delays in flights and discomfort to passengers, sending a clear signal that more investment is needed. As is the case with runways and terminals, boarding bridges are lump sum investments that generate an optimal cycle of underutilization followed by operation at full capacity.

The average airport in LAC has a small number of boarding bridges relative to the number of passengers (and more shuttle transportation) when compared with those in North America, Europe, and East Asia and Pacific. In North America and Europe, the average ratio of number of passengers to boarding bridges in 2005 was less than 300,000. In that same year, the average airport in East Asia and Pacific had 360,000 passengers per boarding bridge. In Latin America there were 560,000 passengers per boarding bridge in the average airport. The data seem to suggest that LAC airports need more investments in boarding bridges. Eleven airports in LAC had a ratio of more than 500,000 passengers per boarding bridge during 2005. The worst case is Congonhas International (CGH), where there were more than 2 million passengers per boarding bridge.

In the case of passengers per square meter of terminal area, we see that the average airport in Latin America is quite similar to that in East Asia and Pacific, but this ratio is lower than the average airports in Europe and North America. Again, the outlier by far is Congonhas International (CGH), where there were 333 passengers per square meter of terminal area. On the other end of the ranking we find another Brazilian airport, Galeão International (GIG) in Rio de Janeiro, with 22 passengers per square meter. This indicator suggests that there are no significant capacity constraints in LAC airports, or in other words, that there have not been overinvestments in the airport sector. However, the limitation of this indicator is that it does not consider specific daily or seasonal capacity constraints. It is usually the case that airports in LAC have a high concentration of flights during a few hours, especially those that serve international passengers. Anecdotal evidence in LAC indicates that several airports suffer from significant concentrations of passengers at some point during the day, resulting in high usage intensity of available capacity, and accordingly, low level of service quality. The problem is that airports are an example of lump-sum investments that should not be planned based only on peak demand periods. Furthermore, in order to regulate congestion and spread the use of facilities throughout the day, economic incentives to airlines and passengers through differentiated tariffs should be put in place.

The partial performance indicators calculated in this section of the report for LAC airports do not allow us to construct a unique performance ranking of airports. However, the indicators showed weak evidence that a couple of airports, Congonhas (CGH) in Brazil and Santiago de Chile (SCL), are more efficient than the other airports in the region, as they show up more times in the top three performers (table 3.3). By no means was it possible, from the calculated indicators, to conclude whether in 2005, airports operated by the private sector were more efficient than those operated by a state-owned company. These results are not surprising due to the problems associated with the use of partial performance indicators in multi-input, multi-output services (explained in detail in the introduction of this chapter). The next section, by studying the evolution through time of partial performance indicators, tests whether it is possible to identify airports that significantly improved their performance and whether privately operated airports improved their performance more than public airports.

Partial Performance Indicators: Time Series

Studying the evolution of partial performance through time gives the opportunity to answer more questions than the calculation of partial performance indicators for one point in time. By tracking the evolution in time of partial performance indicators, short-run macro- (appreciation of exchange rate, economic recession) and microshocks (construction of a new runway, strike in the major airline in a given airport) do not distort comparisons. In addition, and more interestingly for this report, time series data could give valuable information to test the hypothesis that the introduction of private sector participation (PSP) in airports brought about improvements in performance.

The questionnaires prepared for this report and distributed to the main airport operators in Latin America (see appendix A) covered the period from 1995 to 2007. The purpose of asking for data starting in 1995 was to analyze the evolution of airports' performance in the last decade. In addition, the data would provide the opportunity to make a before and after analysis of the introduction of PSP, given that private sector participation in the operation of the major airports in the region began in the late 1990s.

Table 3.3 Summary of Airport Partial Performance Indicators—Top and Bottom Performers, 2005

Partial performance indicator	Top 3 performers	Bottom 3 performers
Passengers per aircraft movement	• Buenos Aires, Argentina (EZE) • Cancún, Mexico (CUN) • Santiago, Chile (SCL)	• São Paulo, Brazil (VCP) • Guatemala City, Guatemala (GUA) • Nassau, Bahamas, The (NAS)
Cargo per aircraft movement (tons)	• São Paulo, Brazil (VCP) • Santiago, Chile (SCL) • Manaus, Brazil (MAO)	• São Paulo, Brazil (CGH) • Cancún, Mexico (CUN) • El Calafate, Argentina (FTE)
Cargo per dedicated aircraft movement (tons)	• Santiago, Chile (SCL) • Lima, Peru (LIM) • Buenos Aires, Argentina (EZE)	• Panama City, Panama (PTY) • Santo Domingo, Dominican Republic (SDQ) • Monterrey, Mexico (MTY)
Passengers per employee	• Santiago, Chile (SCL) • São Paulo, Brazil (CGH) • Cali, Colombia (CLO)	• Manaus, Brazil (MAO) • Panama City, Panama (PTY) • São Paulo, Brazil (VCP)
Aircraft movements per runway	• Mexico City, Mexico (MEX) • São Paulo, Brazil (CGH) • Bogotá, Colombia (BOG)	• Panama City, Panama (PTY) • San Salvador, El Salvador (SAL) • El Calafate, Argentina (FTE)
Labor costs as a share of operating costs	• Guayaquil, Ecuador (GYE) • Buenos Aires, Argentina (AEP) • Cali, Colombia (CLO)	• Barranquilla, Colombia (BAQ) • Guadalajara, Mexico (GDL) • Brasilia, Brazil (BSB)
Labor cost per passenger (US$)	• Cali, Colombia (CLO) • Santiago, Chile (SCL) • São Paulo, Brazil (CGH)	• Panama City, Panama (PTY) • Manaus, Brazil (MAO) • Rio de Janeiro, Brazil (GIG)
Operating cost per passenger (US$)	• Brasilia, Brasil (BSB) • Lima, Peru (LIM) • São Paulo, Brazil (CGH)	• Manaus, Brazil (MAO) • Rio de Janeiro, Brazil (GIG) • Guayaquil, Ecuador (GYE)

(continued next page)

Table 3.3 *(continued)*

Partial performance indicator	Top 3 performers	Bottom 3 performers
Operating cost per aircraft movement (US$)	• São Paulo, Brazil (VCP) • Rio de Janeiro, Brazil (GIG) • Buenos Aires, Argentina (EZE)	• Brasilia, Brasil (BSB) • Lima, Peru (LIM) • São Paulo, Brazil (CGH)
Total revenue per passenger (US$)	• Manaus, Brazil (MAO) • San José, Costa Rica (SJO) • Cancún, Mexico (CUN)	• Buenos Aires, Argentina (AEP) • Brasilia, Brazil (BSB) • São Paulo, Brazil (CGH)
Aeronautical revenue share	• Cali, Colombia (CLO) • Barranquilla, Colombia (BAQ) • Lima, Peru (LIM)	• Manaus, Brazil (MAO) • Santiago, Chile (SCL) • São Paulo, Brazil (VCP)
Aeronautical revenue per aircraft movement (US$)	• Cancún, Mexico (CUN) • Mexico City, Mexico (MEX) • Buenos Aires, Argentina (EZE)	• Santiago, Chile (SCL) • São Paulo, Brazil (CGH) • Brasilia, Brazil (BSB)
Passengers per boarding bridge	• São Paulo, Brazil (CGH) • Buenos Aires, Argentina (AEP) • Cancún, Mexico (CUN)	• Port of Spain, Trinidad and Tobago (POS) • Medellín, Colombia (MDE) • San Salvador, El Salvador (SAL)
Passengers per square meter of terminal area	• São Paulo, Brazil (CGH) • Monterrey, Mexico (MTY) • Buenos Aires, Argentina (AEP)	• Medellín, Colombia (MDE) • São Paulo, Brazil (VCP) • Rio de Janeiro, Brazil (GIG)

Source: Author's compilation.

Note: Top performers for the indicators: labor cost per passenger, operating cost per passenger, and operating cost per aircraft movement are those airports for which the indicators show the *lowest* value. As noted in the text, the *highest* value of the indicators' aeronautical revenue share and aeronautical revenue per aircraft movement should not be directly interpreted as synonymous with top performance.

As was explained in the introduction of this chapter, airport performance in developing countries has seldom been the subject of in-depth research. This has not been the case for other infrastructure sectors in developing countries, in particular in Latin America. This report benefited from a recent research project by Andrés, Guasch, and Lopez (2008), who conducted a thorough evaluation of the impact of PSP on electricity distribution, fixed-line telecommunications, and water and sewerage in Latin America by comparing the evolution of selected indicators before and after the introduction of private sector participation in the management of utilities.[12] These authors identify three distinct periods: (a) the pretransition or preprivatization period, referring to the three years before the transition period; (b) the transition period, starting two years before the privatization or concession was awarded and ending one year after award; and (c) the posttransition or postprivatization period, referring to the four years after the transition. The results indicate that changes in management and ownership generated significant improvements in labor productivity, efficiency, and product/service quality in the three infrastructure sectors analyzed. However, changes are not very remarkable in the posttransition period, suggesting that most of the efficiency gains took place during the transition period.

Unfortunately, very few of the private airport operators that responded to the questionnaire provided data for the years before the change in ownership. The reason cited was that the data are not available and that they could not share the data used for the preparation of the ownership changeover bidding documents. This was an expected although not a desirable outcome of the preparation process of this report. It is usually the case that private operators have limited access to information about the firm before the change of control. Moreover, once private sector participation is introduced, the former state operator, and in some cases the ministerial department that supervised the state operator, are dismantled and human resources and institutional memory lost as a result. Thus, constructing reliable time series of key performance data is a daunting and often impossible task. For those airports under private operation included in our dataset, the available data start in the year the concession was awarded. Hence, it is not possible to undertake a before and after comparison of performance indicators. Given these data constraints, the focus of this section is to identify patterns and major changes, if any, in the evolution of performance indicators in the posttransition or postprivatization period.

Before proceeding to show the results of the calculation of time series partial performance indicators, it is important to make a note about the use of currencies, exchange rates, and inflation. To ensure consistency and comparability between airports from several countries, measures of income and cost used need to be expressed in the same currency. All partial performance measures that are expressed in monetary terms are affected by the exchange rate, which can bias the comparison of these measures among airports located in different countries. For example, the analysis of partial performance measures elaborated for this report for the year 2005 show that the average European airport ranked at the bottom on any of the cost-related partial measures. This result could indicate that a difference in real costs exists between Europe and other regions or it could be the result of a temporary appreciation of the euro during 2005. As figure 3.14 illustrates, that was not the case, since the euro actually suffered a temporary depreciation in 2005. However, if the analysis had been done for the year 2008, it is likely that the cost difference between the average European airport and the average airports in other regions would have been bigger, given the higher value of the exchange rate (U.S. dollar per euro) in 2008.

Also, an analysis based on one point in time (in this case only one year, 2005) might be influenced by the fact that different countries might be at different stages of the economic cycle. For instance, if a country is just coming out of a recession that negatively affected passenger volumes, this will likely bias some partial performance indicators, such as passengers per square meter or passengers per boarding bridge.

When analyzing the evolution of partial performance measures through time, it is necessary not only to express income and cost measures in the same currency, but also to remove the effect of inflation. If costs are not expressed in real prices, a generalized increase in prices could cause an increase in some partial performance measures, such as operating costs per employee or labor costs per passenger, wrongly signaling a decrease in productivity. In addition, by expressing all income and cost measures in U.S. dollars of a given year, the effect of fluctuations in the exchange rate is removed. For these reasons, the income and cost measures used in the analysis were first expressed in local 2005 prices and then in U.S. dollars using the average exchange rate for 2005.[13]

For presentation purposes, only selected partial performance indicators and a representative sample of airports that responded to the questionnaire were used in the time series analysis.[14] The database assembled enables the classification of LAC airports into three groups based on the

Figure 3.14 Evolution of the U.S. Dollar–Euro Exchange Rate, 1999–2009

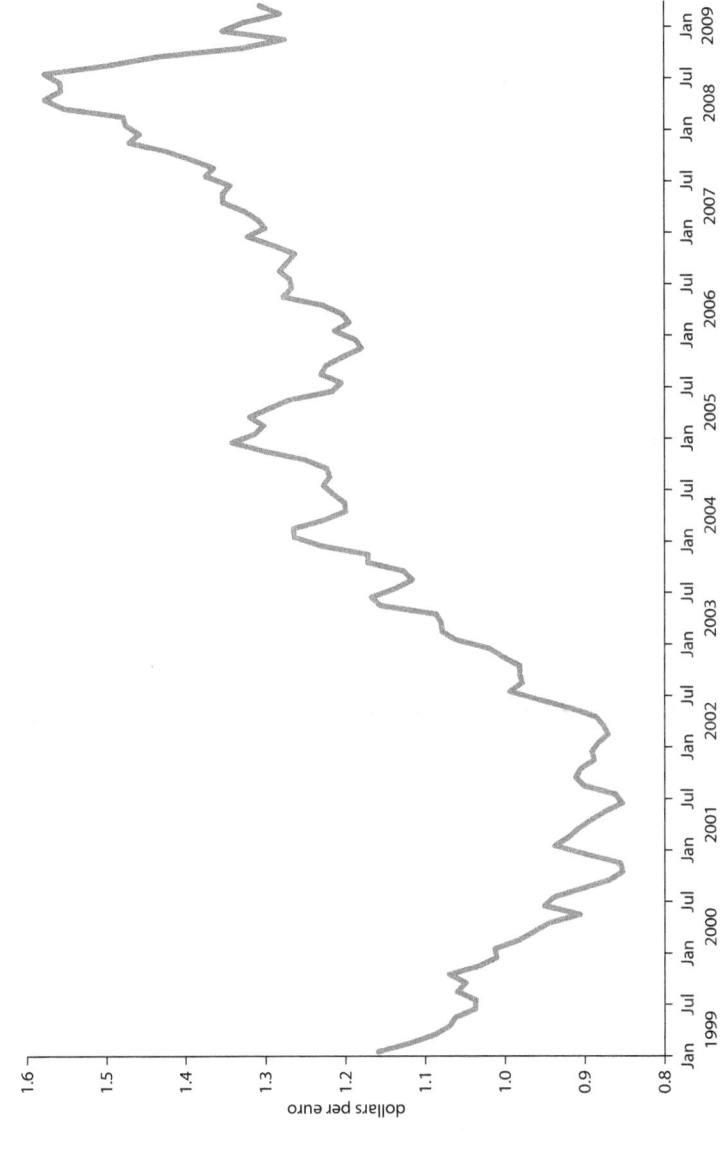

Source: Author's calculation.

number of passengers handled in 2005. The first group, with airports serving more than 15 million passengers, is the smallest and includes only three airports: Mexico City's Benito Juárez International Airport (MEX), Congonhas International (CGH), and Guarulhos International (GRU), both located in São Paulo. The second group consists of 10 airports that served between 5 million and 10 million passengers in 2005, but performance indicators are shown for five airports: Cancún International Airport (CUN), El Dorado International Airport (BOG) in Bogotá, Comodoro Arturo Merino Benítez International Airport (SCL) in Santiago de Chile, Ministro Pistarini International Airport (EZE) in Buenos Aires, and Jorge Chávez International Airport (LIM) in Lima. The third group comprises 14 airports that served less than 5 million passengers in 2005, and results are shown for four airports: Juan Santamaria International Airport (SJO) in San José, José Joaquín de Olmedo International Airport (GYE) in Guayaquil, Tocumen International Airport (PTY) in Panama City, and Piarco International Airport (POS) in Port of Spain.

In the following figures the airports operated by the government or a government-owned enterprise are in light gray, while those under concession are in dark gray,. All graphs also include the average of the partial performance measure for the airports in LAC for the year 2005. Each airport is identified by its code (three letters).

Passengers per Employee

Figure 3.15 shows that, with the exception of a few cases, there is not a clear increase in the number of passengers per employee. The airports in Santiago de Chile (SCL), San José (SJO), Panama City (PTY), and São Paulo (CGH and GRU) had an increase in productive efficiency measured by the indicator passengers per employee. Simple observation of these figures does not make it possible to draw any conclusion about a trend in the evolution of this indicator, as some privately operated airports improved while others did not. Moreover, a similar pattern is observed for publicly operated airports.

The case of Ministro Pistarini Airport (EZE) in Buenos Aires is interesting and illustrates important caveats to the analysis of performance in the airport sector. EZE experienced a significant drop in passengers per employee between 2000 and 2002 (a drop on the order of 50,000 passengers per employee to 16,000). The change was mainly due to a 34 percent decrease in the number of passengers, which was caused by a significant economic crisis after Argentina devalued its

Figure 3.15   Passengers per Employee

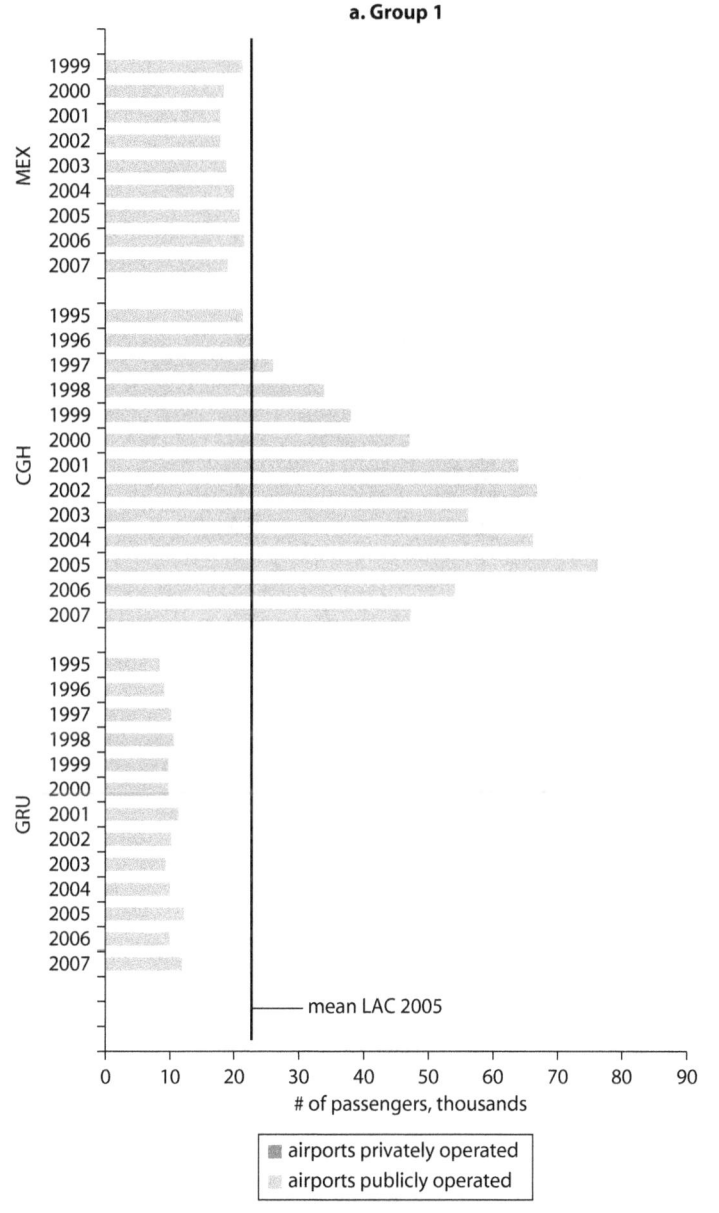

(continued next page)

Figure 3.15 *(continued)*

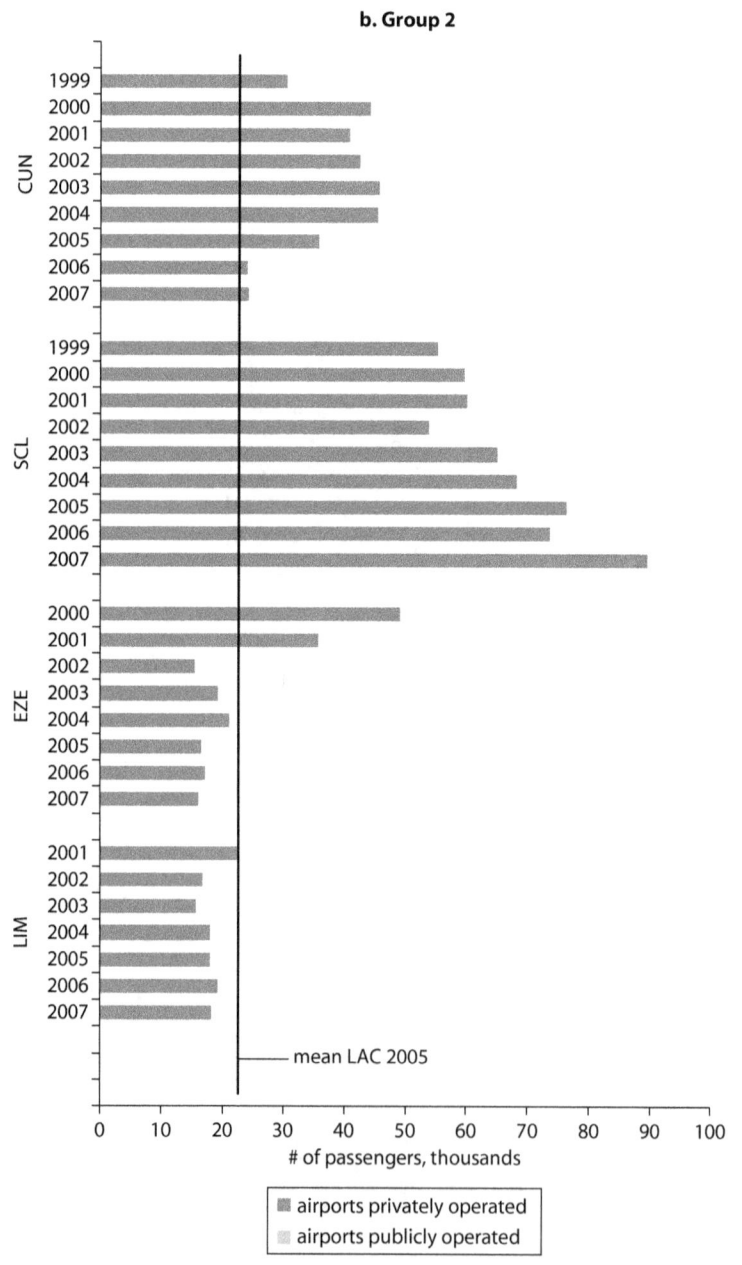

(continued next page)

Figure 3.15 *(continued)*

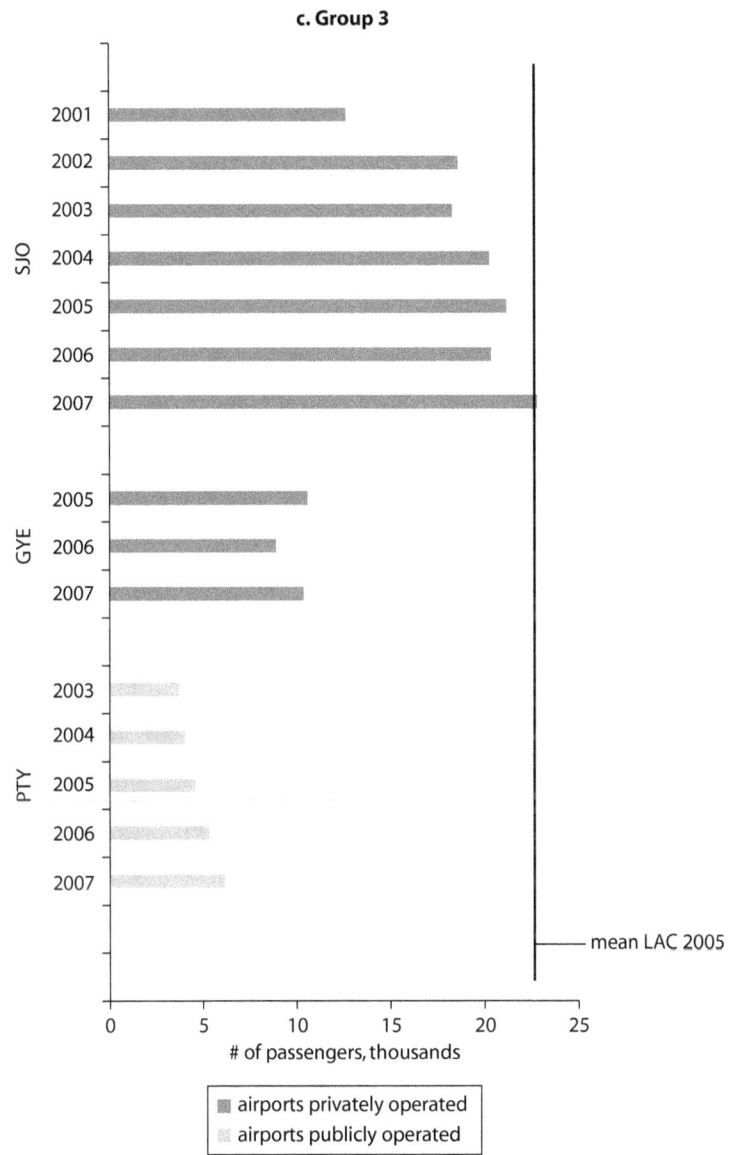

Source: Author's calculation.
Note: For a list of airport codes and the airports they represent, see page xxiii.

currency and defaulted on its external debt. Because airports face a derived demand from the demand for air transport services, it is difficult to adjust production inputs during recessions or negative demand shocks. Accordingly, when benchmarking airports, caution needs to be exercised, as airports could be facing very different economic environments. It could be the case that some of the most commonly cited efficiency performance indicators can deteriorate for reasons out of the airport operator's control. This is one of the main reasons why airport regulators have not fully incorporated benchmarking techniques to set efficiency gain variables in tariff regimes (for a comprehensive justification and discussion of the use of benchmarking techniques to set tariffs, see CAA 2000).

Labor Costs per Passenger

Figure 3.16 depicts labor costs per passenger for the three groups of airports. Most of the airports in the three groups have reduced the amount spent per passenger in labor-related expenses during the period analyzed. In 1996, Guarulhos International (GRU) spent US$2.98 per passenger in labor-related expenses, while in 2006 it spent only US$1.15 per passenger. In Mexico City's airport (MEX), the ratio of labor costs per passenger, measured in 2005 U.S. dollars, shifted from US$1.33 in 2000 to US$0.93 in 2006. In Cancún's airport (CUN) this ratio decreased from US$0.74 in 1999 to US$0.44 in 2004, but then increased to US$0.84 in 2006. In the case of Lima's airport (LIM), data are available for three years (2001–03). During this period the amount spent per passenger in labor-related expenses increased almost 40 percent.

Operating Costs per Passenger

When analyzing a broader measure of cost efficiency, such as operating costs per passenger, only a few airports present a clear trend during the period analyzed (figure 3.17). Only Guarulhos International (GRU) and the airport in Guayaquil (GYE) experienced a steady decrease in the ratio of operating costs to number of passengers. The airport in San José (SJO) also experienced a decrease in this ratio for all but one of the years analyzed, while for Congonhas International (CGH), the ratio of operating costs to number of passengers decreased for most of the years until 2005, but started increasing in 2006. At the Ministro Pistarini (EZE) airport in Argentina, the operating costs per passenger, measured in 2005 U.S. dollars, ranged from US$7.51 to US$32.35 during the eight-year

Figure 3.16 Labor Costs per Passenger

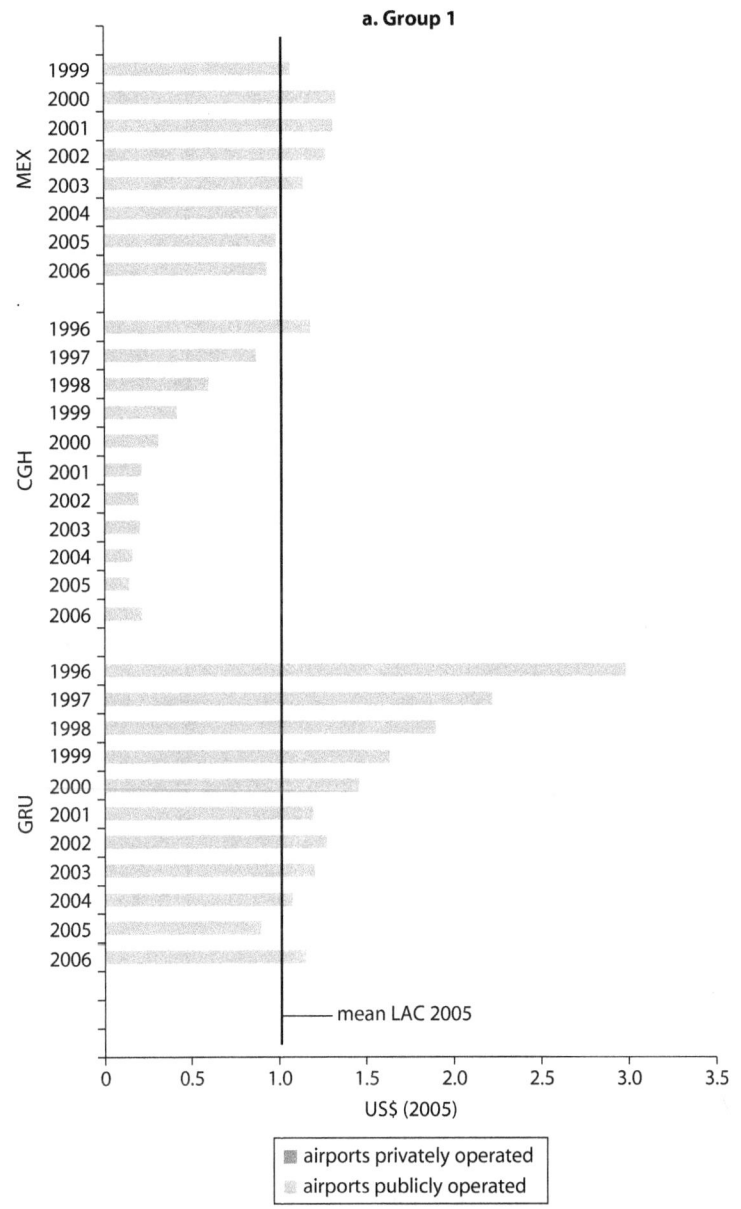

a. Group 1

(continued next page)

96 Airport Economics in Latin America and the Caribbean

Figure 3.16 *(continued)*

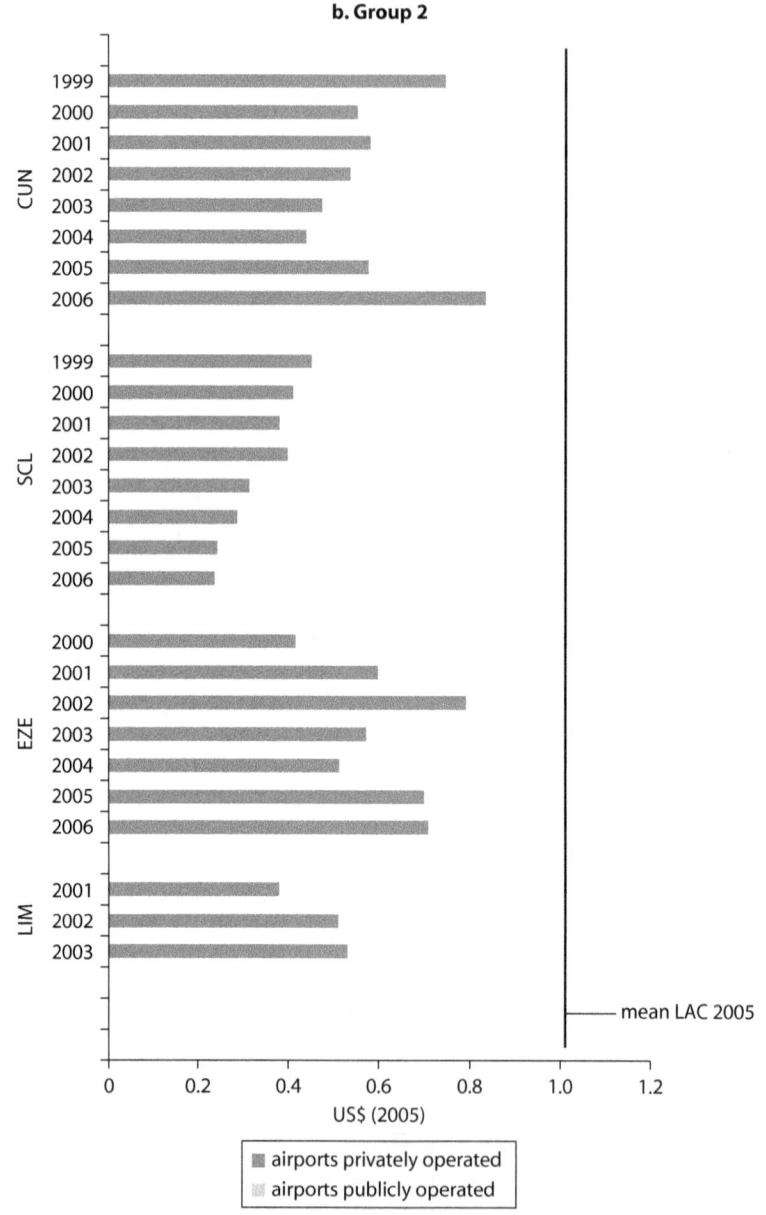

(continued next page)

Figure 3.16 *(continued)*

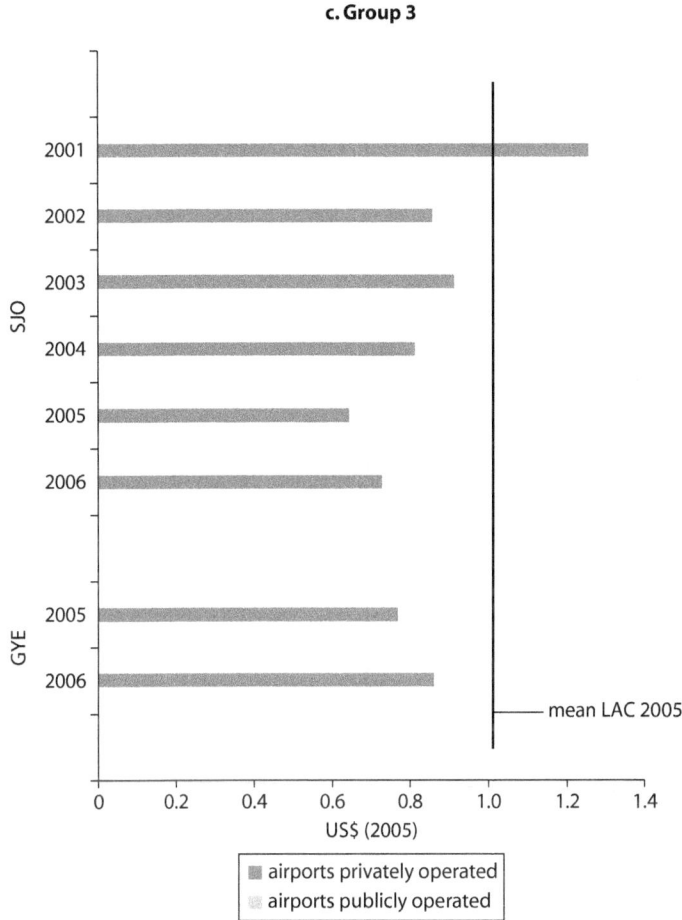

Source: Author's calculation.
Note: For a list of airport codes and the airports they represent, see page xxiii.

period starting in 2000. In the case of Santiago de Chile's (SCL) airport, this same partial performance measure ranged from US$2.00 to US$3.30 between 1999 and 2007.

The evolution of the two cost efficiency measures, labor costs per passenger and operating costs per passenger, does not enable us to draw definite conclusions. It appears the airports experienced an overall reduction in both cost indicators between 1996 and 2007. However, there are wide differences across airports. No conclusion can be drawn

Figure 3.17 Operating Costs per Passenger

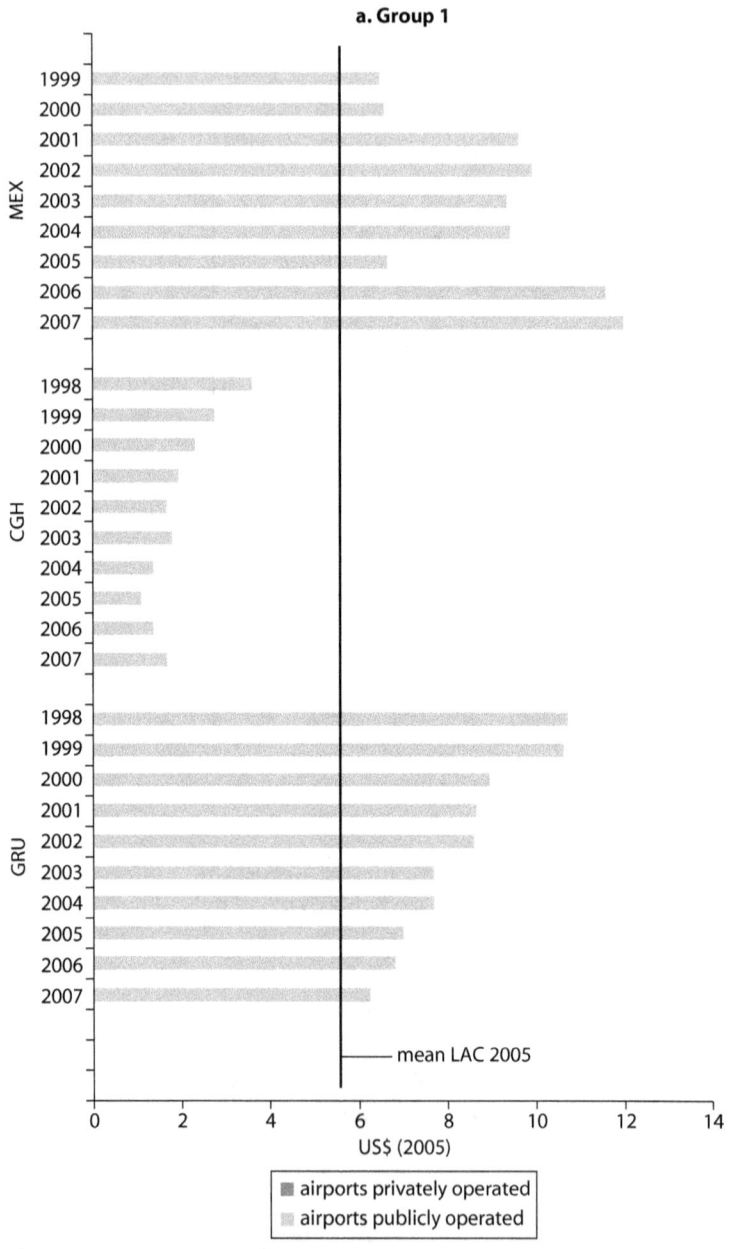

(continued next page)

Figure 3.17 *(continued)*

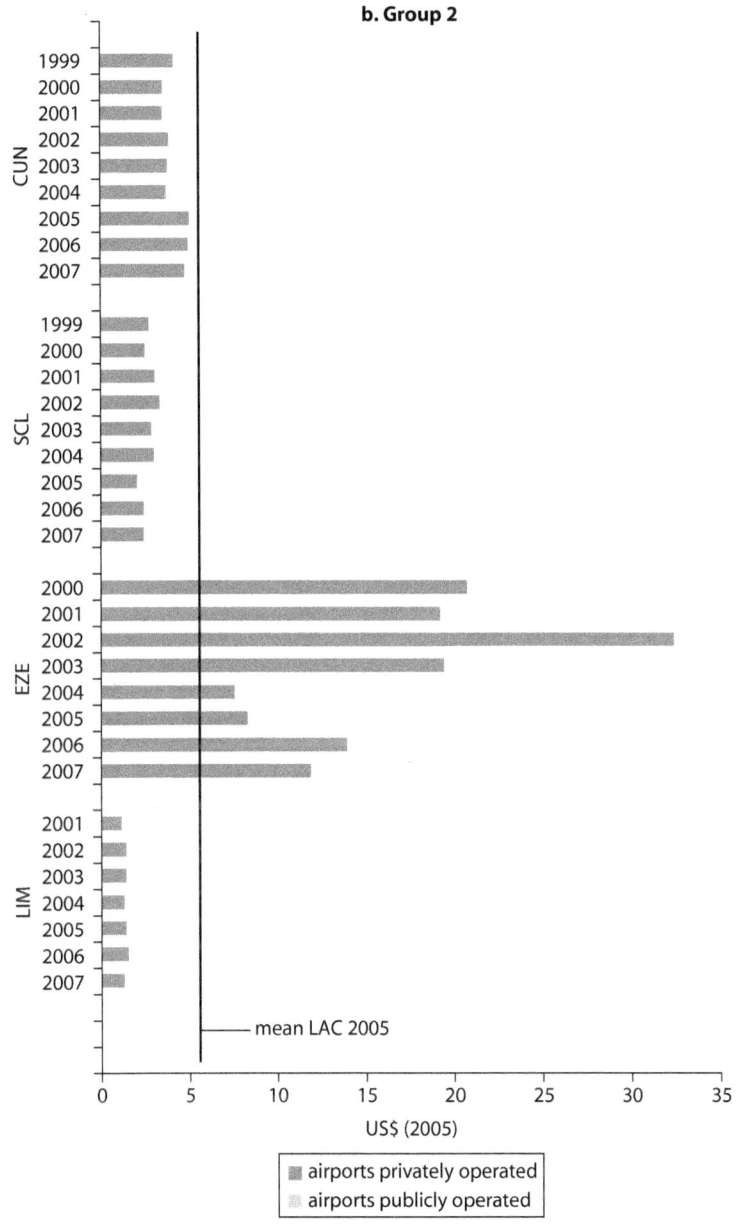

(continued next page)

Figure 3.17 *(continued)*

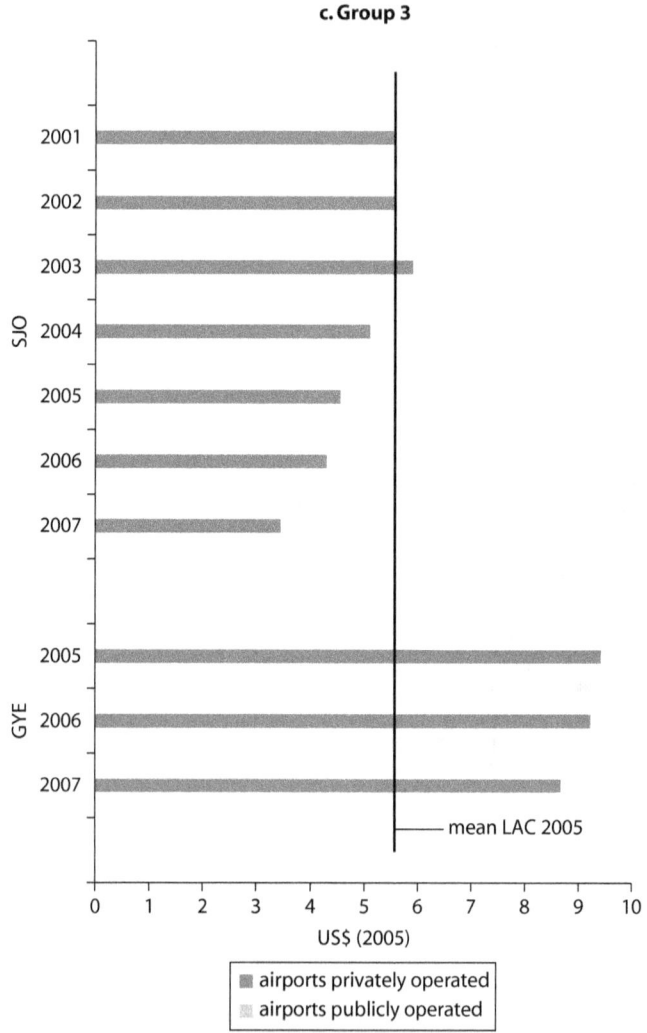

Source: Author's calculation.
Note: For a list of airport codes and the airports they represent, see page xxiii.

when airports are divided by type of operator (public or private) or even by size.

Revenue Indicators

Revenue indicators are important for efficiency analysis, as they provide a signal on how well an airport is generating revenues with the same or even fewer inputs than its competitors (figure 3.18). Considering the airports included in our dataset, only one airport (Cancún) shows a steady growth trend of the ratio of total revenues to passengers. The evidence for the other airports is mixed, with some airports showing important gains and others showing a significant reduction. As with the previous indicators, it is not possible to draw conclusions on the behavior of the ratio of total revenues per passenger across size of airport or type of operator (public or private).

Revenue per Employee

When analyzing the total revenue generated by the average employee in each airport (figure 3.19), a contrast can be observed between the airports in Santiago de Chile (SCL) and in Buenos Aires (EZE). The total revenue per employee in SCL was increasing from 1999 to 2007, with only small decreases in 2002 and 2006. In contrast, the total revenue per employee in EZE significantly decreased from 2000 to 2007, and particularly between 2000 and 2003. Congonhas International (CGH) and Guarulhos International (GRU) both in Brazil have also experienced a decrease in the total revenue per employee, but these have been more moderate than the decrease in EZE. In CGH and GRU, the total revenue per employee decreased 12 percent and 27 percent, respectively, between 2000 and 2007, while in EZE it decreased 67 percent during the same period. In Cancún (CUN) the total revenue per employee had an erratic behavior, while in Mexico City's airport (MEX) as well as in Lima's (LIM) it has remained stable.

According to the information gathered in the database, the fluctuation of this indicator is explained mostly by changes in revenues rather than in the quantity of employees. That is expected, as employment is difficult to adjust. Even though it is not possible to provide a robust conclusion regarding the relationship between ownership and the level and trend of this indicator, it seems that private operators perform better, both in the improvement through time of this indicator and the absolute level (that is, revenue per employee is higher in airports operated by the private sector).

Quality Indicators

There are several other partial performance indicators that can be studied. Ideally, revenue and cost indicators should be complemented and expanded with quality indicators. However, there are very few airports and virtually no regulator that releases data on the evolution of quality variables. There are, nonetheless, certain measures that give a proxy of the

Figure 3.18 Total Revenue per Passenger

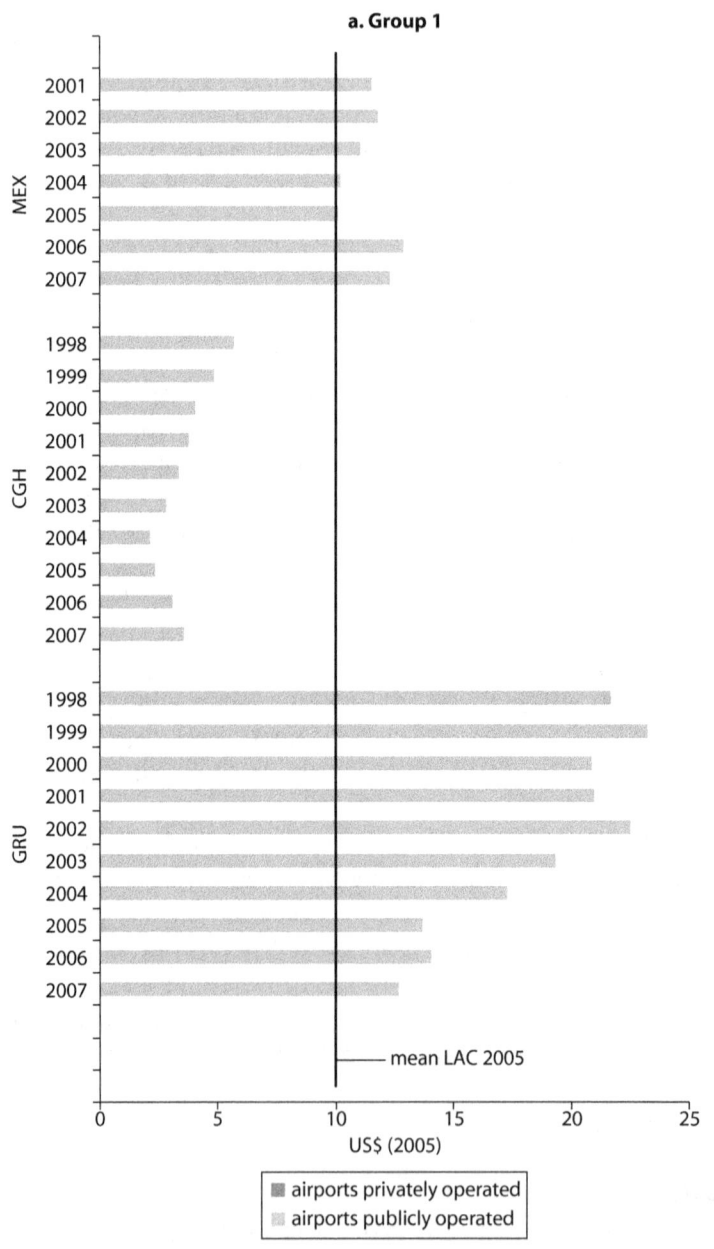

(continued next page)

Figure 3.18 *(continued)*

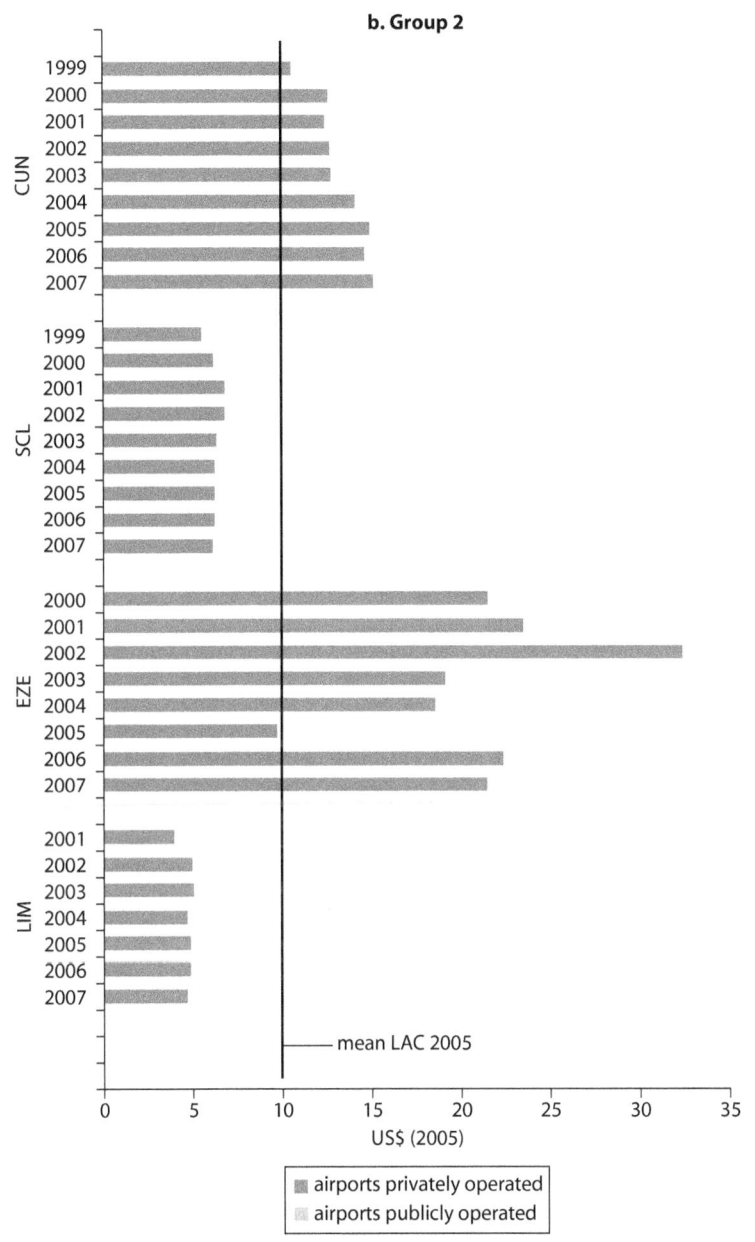

(continued next page)

Figure 3.18 *(continued)*

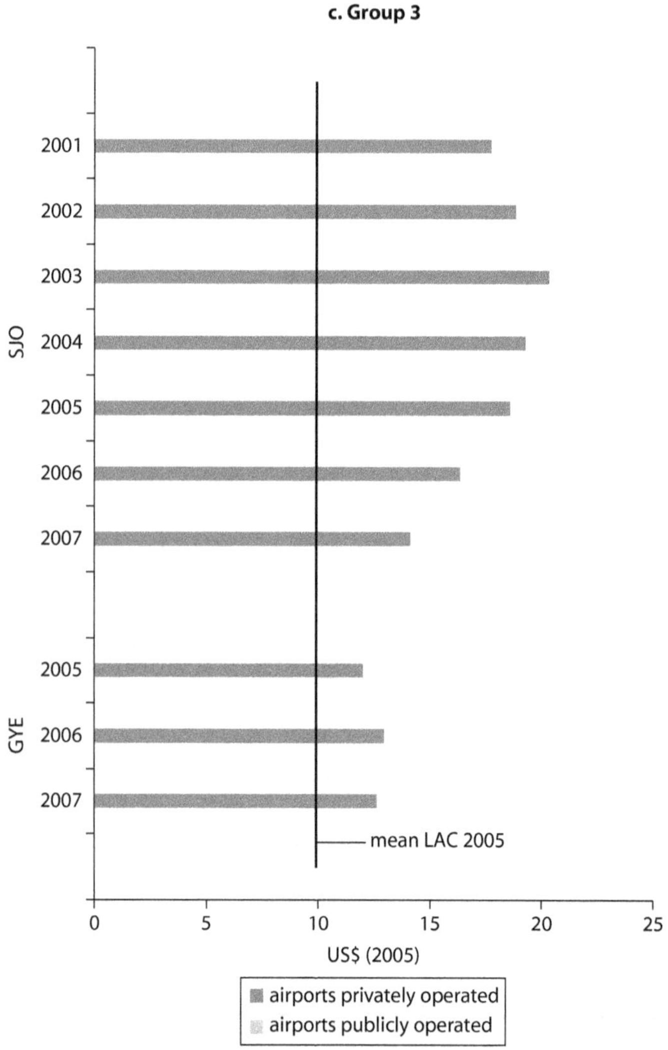

c. Group 3

Source: Author's calculation.
Note: For a list of airport codes and the airports they represent, see page xxiii.

quality of service provided by the airport, such as the previously described passengers per boarding bridge and passengers per square meter of terminal area.

Figure 3.20 shows the evolution of passengers per boarding bridge. Noteworthy are the large drops in the number of passengers per boarding bridge in Mexico City (MEX), Cancún (CAN), Santiago de Chile (SCL), Bogotá (BOG), Guayaquil (GYE), and Panama City (PTY). The decrease in the number of passengers per boarding bridge observed in Mexico City's airport (MEX) in 2001 and 2007 are the consequence of an addition of eight and twenty-three new boarding bridges, respectively. On the

Figure 3.19 Total Revenue per Employee

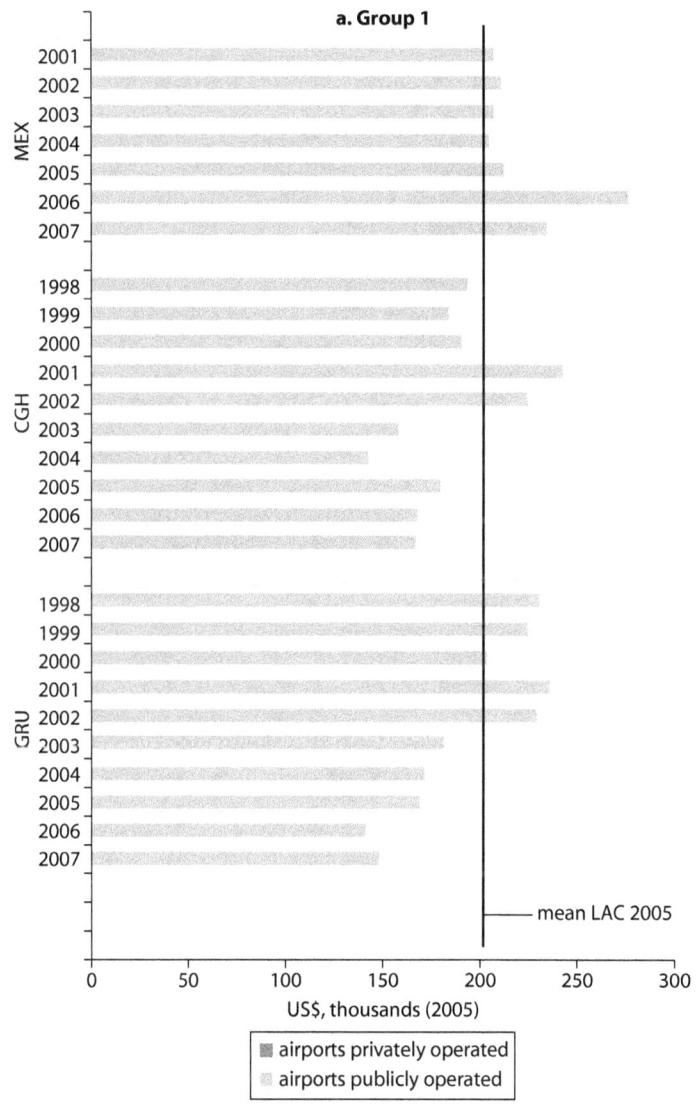

(continued next page)

Figure 3.19 *(continued)*

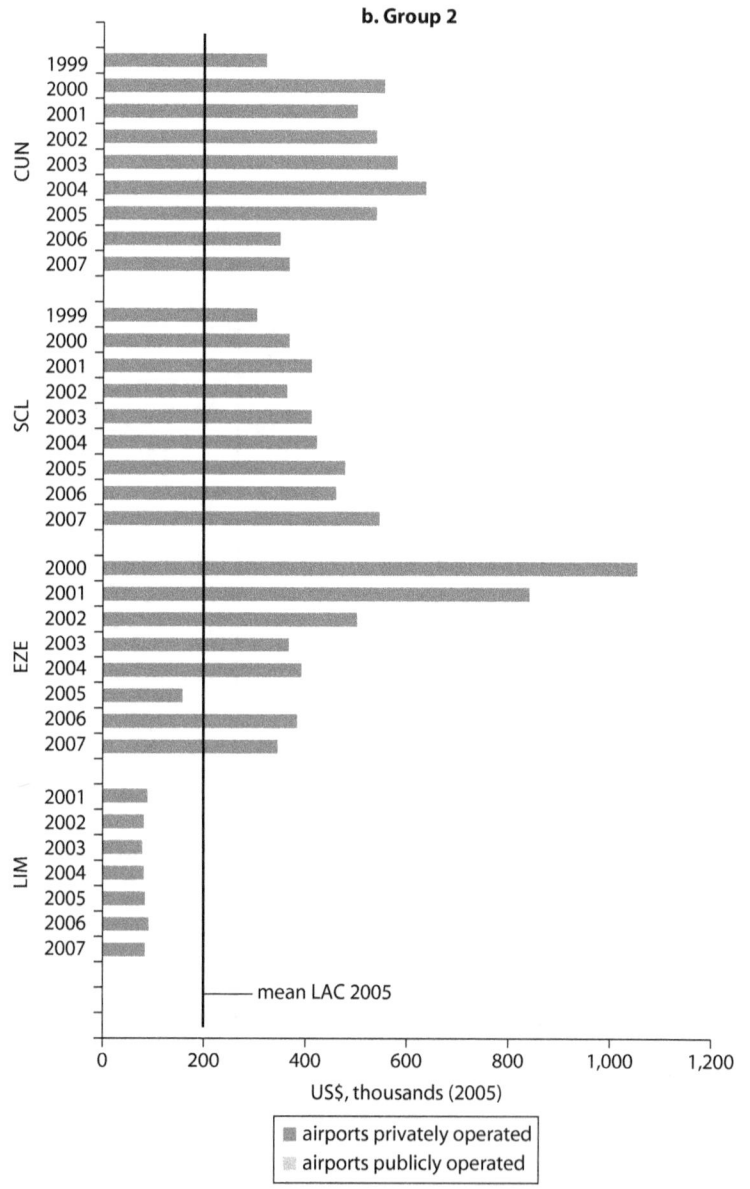

(continued next page)

Figure 3.19 *(continued)*

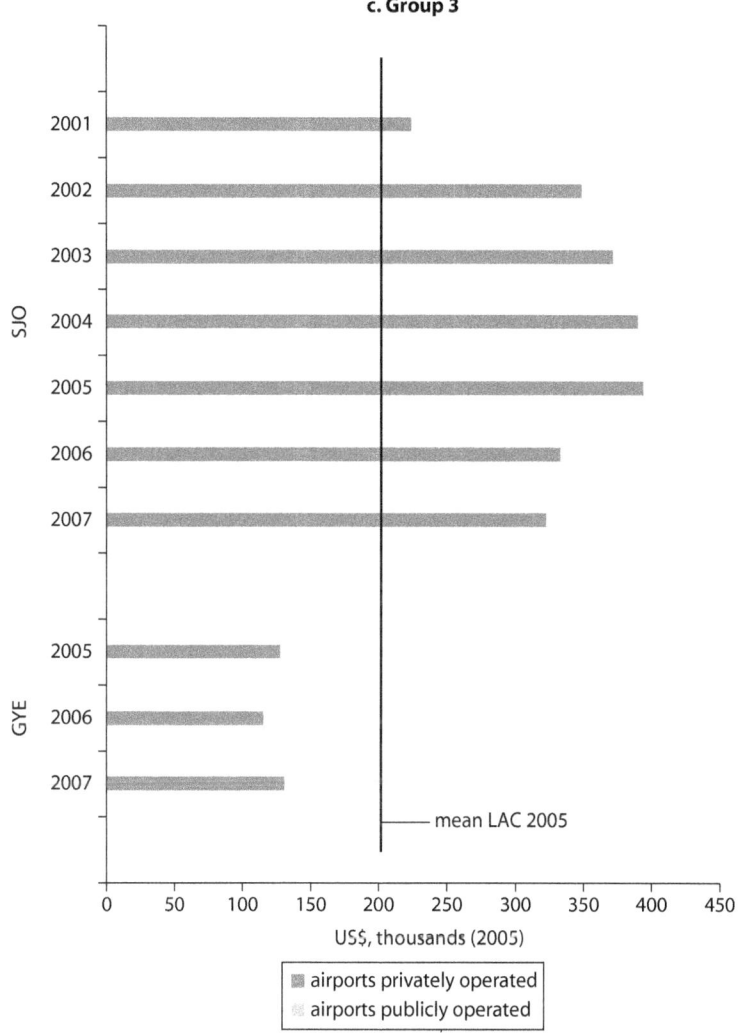

Source: Author's calculation.
Note: For a list of airport codes and the airports they represent, see page xxiii.

other hand, Cancún's airport added 11 new boarding bridges in 2007, while Santiago de Chile's airport added 6 boarding bridges in 1999 and 7 in 2001. This was also the case in Bogotá's airport in 2001 and Guayaquil's and Panama City's airports in 2006.

The calculation of the time evolution of partial performance indicators carried out in this section provided more information to assess airports' performance. To facilitate the presentation, airports were divided in groups using size as the grouping criterion. As was the case with the comparison of partial performance indicators for the year 2005, the time series evolution of partial performance indicators does not allow the

Figure 3.20   Passengers per Boarding Bridge

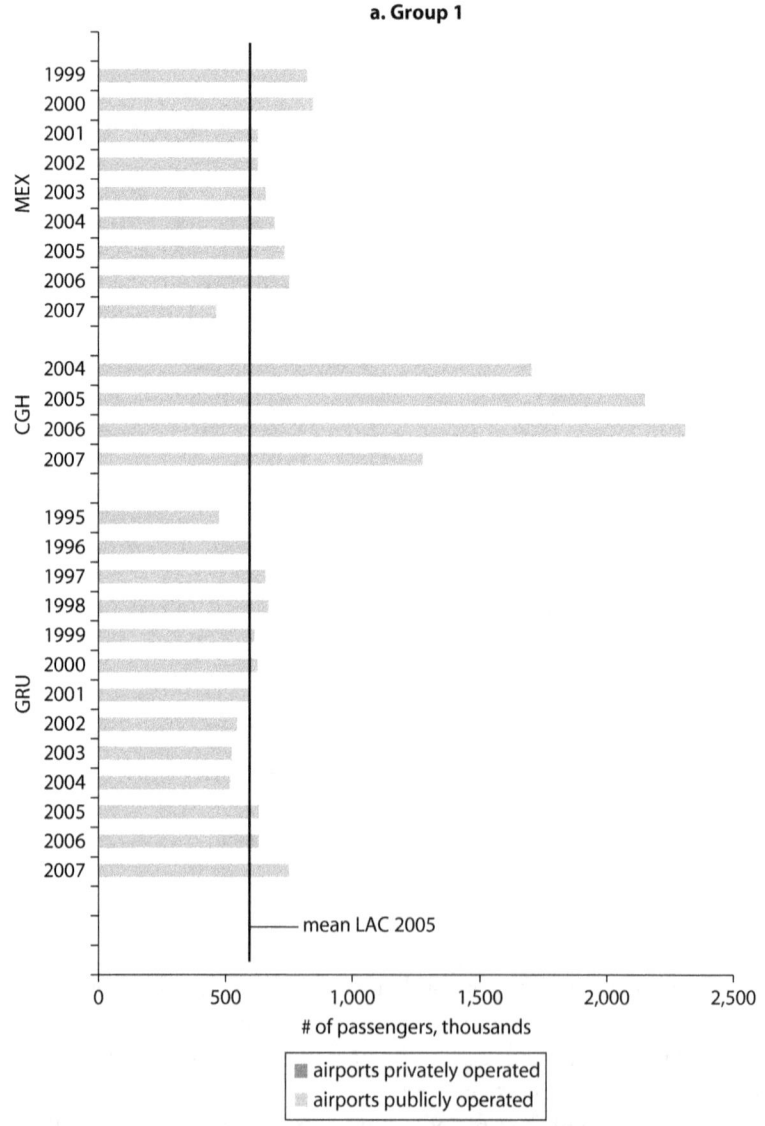

(continued next page)

Efficiency Estimation 109

Figure 3.20 *(continued)*

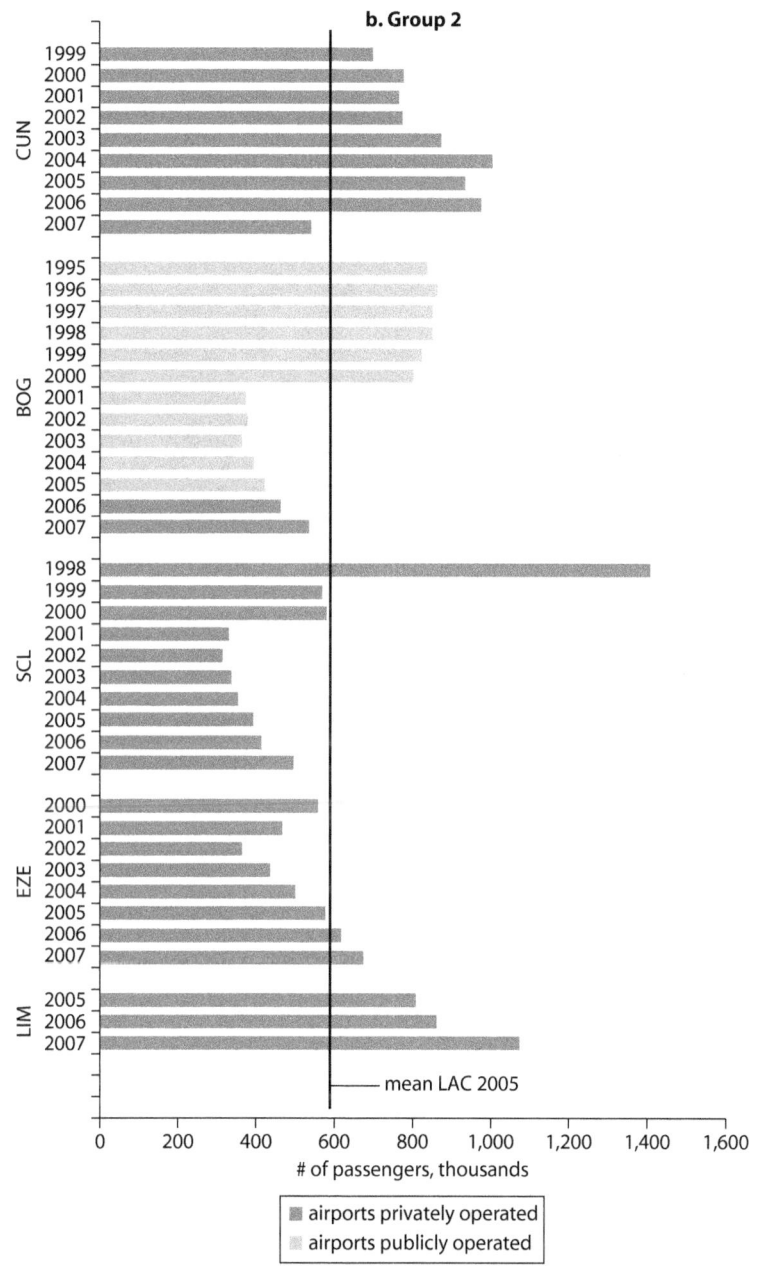

(continued next page)

Figure 3.20 *(continued)*

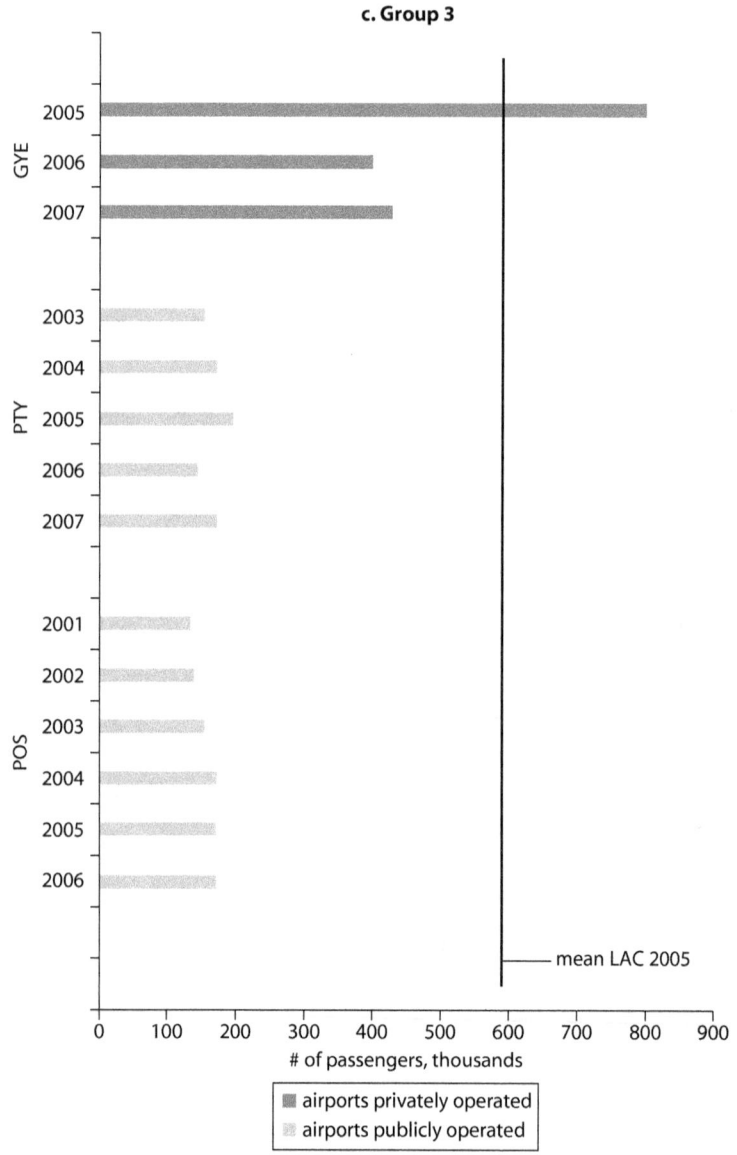

Source: Author's calculation.
Note: For a list of airport codes and the airports they represent, see page xxiii.

generation of a single measure of efficiency to rank the performance of airports. To that end and following the recent evolution in the specialized literature, the next section calculates aggregate measures of efficiency and compares its evolution for LAC airports.

Measuring Technical Efficiency of Airports in LAC Countries

In order to overcome the shortcomings of partial performance indicators, this section computes aggregate productivity measures. By taking advantage of a database collected by the Air Transport Research Society for the main airports in Asia, Europe, and North America and the use of the responses received to the questionnaire sent to Latin American airports, this section presents the computation of a worldwide benchmark for Latin American airports.

The content of this section is quite technical, as it reflects the latest developments in the specialized literature on the computation of efficiency frontiers. To the extent possible, the intuition behind the results is laid out, and an introduction based on graphical representations of theoretical concepts precedes the results.[15]

The DEA approach was chosen among the different productivity measures most frequently used to compute technical efficiency scores. The selection of DEA is explained by the availability of data and their quality. Ideally, further research should be conducted with other approaches to test whether the results are consistent across estimation techniques.

This section is divided into three parts. The first computes a DEA frontier for commercial airports around the world using data for the years 2005 and 2006. This estimation allows the identification of the performance of LAC airports relative to the best practices in the sector. For each airport in the LAC region, it was possible to assess if it is on the frontier that is defined by the most efficient airports in the sample. If it is not, then the set of airports (referred to as peers) with similar productive characteristics that make up the frontier for each airport is identified.

The second part of this section attempts to identify factors that drive the differences in observed efficiency in the airport sector. In order to do this a truncated regression model is estimated, using the efficiency scores obtained from the DEA efficiency frontier estimation as dependent variables. Several variables that attempt to capture the institutional framework and socioeconomic environment in which the airport operates, as well as specific characteristics of each airport (share of aeronautical revenues, hub airport, among others) are included as independent, or explanatory, variables.

Finally, the third part measures the total factor productivity change (TFPC) for LAC airports over the period 1995–2007. The methodology used, which is explained in detail below, consists of the computation of a Malmquist quantity index of TFPC based on the nonparametric DEA approach.

Computing a Worldwide Airport Efficiency Frontier

In this subsection, technical efficiency scores for 148 airports worldwide are computed and a DEA activity frontier is built. The data comprises the years 2005 and 2006 from 22 LAC airports, 23 airports from East Asia and Pacific, 40 from Europe, and 63 from Canada and the United States.

DEA is a deterministic nonparametric approach used to build a benchmark, the best practice frontier, based on available information. One of the main advantages of this approach is that it takes into account the multi-output and multi-input dimensionality of production, which is a characteristic of the production function of airports. Another advantage is that computations are based exclusively on measures of physical outputs and inputs, without the need to use prices, which are very difficult to collect and compare, particularly at the international level.

Two models are estimated under the competing assumptions: constant returns to scale (CRS) and variable returns to scale (VRS).[16] This allows us to compute scale efficiencies and to identify for each airport the returns-to-scale region—increasing, constant, or decreasing—in which it operates. The calculations of this report assume that airports have as a production target the maximization of outputs for a given input combination; therefore, an output-oriented framework is used.

Figure 3.21 illustrates CRS and VRS frontiers in a simple one-output (y) one-input (x) setting. The points P, Q, R, S, and T illustrate the observed quantities of input used and output produced by different production units (in our case airports). Two frontiers, *best practice convex envelope* in the DEA terminology, are computed assuming constant and variable returns to scale (CRS and VRS). R is the only point at which a production unit is technically efficient under both CRS and VRS. In other words, the production unit at R operates at the optimum constant returns scale. S and T are efficient under the VRS assumption, with S in the region of increasing returns to scale and T in the region of decreasing

Figure 3.21 DEA-CRS and DEA-VRS Frontiers

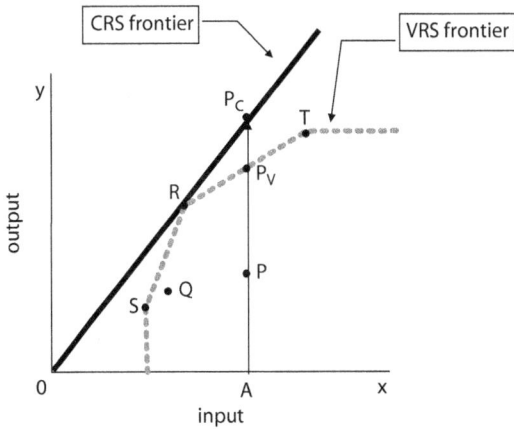

Source: Coelli et al. 2003.

returns to scale. Finally, P and Q are technically inefficient. They would be able to produce more output units using the same input quantities. For instance, production unit P uses quantity A of input x to produce quantity $\overline{AP}$ of output y. The vector $\overline{PP}_C$ measures the distance to the best practice frontier. It can be decomposed into two parts: the distance $\overline{PP}_V$ corresponds to the pure technical inefficiency, while the distance $\overline{P_V P_C}$ denotes technical inefficiency due to the scale of operation. As can be seen from figure 3.21, production unit P is compared with firms R and T (its peers), which form the piecewise linear combination benchmark to which unit P is compared. Similarly, the peers for production unit Q are R and S. Finally, note that under the CRS hypothesis, production unit R is the benchmark for all the other production units.

The literature that estimates aggregate airport efficiency measures is very recent but has grown quickly in the decade thanks to the availability of comparable data, mostly in developed countries. Pestana Barros and Dieke (2008) present an overview of this literature, showing that most studies use the DEA approach, which takes into account the multi-output and multi-input nature of the business. However, there are considerable differences across studies in defining inputs and outputs. On the outputs side, the more complete and often-used model specification includes three output dimensions: passenger, freight, and aircraft movements. On the inputs side there is lesser consensus in the literature, mainly due to data availability problems. In any case, most studies include a bundle of variables representing labor and capital inputs. The most commonly used variables are the number of employees, as proxy for labor input, and the number or size of runways, terminal size, and number of boarding bridges, as proxies for capital. When comparable accounting data are available, inputs are represented by operating costs and capital stock.

In addition to physical variables, the data available for the preparation of this report also include information on airport revenues and operating expenditures and in some cases valuation of capital investments. However, given the lack of homogeneity in the definition of these variables and the fact that they were gathered from different sources, they were excluded from the analysis. Consequently, the use of physical input quantities remained as the only possible choice for the calculation of the efficiency frontier. This may be an inferior solution but one that seems to have fewer potential measurement biases.

In summary, the availability and comparability of data at an international level allow the specification of the airport business as a three-output and three-input production function:

Outputs   Passengers
                Tons of freight
                Aircraft movements

Inputs   Employees
                Runways
                Boarding bridges

The data, corresponding to the years 2005 and 2006, are well balanced for the 22 LAC airports but unbalanced for the other regions of the world, particularly for European airports.[17] For this reason, the data were pooled to carry out the benchmark study. In other words, a single DEA frontier was computed for the period 2005–06.

Table 3.4 presents descriptive statistics for outputs and inputs by region. LAC airports are on average smaller than those from other regions in terms of the three outputs: passengers, tons of freight, and aircraft movements. Despite these differences in the scale of production, on average, LAC airports employ nearly as much staff as Canadian and U.S. airports. At the same time, in terms of capital investments, the number of runways and boarding bridges is several times lower in LAC airports than in Canadian and U.S. airports.

Table 3.5 presents the technical efficiency (TE) results for the airports in the four regions, which were calculated by performing DEA computations using the Data Envelopment Analysis (Computer) Program (DEAP;

Table 3.4 Descriptive Statistics by World Region, 2005–06

	Outputs (× 1,000)			Inputs		
Statistics	Passengers	Tons of freight	Aircraft movements	Employees	Runways	Boarding bridges
LAC (22 airports, 44 observations)						
Mean	6,430.6	117.2	96.1	424.0	1.5	11.3
STD	6,033.6	119.0	82.9	412.0	0.5	9.7
Min.	181.0	0.2	1.9	20.0	1.0	0.0
Max.	24,727.0	470.9	356.0	1,568.0	2.0	38.0
East Asia and Pacific (23 airports, 39 observations)						
Mean	18,776.7	836.0	148.2	1,044.0	1.7	52.3
STD	12,432.4	970.7	82.7	1,107.3	0.6	35.5
Min.	1,293.3	10.3	10.5	137.0	1.0	0.0
Max.	45,100.0	3,600.0	286.5	4,873.0	3.0	143.0
Europe (40 airports, 66 observations)						
Mean	19,305.0	318.3	211.8	2,029.4	2.3	67.9
STD	15,728.4	515.7	127.8	2,982.6	1.0	58.3
Min.	1,218.9	3.6	29.8	298.0	1.0	6.0
Max.	67,915.0	2,131.0	533.0	17,528.0	6.0	264.0
Canada and the United States (63 airports, 125 observations)						
Mean	21,318.4	406.5	310.9	549.9	3.4	69.9
STD	17,976.6	641.8	196.7	480.7	1.2	42.6
Min.	2,657.1	3.6	60.5	119.0	1.0	14.0
Max.	85,907.4	3,713.4	980.4	3,000.0	7.0	178.0

Source: Author's compilation using World Bank Airports LAC Benchmarking Database and ATRS 2008.
Note: STD = standard deviation; min = minimum value, max = maximum value.

Table 3.5 Average Technical Efficiency Scores and Scale Efficiency by Region, 2005–06

	Technical efficiency			Returns to scale diagnosis (% of observations)		
World region	CRS	VRS	SE	IRS	CRS	DRS
Latin America	0.532	0.690	0.801	70.5	9.1	20.5
East Asia and Pacific	0.670	0.771	0.869	84.6	12.8	2.6
Europe	0.490	0.530	0.927	43.9	6.1	50.0
Canada and the United States	0.540	0.616	0.875	23.2	8.0	68.8
All	0.545	0.629	0.875	44.5	8.4	47.1

Source: Author's estimation.
Note: CRS = constant returns to scale; DRS = decreasing returns to scale; IRS = increasing returns to scale; SE = scale efficiency; VRS = variable returns to scale.

Coelli 1996). The average TE score of airports in all regions is 0.545 under the constant returns to scale (CRS) assumption. This means that, on average, the airports included in the sample could almost double their outputs (passengers, tons of freight, and aircraft movements) with the same quantity of inputs they currently use.

However, part of the distance to the best practice CRS frontier is explained by the scale of operation. Under the variable returns to scale (VRS) assumption, the average TE is 0.629 and the average scale efficiency is 0.875.[18] Table 3.5 also shows the distribution of airports in each region according to the type of production scale (increasing, constant, or decreasing). The last three columns of table 3.5 report the percentage of airports corresponding to this classification. Grouping all regions, 44.5 percent, 8.4 percent, and 47.1 percent of the airports in our dataset operate under increasing, constant, and decreasing returns to scale, respectively.

LAC airports appear to be the ones that suffer the most from a suboptimal scale operation. Scale inefficiency is close to 20 percent (scale efficiency [SE] = 0.801), mainly concentrated in the increasing returns to scale area (70.5 percent of observations). This means that on average, airports in LAC could improve their efficiency 20 percent if they were to increase their scale of operation to the optimal scale. Contrary to that finding, nearly 70 percent of Canadian and U.S. airports operate in the decreasing returns to scale region. The results of returns to scale diagnosis coincided with the intuition: airports in LAC are smaller, and given that the production technology of airports is characterized by large fixed investments (runways, terminals), it is logical to expect that smaller airports are still in the increasing returns to scale zone of the production function. It should be noted that airports identified as operating at the optimal scale (CRS) in our database handle between 20 and 30 million passengers each year, a result that exceeds previous estimates.[19] The relevant policy question is whether airports can influence the scale of operations. The answer depends on many factors, including the availability of land to build new facilities, existence of competition, congestion of existing facilities, and the possibility of changing airport tariffs. However, airports have strong limitations in the extent of influence on the demand they face. It is a well-accepted fact that airports face a derived demand, and consequently, they cannot significantly alter the outputs when they change inputs. Notable exceptions are airports that suffer strong congestion, but the argument is valid only for airport expansion (increase in inputs). When airports face a scenario of output contraction caused by a macroeconomic crisis (for instance, the financial crises that began in 2008), there is not much they can do to adjust the scale of operation because inputs remain constant (runways, terminals[20]) when output falls due to factors completely out of their control.

Table 3.6 presents detailed results for LAC airports.[21] Only two airports in the region are technically efficient under both CRS and VRS: Congonhas (CGH) and Viracopos (VCP), both in São Paulo. However, it is important to highlight that VCP is a special case: it is an efficient unit in DEA by default, which occurs when a production unit has no peers to which it can be compared. VCP is an airport that during our sample period can be characterized as a dedicated freight airport, as it has virtually no passenger

Table 3.6   Average Technical Efficiency Scores for LAC Airports, 2005–06

Country	Airport	CRS	VRS	Scale efficiency
Argentina	AEP	0.612	0.998	0.614
	EZE	0.414	0.417	0.993
	FTE	0.115	1.000	0.115
Brazil	BSB	0.498	0.536	0.931
	CGH	1.000	1.000	1.000
	GIG	0.318	0.320	0.994
	GRU	0.677	0.678	0.998
	MAO	0.377	0.692	0.544
	VCP	1.000	1.000	1.000
Chile	SCL	0.786	1.000	0.786
Colombia	BAQ	0.329	0.524	0.628
	CLO	0.496	0.734	0.676
Costa Rica	SJO	0.594	0.983	0.605
Dominican Republic	SDQ	0.260	0.372	0.699
Ecuador	GYE	0.472	0.646	0.739
El Salvador	SAL	0.114	0.127	0.900
Mexico	CUN	0.860	1.000	0.860
	GDL	0.643	0.649	0.991
	MEX	0.961	0.963	0.998
	MTY	0.403	0.410	0.982
Panama	PTY	0.164	0.178	0.926
Peru	LIM	0.621	0.961	0.646
All		0.532	0.69	0.801

Source: Author's estimation.
Note: CRS = constant returns to scale; TE = technical efficiency; VRS = variable returns to scale.
For a list of airport codes and the airports they represent, see page xxiii.

movement and no boarding bridges. Other results of table 3.6 can be summarized as follows: (a) TE scores for LAC airports show notable variations, from airports on the frontier (with a value of 1) to airports that have TE scores close to 0; (b) when assuming CRS, only two airports, CGH and VCP, are on the frontier; and (c) when VRS is assumed and, consequently, scale efficiency is isolated, the TE of LAC airports improves. Out of 22 airports, 6 are on the frontier. The later subsection on sources of technical efficiency tries to identify the variables that explain the observed differences in TE scores across airports.

As previously mentioned in this subsection, the DEA approach allows the identification of peers for each airport, which are the set of efficient airports that make up the relevant frontier for a given airport. Table 3.7 presents the peers for LAC airports in 2005 under the DEA VRS model. It should be noted that, by construction, technically efficient airports do not have other airports as peers. Technically inefficient airports have, on the contrary, a benchmark composed by other units. Given the three-output and three-input dimensionality of the production setting, the maximum number of peers is six, but an airport can have fewer than six peers.

It is important to remark that some LAC airports are peers for other airports. They serve as peers not only for other airports in the LAC region but also for other airports around the world. This is the case mainly of CGH (Congonhas, São Paulo), which is a peer for 28 observations (2005 and 2006 airport observations taken together). Other airports playing the same role of peers are AEP (Aeroparque Jorge Newbery, Buenos Aires), SCL (Comodoro Arturo Merino Benítez, Santiago de Chile), CUN (Cancún), and, to a lesser extent, FTE (Calafate, Argentina) and SJO (San José, Costa Rica). An interesting result is that all LAC airports in our sample, with the exception of MAO (Manaus, Brazil), have at least one LAC airport as a peer. Eight airports from outside the LAC region act as peers for LAC airports: XMN (Xiamen), ICN (Seoul), SDF (Louisville), LAX (Los Angeles), MEM (Memphis), SNA (Santa Ana, California), ATL (Atlanta), and MFM (Macao SAR, China).[22]

For illustration purposes, consider in more detail one observation: BSB airport (Juscelino Kubitschek, Brasilia). For this airport, the computed DEA TE score was 0.552, which corresponds to a 45 percent output inefficiency diagnosis. The airports identified as peers for BSB are CGH (Congonhas, São Paulo) and three U.S. airports: LAX (Los Angeles), MEM (Memphis), and SNA (Santa Ana, California). If BSB is compared with CGH, its only LAC peer, and one looks at some of their main

Table 3.7 Peer Analysis, DEA VRS, 2005

Country	Airport	TE VRS 2005	As peer for other airports	Peers 1	2	3	4	5
Argentina	AEP	1.000	9	AEP				
	EZE	0.404	0	CGH	(CGH)	(XMN)	(ICN)	(SDF)
	FTE	1.000	7	FTE				
Brazil	BSB	0.552	0	CGH	LAX	MEM	SNA	
	CGH	1.000	28	CGH				
	GIG	0.316	0	(CGH)	(XMN)	(ICN)	ATL	
	GRU	0.680	0	(CGH)	(XMN)	(ICN)	ATL	
	MAO	0.680	0	SJO	(XMN)	MFM	SNA	
	VCP	1.000	0	VCP				
Chile	SCL	1.000	10	SCL				
Colombia	BAQ	0.507	0	FTE	SJO	(XMN)	SNA	
	CLO	0.747	0	(FTE)	SCL	SNA		
Costa Rica	SJO	1.000	6	SJO				
Dominican Republic	SDQ	0.386	0	AEP	(LIM)	(SCL)	SNA	(XMN)
Ecuador	GYE	0.814	0	(FTE)	SJO	(XMN)	SNA	
El Salvador	SAL	0.131	0	(CGH)	LAX	MEM	SNA	
Mexico	CUN	1.000	11	CUN				
	GDL	0.615	0	CGH	FTE	(XMN)	(SDF)	
	MEX	0.947	0	CGH	ICN	(XMN)	ATL	SNA
	MTY	0.424	0	CGH	(FTE)	(ATL)	MEM	SNA
Panama	PTY	0.188	0	CGH	ICN	(XMN)	(SDF)	SNA
Peru	LIM	0.922	0	AEP	(LIM)	(SCL)	(XMN)	SNA

Source: Author's estimation.
Note: DEA = Data Envelopment Analysis; VRS = variable returns to scale. Underlined peers are LAC airports. Observations in parentheses are 2006 observations. Other airports: ICN (Seoul, Republic of Korea); MFM (Macao SAR, China); XMN (Xiamen, China); ATL (Atlanta, Georgia); SDF (Louisville, Kentucky); MEM (Memphis, Tennessee); LAX (Los Angeles, California); SNA (Santa Ana, California). For a list of airport codes and the airports they represent, see page xxiii.

output-input features (for the year 2005), DEA results are confirmed. On the output side, BSB handles 9.4 million passengers per year, against the 17.1 million passengers of CGH. Similarly, BSB had 171,600 aircraft movements in 2005, against 282,600 aircraft movements in CGH. Finally, on the input side, BSB had 365 employees and 13 boarding bridges, while CGH had 225 employees and eight boarding bridges.

Identifying Sources of Technical Efficiency

The previous subsection presented the estimation of technical efficiency for 148 airports in the world and showed the results for the LAC airports included in the sample. With the TE scores in hand, the logically subsequent question is: What are the variables that explain the observed differences in technical efficiency across airports?

The previous subsection showed that a fraction of the variation in TE scores can be explained by the scale of operation. However, even when a VRS model, which isolates the scale component of technical inefficiency, is used, significant differences in technical efficiency exist.

A potential factor behind the observed differences in efficiency is quality. It is likely that, other things being equal, airports operating with a large staff and/or a large number of boarding bridges provide better service quality to passengers. Unfortunately, survey data on users' satisfaction are not yet available at an international scale, so we were not able to include quality indicators in our analysis.

It is possible to divide the measurable potential drivers of efficiency into two groups that can be distinguished by the degree of control that each airport has over these variables. Among the exogenous (out of airports' control) drivers, the institutional setting or the demographic and socioeconomic environment in which airports operate can be included. Within the group of variables for which airports have a higher degree of control (endogenous), the percentage of passengers in transit (an attribute of hub airports), and the importance of nonaeronautical activities (duty-free shops, parking, local transportation, and so forth) can be included.

This subsection tests the effects of some of these potential factors using available information from different sources. To that end, a truncated regression model is estimated using the airport TE scores of the previous subsection as dependent variables and the exogenous and endogenous drivers as explanatory variables. The choice of a truncated model is dictated by the nature of the TE measure (which is by definition truncated at 1.0) and by the use of this model in the most recent academic literature (Simar and Wilson 2007).[23]

Table 3.8 presents average values by region for the candidate variables to account for observed differences in technical efficiency. Starting with the institutional setting, table 3.8 shows that, on average, LAC airports operate under a more liberalized framework. Indeed, more than half of LAC airports (54.5 percent) in the sample operate as private concessions, and 31.8 percent are regulated by an independent regulatory agency. In

Table 3.8 Potential Explanatory Factors of Technical Inefficiency, 2005–06

Explanatory factors	Latin America	Asia	Europe	Canada and United States
Institutional framework				
Private airport (%)	54.5	25.6	37.9	0
Independent regulatory agency (%)	31.8	10.3	16.7	0
Socioeconomic environment				
GDP per capita (US$)	5,442	17,397	32,598	42,219
Tourism expenditures per capita (US$)	69	532	943	393
Population concentration				
Population in the area (1,000s)	7,719	6,709	3,200	3,984
Population > 5 million (% of observations)	45.5	48.7	22.7	34.4
Airport characteristics				
Hub airport (%)	9.1	17.9	40.9	27.2
Passengers connecting (% of passengers)	7.9	9.5	32.8	23.4
Aeronautical revenues (% of total revenue)	56.9	53.8	51.6	49.2

Source: Author's estimation.
Note: The value of 5 million corresponds to the mean of the population of the cities where airports are located.

contrast, only 25.6 percent of Asian airports and 37.9 percent of European airports are under private management, while 10.3 percent and 16.7 percent of Asian and European airports, respectively, are regulated by an independent regulatory agency. Finally, all airports in Canada and the United States are operated by state-owned enterprises, and regulatory agencies in those two countries still depend directly on a political authority (a ministry or a government agency).

Another potential factor that could have a role in the explanation of airport performance is the socioeconomic environment in which airports operate. This effect is incorporated with two indicators: GDP per capita (measured in nominal U.S. dollars) and tourism expenditures (also measured in nominal U.S. dollars). However, it is worth stressing that these variables are only available at the country level and do not necessarily correspond to the area of influence of the airports.[24]

The demographic environment is represented by the concentration of population in the area served by the airport. On average, LAC airports appear to serve very large urban agglomerations (45.5 percent of airports), like their Asian counterparts (48.7 percent). Compared to European and North American airports, which are on average located in cities with 3 million to 4 million inhabitants, LAC airports are on average located in cities with 8 million people. In the regression analysis, this information will be incorporated with a binary (dummy) variable that takes a value of 1 for airports located in cities with more than 5 million people and of 0 otherwise.

Finally, a set of variables that represent characteristics that are particular to each airport is introduced. One of them is their specialization as a hub, represented by the percentage of connecting passengers. LAC airports have the lowest percentage of connecting passengers, with 7.9 percent (and also have the lowest percentage of hubs—9.1 percent), followed by Asian airports. The highest percentage is observed among European airports, where nearly one-third of passengers are connecting. Another variable that is particular to each airport is the share of aeronautical revenues in total revenues. Table 3.8 shows that aeronautical revenues are on average more important for LAC airports (where they represent almost 60 percent of total revenues) than for airports in any other region.

Table 3.9 reports the results, in the form of marginal effects, of estimations for alternative truncated regression models. The first two columns show the estimates of two models with VRS TE scores as dependent variables, with and without dummies, for each world region. The third column presents the estimates of a model with CRS TE scores as dependent variables, without regional dummies. The Likelihood Ratio Tests (LT) indicate that in all three cases, the explanatory variables included in the model, taken all together, have a statistically significant effect on the dependent variable. Even though the results are sensitive to the returns to scale assumption, overall, the sign and magnitude of marginal effects are comparable for VRS and CRS assumptions. The main difference concerns the statistical significance of most explanatory variables, which tend to be nonsignificant when CRS is assumed.

Several results are worth highlighting. First, it should be noted that there are two variables that appear as the main drivers of technical efficiency in the airport sector. On the one hand hub airports are, on average, 10 percent to 15 percent more efficient than other airports. On the other hand, the population size in the area served by the airport also seems to matter: airports located in areas with more than 5 million inhabitants are 17 percent to 20 percent more efficient than airports that serve less-populated areas.

Second, the results show that the institutional variables (whether the airport is private or public and whether it is regulated by an independent regulatory agency) are associated with positive marginal effects. However, these variables are not statistically significant, with the exception of the dummy for private airports under the VRS assumption. According to these results, privately operated airports tend to be more efficient, with a

Table 3.9 Truncated Regression—Marginal Effects

	VRS TE with regional dummies		VRS TE without regional dummies		CRS TE without regional dummies	
Explanatory factors	Marginal effect	(std)	Marginal effect	(std)	Marginal effect	(std)
Institutional framework						
Private airport (dummy)	0.064	(0.036)*	0.082	(0.035)**	0.068	(0.041)
Regulation authority (dummy)	0.048	(0.048)	0.041	(0.050)	0.083	(0.059)
Socioeconomic environment						
GDP per capita	0.006	(0.002)***	0.001	(0.001)	0.001	(0.001)
Tourism expenditures per capita	−0.033	(0.049)	−0.005	(0.033)	−0.045	(0.036)
Population concentration						
Population > 5 million (dummy)	0.169	(0.025)***	0.201	(0.027)***	0.173	(0.031)***
Airport characteristics						
Hub airport (dummy)	0.122	(0.028)***	0.099	(0.031)***	0.153	(0.031)***
Aeronautical revenues	−0.150	(0.081)*	−0.183	(0.085)**	−0.134	(0.102)
Control variables (dummies)						
Asia	0.059	(0.047)	—	—	—	—
Europe	−0.200	(0.059)***	—	—	—	—
Canada and the United States	−0.201	(0.069)***	—	—	—	—
Year 2006	−0.023	(0.023)	−0.107	(0.024)	−0.210	(0.274)
LR test	Chi^2 (11)	110.3***	Chi^2 (8)	80.8***	Chi^2 (8)	56.7***
Observations	251		251		251	

Source: Author's estimation.
Note: LR = likelihood ratio; CRS = constant returns to scale; VRS = variable returns to scale; — = not applicable.
Significance level: * = 10 percent, ** = 5 percent, *** = 1 percent.

TE score that is on average 6 percent to 8 percent points higher than publicly operated airports.

Another important feature that distinguishes airports is the importance of aeronautical activities in their operation. As expected, the importance of these activities, summarized by the share of aeronautical revenues in the total airport revenue, plays a negative effect on efficiency (although this effect is statistically significant only when we use VRS TE scores as the dependent variable). In other words, airports in which nonaeronautical (that is, commercial) activities are more important tend to be more efficient. The estimated marginal effect indicates that, on average and holding the other variables constant, a 10 percent increase in the share of aeronautical revenues produces a loss in technical efficiency of nearly 2 percent.

GDP per capita seems to have a positive effect on airport efficiency. However, this estimate is only significant in the VRS model (with regional dummies). In this case, when GDP per capita increases by US$10,000, the technical efficiency of airports is expected to increase 6 percent. Finally, tourism expenditures are not significant in the three specifications.

Measuring Productivity Change of LAC Airports

The objective of this subsection is to assess how airport productivity evolved in Latin America and the Caribbean. This exercise tracks the evolution of productive efficiency among LAC airports. It is possible, then, to identify those airports that experienced the largest efficiency gains and that can be categorized as best performers. To that end, total factor productivity change (TFPC) for LAC airports over the period 1995 to 2007 is computed. The period covered was determined by the data compiled through the questionnaires distributed for the elaboration of this report.

The computation relies on the same three-output three-input model specification used in the international benchmark study presented above, and the methodology consists of the computation of a Malmquist quantity index of TFPC based on the nonparametric DEA approach (Färe et al. 1994).

Figure 3.22 illustrates the computation of the Malmquist index in a simple one-output (y) and one-input (x) setting. Points M_t and M_{t+1} correspond to consecutive observations of production unit M at period t and $t+1$, respectively. Based on available information for the sector, two DEA frontiers are computed, one for period t and another one for period $t+1$, under the assumption of constant returns to scale.

The technical efficiency (TE) of unit M in period t corresponds to the ratio AM_t/AB, an output-oriented distance function in the production activity terminology. In period $t+1$, the TE of unit M is given by the distance function DM_{t+1}/DF. Proceeding in the same way, and using the same information, it is possible to compute two auxiliary distance functions. One measures the distance separating M_t from the frontier in period $t+1$, given by AM_t/AC, and the other measures the distance separating M_{t+1} from the frontier computed in period t, given by DM_{t+1}/DE.

Figure 3.22 Malmquist Index of Total Factor Productivity Change

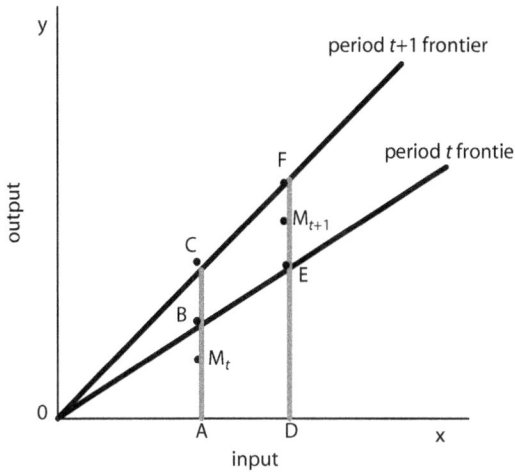

Source: Färe et al. 1994.

Färe et al. (1994) show how to compute a Malmquist index of TFPC, based on the four distance functions introduced above. In terms of figure 3.22, total factor productivity change of firm M from period t to period $t+1$ is computed as follows:

$$TFPC_M = \left(\frac{DM_{t+1}}{DE} \Big/ \frac{AM_t}{AB} \times \frac{DM_{t+1}}{DF} \Big/ \frac{AM_t}{AC} \right)^{0.5} \quad (1)$$

After some simple algebraic manipulations, this formula can be restated as:

$$TFPC_M = \left(\frac{DM_{t+1}}{DF} \Big/ \frac{AM_t}{AB} \right) \times \left(\frac{AC}{AB} \times \frac{DF}{DE} \right)^{0.5} \quad (2)$$

From figure 3.22 it can be easily verified that the first term in brackets in the right side of equation 2 corresponds to the productivity improvement of unit M, from period t to period $t+1$, in terms of technical efficiency. This term is known as technical efficiency change (TEC). The second term in brackets, known as technical change (TC), measures the frontier shift between period t and period $t+1$. It corresponds to the frontier shift computed as the geometric mean of the change in technology between the two periods.

The Malmquist index of TFPC presents two advantages with respect to traditional index numbers. On the one hand, prices are not needed in order to calculate this index. On the other hand, the index can be decomposed into a measure of technical progress (TC) of the activity level taken as a whole, and another measure (TEC) that captures how each unit is catching up with respect to the technological frontier. Its main disadvantage compared with traditional index numbers is that it cannot be computed separately for each unit. Its computation relies on the estimation of sequential frontiers. And for this purpose, panel data must be available for representative units operating in the sector.

This section of chapter 3 relies on a panel composed exclusively of LAC airports for the period 1995–2007. Unfortunately, the international panel including airports around the world is only available for the years 2005 and 2006, and consequently the computation of TFPC could not be done and used as a benchmark for LAC airports.

Table 3.10 presents descriptive statistics for the three subperiods in which the sample is decomposed: 1995–99, 2000–03, and 2004–07. For each of these three subperiods, the number of airports in the sample varies noticeably, from 7 to 22. As a consequence, the benchmark

Table 3.10 Descriptive Statistics by Period

Statistics	Outputs (× 1,000)			Inputs		
	Passengers	Tons of freight	Aircraft movements	Employees	Runways	Boarding bridges
1995–99 (7 airports, 26 observations)						
Mean	5,039.7	145.4	119.1	723.5	1.5	9.7
STD	4,586.1	125.7	80.9	690.0	0.5	10.1
Min.	250.6	21.4	30.5	77.0	1.0	0.0
Max.	14,705.1	409.2	293.8	2,056.0	2.0	38.0
2000–03 (17 airports, 60 observations)						
Mean	6,136.6	132.8	112.4	429.3	1.5	11.8
STD	5,314.4	124.2	88.0	465.8	0.5	10.9
Min.	654.8	10.4	29.5	56.0	1.0	0.0
Max.	21,694.0	418.9	334.5	1,940.0	2.0	38.0
2004–07 (22 airports, 85 observations)						
Mean	6,579.4	121.1	99.1	433.9	1.5	12.0
STD	5,992.7	120.6	83.6	421.9	0.5	10.7
Min.	157.9	0.0	1.9	20.0	1.0	0.0
Max.	25,882.0	470.9	379.0	1,598.0	2.0	56.0

Source: Author's estimation based on World Bank Airports LAC Benchmarking Database and ATRS 2008.
Note: STD = standard deviation; min = minimum value; max = maximum value.

used for TFPC computations varies as well, and the results should be interpreted carefully, mainly for the TFPC decomposition into TEC and TC.[25]

Table 3.11 presents the estimation of TFPC by subperiod and by LAC airport.[26,27] Average productivity growth oscillated over the three subperiods. Between 1995 and 1999 airports in the region posted an average annual productivity growth of –2.7 percent. However, it should be noted that this growth corresponds to the average scores of Brazilian airports and the airport in Barranquilla, Colombia, the only airports for which data are available for this period. The results are driven by the strong negative growth of the airport in Barranquilla.

Table 3.11 Average Annual Total Factor Productivity by Airport and Subperiod
percentage

Country	Airport	1995–99	1999–2003	2003–07
Argentina	AEP	—	–7.0	–3.0
	EZE	—	–18.9	4.0
	FTE	—	—	22.9
Brazil	BSB	10.0	5.4	2.9
	CGH	13.8	2.6	–4.0
	GIG	7.4	–5.5	16.3
	GRU	3.5	–0.9	2.7
	MAO	–2.3	0.3	6.8
	VCP	0.9	–7.6	–0.8
Chile	SCL	—	1.3	2.0
Colombia	BAQ	–23.0	–8.4	1.5
	CLO	—	–6.2	–5.1
Costa Rica	SJO	—	22.1	0.0
Dominican Republic	SDQ	—	—	–3.7
Ecuador	GYE	—	—	8.1
El Salvador	SAL	—	2.7	1.4
Mexico	CUN	—	6.6	–0.3
	GDL	—	–6.1	9.5
	MEX	—	1.1	4.9
	MTY	—	5.8	4.7
Panama	PTY	—	—	7.4
Peru	LIM	—	—	9.7
All		–2.7	–1.2	3.9

Source: Author's estimation.
Note: For a list of airport codes and the airports they represent, see page xxiii.

Productivity growth during the intermediate subperiod (1999–2003) was negative (−1.2 percent per year on average) and was driven mainly by some airports that experienced dramatic losses in productivity, like EZE (Ministro Pistarini, Buenos Aires) which showed a loss in productivity of −18.9 percent per year over this period as a direct consequence of the economic and financial crisis Argentina suffered during 2001/02.

Conversely, positive rates of growth appear to be the norm (with only some exceptions) during the last subperiod (2003 to 2007). The average TFPC rate was 3.9 percent during this period, with many airports experiencing annual productivity growth rates close to, or even higher than, 10 percent. Different complementary explanations could be driving the high rates of TFPC of this period. But, as negative economic shocks are a likely explanation of the reduction in productivity between 1999 and 2003, the strong economic growth enjoyed by LAC economies in the period 2003–07 is a strong driver of improvements in airports' TFPC.

One of the main questions that motivated the elaboration of this report was whether privately operated airports in LAC, a region that has experimented with a wide variety of private sector participation schemes for the operation of airports, have higher productivity levels. Table 3.12 presents the evolution of airport productivity by type of ownership and size. To avoid reaching biased conclusions caused by differences in airport size, airports are weighted using the workload unit (WLU) measure.

The results reported in table 3.12 show that the largest airports are the ones that registered faster productivity growth. In particular, those airports that handle between 7.5 million and 10 million passengers per year posted an average annual growth rate of 5.4 percent for the whole period, and an even higher growth of 7.0 percent during the last subperiod. Interestingly, the category made up by the three biggest airports in the region (CGH, GRU, and MEX, which handle more than 10 million passengers per year) grew faster during the first subperiod but then grew at a rather low rate over the two last subperiods.

Public airports appear to have performed better on average over the whole period compared to private airports (annual productivity changes of 2.9 percent and 0.7 percent, respectively). Nevertheless, if the analysis focuses on their evolution over the last two subperiods, for which the available information is more complete, both groups behaved quite similarly, registering negative productivity growth during the period

Table 3.12 Average Total Factor Productivity by Airport Categories
annual percent change

Airport categories	1995–99	1999–2003	2003–07	ALL
		Nonweighted		
Size (million passengers)				
< 5.0	−5.6	−1.8	3.5	0.4
5.0 to 7.5	–	−4.3	3.7	0.5
7.5 to 10.0	8.9	1.7	7.0	5.4
> 10.0	8.5	0.9	1.8	3.4
Private vs. public				
Private	−23.0	−1.6	3.4	0.7
Public	5.3	−0.8	4.5	2.9
All	2.7	−1.2	3.9	1.9
		Weighted		
Private vs. public				
Private	−23.2	−0.5	2.7	1.3
Public	6.1	0.2	4.4	3.2
All	5.5	0.0	3.7	2.6

Source: Author's estimation.
Note: Weighted using workload units. Airport categories are composed as following: Public: BSB, CGH, GIG, GRU, MAO, and VCP (Brazil); SAL (El Salvador); MEX (Mexico); and PTY (Panama). Private airports: AEP, EZE, FTE (Argentina); SCL (Chile); BAQ and CLO (Colombia); SJO (Costa Rica); GYE (Ecuador); CUN, GDL, and MTY (Mexico); and LIM (Peru).
Airport size: less than 5.0 million passengers: BAQ, CLO, FTE, GYE, MAO, PTY, SAL, SDQ, and SJO; 5.0–7.5 million passengers: AEP, EZE, GDL, LIM, MTY, and SCL; 7.5–10.0 million passengers: BSB, CUN, and GIG; more than 10.0 million passengers: CGH, GRU, and MEX.

1999–2003 and positive growth between 2003 and 2007 (although with a slightly more favorable profile for public airports). These results are confirmed when TFPC averages are weighted using WLU as the weight variable.

Finally, table 3.13 presents the decomposition of the Malmquist TFPC index into its two main components, TEC and TC. The table presents both nonweighted and weighted (by WLU) averages. Note that weighted averages give a better approximation of the average productivity growth for the airport activity in the region. Since larger airports performed better than smaller ones, the weighted average TFPC is higher than the nonweighted average (2.6 percent compared to 2.2 percent).

Despite these differences, in general, the results are very similar when nonweighted and weighted averages are used. Both averages show that

Table 3.13 Malmquist Total Factor Productivity Index Decomposition—Averages by Period
annual percent change

	Nonweighted			Weighted		
Period	TEC	TC	TFPC	TEC	TC	TFPC
			By period			
1995–99	−1.5	6.0	4.4	−0.6	6.1	5.5
1999–2003	2.3	−3.3	−1.2	1.1	−1.1	0.0
2003–07	6.4	−2.4	3.9	4.3	−0.6	3.7
			All			
1995–2007	3.6	−1.4	2.2	2.4	0.2	2.6

Source: Author's estimation.

the airport industry in the LAC region did not experience any improvement in productivity due to technical change over the period. In other words, there was no significant change in the production frontier of the industry between 1995 and 2007, as the estimated TC index is near zero or even negative, except for the first subperiod. In fact, the table shows that the main source of TFPC corresponds to improvements in TEC, particularly during the last subperiod. This result has to be interpreted in terms of a catching-up process. Most LAC airports grew during the sample period (1995–2007), mainly by better allocating inputs in a framework of well-known technologies and production processes. This process allowed them to position themselves closer to the activity frontier than they were at the beginning of the period.

Conclusion

This chapter presented a detailed analysis of LAC airports' performance. It starts by a comparison of the most frequently used partial performance indicators. More than 20 airports in LAC are compared using 2005 data. The graphs that illustrate the partial performance indicators include the average values observed in other regions of the world (Asia, Canada and the United States, and Europe) and the accompanying text explain the main findings and caveats necessary to consider when linking the results of partial performance indicators and coming up with a conclusion about the performance ranking of airports. To enrich the analysis of partial performance indicators, the evolution in time of these indicators was carried out whenever data were available. Airports were divided by size to facilitate the graphical presentation.

Overall it is difficult and not always correct to obtain clear-cut conclusions about airport performance solely by considering partial performance indicators. The text presents several examples of why reaching conclusions about performance just by looking at selected indicators could give misleading conclusions. Still, an effort to rank airports was produced and reflected in table 3.3, which identifies best and worst airport performers in LAC.

Relying on some of the most advanced techniques currently in use by specialists in the measurement of productivity, this report presents aggregate measures of efficiency. The literature review carried out for the preparation of this report did not identify any publicly available attempt to measure productive efficiency for a representative sample of LAC airports using aggregate productivity measurement techniques. Thus, this report presents the first comprehensive calculation of technical efficiency of airports in the Latin America and Caribbean region.

The results indicate that technical efficiency for LAC airports show notable variations: from airports on the frontier (with a value of 1) to airports that have technical efficiency scores close to 0. In the best-case scenario, when variable returns to scale are assumed, out of the 22 LAC airports in the sample, 6 are on the frontier. The results obtained when using aggregate measures of efficiency tend to coincide with comparisons using partial performance indicators.

On average, LAC airports are less efficient than Asian and North American airports when constant returns to scale are used, but they are more efficient than European airports. However, when boarding bridges are excluded and not considered proxy for capital investments, LAC airports are on average significantly less efficient than in the other regions included in the study.

Using information for more than 148 airports worldwide, several factors that explain the observed differences in airport efficiency were identified using regression analysis. As expected, the regression analysis shows that airports that serve as hubs tend to be more efficient. Moreover, airports that are located in cities with more than 5 million inhabitants are also more efficient than airports located in smaller cities. The level of income (GDP per capita) also seems to positively influence productive efficiency. Airports that rely more on revenue sources other than aeronautical tariffs also tend to be more efficient, a finding consistent with the recent literature (ATRS 2008). Finally, airports that are privately operated tend to stand closer to the efficient frontier than their publicly operated counterparts, although this effect is not significant across all the different specifications tested.

When analyzing in more detail how LAC airports' productivity evolved between 1995 and 2007, the calculations indicate that productivity growth has been driven mainly by improvements in technical efficiency and not by pure technical change. This finding implies that the efficient production frontier of the sector did not experience any major shift between 1995 and 2007, but many airports were able to raise their efficiency level and become more productive, a process by which they were able to come closer to the efficient frontier. Probably the most unexpected result is that privately operated airports in LAC have not outperformed publicly operated airports. Given the wide variety of private participation schemes used by LAC countries, this result should lead to more detailed, case-by-case research to assess the effects of private participation on airport performance. In addition, future research should also assess financial efficiency as well as the impact of private participation on the quality of service delivered.

Notes

1. Gillen and Lall (1997), Parker (1999), and Murillo Melchor (1999) are among the first published papers that measure performance of airports using aggregate measures of efficiency.
2. Flor and de la Torre (2008) use Data Envelopment Analysis (DEA) methods to analyze efficiency and total factor productivity of airports in Peru. Similarly, Fernandes and Pacheco (2002) also employ DEA methods to compute a production frontier using data for Brazilian airports. Gómez-Lobo and González (2008) use DEA to compare the airport of Santiago de Chile with airports in developed countries. The literature review conducted for this report did not identify other papers that use efficiency estimation techniques applied to airports in Latin America.
3. This report would have benefited from an analysis of perception of quality, but the lack of public information regarding passengers' and airlines' experience during the consumption of airport services did not allow us to pursue such analysis.
4. See Andrés et al. (2008) for a survey of the recent literature and an application of partial performance indicators in the electricity, water distribution, and fixed telecommunications sectors.
5. The book *A Primer on Efficiency Measurement for Utilities and Transport Regulators* by Coelli et. al. (2003) provides an excellent introduction to aggregate productivity measurement methods.
6. The Airport Performance Indicators by Jacobs Consultancy was formerly known as TRL Airport Performance Indicators.

7. Though information is available for cargo per cargo-dedicated aircraft movements for most of the LAC region, regional averages for North America, Europe, and Asia Pacific were not available, nor were data for Brazil's airports, including Viracopos-Campinas International (VCP). Without this information, a graphical representation of this indicator would not have been sufficient to represent the region or provide a basis for global comparison.
8. The questionnaire developed for this report asked the operator to provide information about staff directly employed by the airport operator and total employees in the airport. Most operators provided data for the former category of staff but provided virtually none for the latter. The same problem with staff information was reported by ATRS for airports in Europe, North America, and Asia. It is difficult for airport operators to have information about staff employed by companies in charge of outsourced services.
9. Even though our data set does not contain labor (staff) data before and after concessions took place, anecdotal evidence suggests that when operation and management are transferred to the private sector, airports tend to increase outsourcing through service contracts, mainly for security and cleaning. It is interesting to note that from figure 3.3, it is not possible to assert that privately managed airports in LAC show higher values for the ratio of passengers per employee.
10. For this partial performance indicator, the ATRS report split the region East Asia and Pacific in two: Asia and Australia–New Zealand.
11. The use of buses instead of boarding bridges is particularly uncomfortable for handicapped passengers.
12. Most of the literature uses before and after time comparisons to evaluate the impact of privatization, even though the ideal strategy would be to compare utilities under private operation with publicly operated utilities sharing similar characteristics. The reason for most researchers' selection of the before and after methodology lies in the difficulty of identifying comparable firms (firms with identical characteristics) operating under different ownership regimes. Even a comparison using before and after scenarios for a given firm is a difficult exercise to carry out due to lack of available and reliable data.
13. That is, nominal prices were adjusted by local inflation and expressed in 2005 constant prices and then converted to U.S. dollars using the average value of the exchange rate in 2005.
14. Time series of the partial performance indicators for those airports not presented in this section are available upon request. The selection of airports was somewhat arbitrary but was made looking for a balance among size, ownership, and country coverage.

15. The nonexpert readers interested in efficiency estimation are encouraged to read *A Primer on Efficiency Measurement for Utilities and Transport Regulators*, Coelli et al. (2003).
16. *Constant returns to scale* implies that when all production inputs are increased by 10 percent, the output increases by 10 percent. When DEA is used and CRS technology is used, it is assumed that all airports operate under constant returns to scale. *Variable returns to scale*, on the other hand, calculates technical efficiency and isolates the scale component (that is, it allows identification of whether an airport is inefficient because it operates at a scale other than constant returns to scale).
17. A balanced sample in this context means we have observations for years 2005 and 2006 for all airports.
18. By construction, TE under VRS multiplied by scale efficiency (SE) equals TE under CRS. Table C.3 in appendix C replicates table 3.5 but adds the results of computing average TE scores using a model with two inputs (leaving in runways and staff and removing boarding bridges). Investment in boarding bridges shows a significant underinvestment in LAC (569,000 passengers per boarding bridge, compared with 359,000, 284,000, and 305,000 in Asia, Europe, and North America, respectively), and given that DEA cannot measure quality of service, it tends to reward airports that underinvest in capital. When removing boarding bridges from the calculation, the average TE score for LAC airports falls significantly relative to the average in other regions.
19. Doganis (1992) found that airports experience significant increasing returns to scale up to 1 million passengers and that unit costs continue to decline up to 3 million passengers, but that they level off thereafter. Our estimates indicate that constant returns to scale are reached at a much higher volume of passengers.
20. It could be argued that airports can close a runway or terminal, but this is usually not the optimal strategy. It is better for airports to maintain assets in proper condition rather than abandon them and then invest in rehabilitation.
21. Table C.1 in appendix C presents detailed results for the calculation of TE scores for all airports other than those in Latin America.
22. Peer airports are the equivalent of points R, T, and S in figure 3.21.
23. We estimate truncated regressions using the "truncreg" procedure of STATA 9.0.
24. Given that our data set contained a lot of airports in the United States, and given the availability of data for these airports, we used GDP per capita of the state in which each airport is located instead of GDP per capita for the country as a whole.

25. The only criterion used to split the data was to obtain three subperiods with an equivalent number of years. The sample covers a large range of airport sizes. Measuring size by the number of passengers per year, the sample ranges from 158,000 to 25.8 million passengers. Zero values are reported for some variables. On the output side, this is the case for freight transportation for at least one airport. On the input side, at least one airport was still not equipped with boarding bridges in 2007.
26. In order to avoid potential biases due to the presence of an unbalanced panel, Malmquist index computations were performed separately for each two-year sequential period using in each case a balanced panel of airports.
27. The TFPC index values reported in tables 3.11–3.13 exclude 14 observations (out of a total of 154). The excluded observations correspond to airports that introduced major changes in their capital stock in a particular year. These changes, given by increases in either the number of runways or boarding bridges, are reported in a given year and thus represent a significant discrete change in the inputs of production (the moment where the investment is ready to use). Given that these types of investments are lumpy by nature, they tend to have a big negative impact on the measures of productivity change (for instance, when one runway is added in year X, it is expected that the quantity of aircraft movements per runway will go down significantly in year X). Appendix C reports the results for all airports and years. In table C.2 values in bold indicate the year of changes in the capital stock of either the number of runways or boarding bridges. In most cases the TFPC index corresponding to these observations are, as expected, highly negative.

References

Andrés, L., J. L. Guasch, and A. S. Lopez. 2008. "Regulatory Governance and Sector Performance: Methodology and Evaluation for Electricity Distribution in Latin America." Policy Research Working Paper 4494, World Bank, Washington, DC.

ATRS (Air Transport Research Society). 2008. "2008 Airport Benchmarking Report." ATRS, Vancouver, Canada.

CAA (Civil Aviation Authority). 2000. "The Use of Benchmarking in the Airport Reviews." Background paper, CAA, London.

Coelli, T. 1996. "A Guide to DEAP: A Data Envelopment Analysis (Computer) Program." Department of Econometrics, University of New England, Armidale, Australia.

Coelli, T., A. Estache, S. Perelman, and L. Trujillo. 2003. *A Primer on Efficiency Measurement for Utilities and Transport Regulators.* Washington, DC: World Bank Institute.

Doganis, R. 1992. *The Airport Business*. New York: Routledge.

Färe, R., S. Groskskopf, and C. Lovell. 1994. *Production Frontiers*. Cambridge, U.K.: Cambridge University Press.

Fernandes, E., and R. R. Pacheco. 2002. "Efficient Use of Airport Capacity." *Transportation Research Part A: A Policy and Practice* 36: 225–38.

Flor, L., and B. de la Torre. 2008. "Medición no paramétrica de eficiencia y productividad total de los factores: El caso de los aeropuertos regionales de Perú." *Revista de Regulacion en Infraestructura de Transporte* 1 (1): 99–114.

Gillen, D., and A. Lall. 1997. "Developing Measures of Airport Productivity and Performance: An Application of Data Envelopment Analysis." *Transportation Research* 33 (4): 261–73.

Gómez-Lobo, A., and A. González. 2008. "The Use of Airport Charges for Funding General Expenditures: The Case of Chile." *Journal of Air Transport Management* 14: 308–14.

Jacobs Consultancy. 2007. "Airport Performance Indicators 2007." London.

Murillo Melchor, C. 1999. "An Analysis of Technical Efficiency and Productive Change in Spanish Airports Using Malmquist Index." *International Journal of Transport Economics* 26: 271–92.

Parker, D. 1999. "The Performance of BAA before and after Privatization." *Journal of Transport Economics and Policy* 33 (2): 133–46.

Pestana Barros, C., and P. U. C. Dieke. 2007. "Performance Evaluation of Italian Airports: A Data Envelopment Analysis." *Journal of Air Transport Management* 13: 184–91.

Simar, L., and P. W. Wilson. 2007. "Estimation and Inference in Two-Stage, Semi-Parametric Models of Production Processes." *Journal of Econometrics* 136 (1): 31–64.

CHAPTER 4

Institutional Design and Governance of Airport Regulators in Latin America

A wave of structural reform, market liberalization, and privatization swept across Latin America and the Caribbean (LAC) during the 1990s. The airport sector was not spared. By mid-2000, several LAC countries had begun introducing private sector participation in the management of airport services. Yet ownership change was not uniform; different modes and arrangements were adopted. While Argentina opted to concession its airport network to a single operator, Chile adopted a case-by-case strategy, and Mexico concessioned its airports by groups (Lipovich 2008). Colombia, Costa Rica, and Peru are among other countries that embarked on reforming their airport sector.

Countries that introduced private sector participation in the airport sector had faced the most challenging aspect of the privatization model in Latin America: how to design and implement effective and efficient economic regulation. The debate about the necessary conditions to implement sound regulatory decisions included not only the content of regulatory policies (for instance, tariff methodologies) but also the institutional design of the government authority (as independent commissions or government departments). This chapter focuses primarily on the latter. It addresses the realities and challenges of airport regulators from a public sector governance perspective and analyzes the institutional design of regulators in terms of their autonomy from authorities formulating policies, the transparency of their procedures, and the quality of their bureaucracy. The analysis does not cover areas related to sector planning, safety, security, licensing of airlines and pilots, and other areas that require a sound regulation; it concentrates only on governance aspects directly related to economic regulation.

International practices exemplify two main typologies of airport regulators. The first approach may be characterized by the presence of an independent regulator as the main decision maker in the sector. In the second approach, using primarily competition law, the policy framework dispenses with any kind of direct regulation, relying heavily on consultations between an airport and its users. Legal provisions enable competition authorities to control anticompetitive behavior, including the possibility of imposing tighter regulation and price controls when consultations do not prove satisfactory. A third approach, a blend of the two mentioned above, exists in Australia. The Australian Competition and Consumer Commission has broad responsibility for administering competition policy as well as regulation in all sectors with essential facilities.

Latin American countries demonstrate a governance design that matches more closely with the first typology of regulators, the independent regulator. Most countries that concessioned airport services had created regulatory agencies as their preferred institutional arrangement to enforce concession contracts and the quality of services. In cases where the bulk of airport services remained as state owned, the role of regulator was placed in the hands of government departments with limited independence from sector authorities. The region also demonstrated the presence of independent regulators in the context of state-owned enterprises. This is the case of Brazil, where the national airport administrator (INFRAERO) is regulated by the National Civil Aviation Agency (ANAC).

Independent regulatory agencies in the airport sector, as in other infrastructure industries, were given the highest levels of administrative and legal independence and subject to accountability before the congress. Their decision-making authority was placed within a board of directors, which would be composed of technical and nonpolitical members. The agencies were also given significant regulatory competencies to determine tariffs and minimum requirements for quality of service.

In countries where airports remained publicly owned, regulatory functions were kept in the hands of nonindependent agencies (usually under the name of *administraciones aeronauticas*). These institutions, sometimes having a separate status from the government, possess overall policy implementation responsibilities, although decisions are made by policy formulators such as the line ministry.

In this chapter, institutional attributes of independent regulatory agencies (IRAs) are compared with nonindependent regulatory agencies or government departments (non-IRAs) in the airport sector. The goal is to identify under which arrangement regulatory governance can be enhanced. Moreover, the multidimensional approach of this chapter allows the disentanglement of different aspects of regulatory governance to test their individual strengths in both IRAs and non-IRAs.

Literature Review

The literature on independent regulators in Latin America has mainly focused on the electricity and water sectors, where the highest number of IRAs have been set up. This section reviews this literature as it contributed to the development of the methodology used in this study because no previous paper has conducted a cross-country assessment of the governance structure of airport regulators in Latin America.

Literature on IRAs in the LAC region has adopted two main approaches. The first approach has been quantitative, establishing correlations between different indexes of agencies' autonomy, transparency, and accountability, and sector performance indicators, such as coverage, quality, and labor productivity. The second approach has been qualitative, making use of institutional mapping and benchmarking techniques to assess the presence of several institutional attributes in regulatory agencies. Studies addressing IRAs in a more comprehensive manner are limited.

Andrés et al. (2008), an example of the first approach, explore the correlations between different measures of the governance of regulatory agencies and sector indicators (company level) in the electricity sector of the LAC region. Through principal component analysis (PCA), they develop different indexes of agencies' governance, establishing links between utilities' performance and the existence of a regulatory agency, the experience of the regulatory agency (given by the years of the regulators since establishment), and the governance levels of regulatory agencies. (An aggregated index of governance in regulatory agencies produced weighting of several dimensions of governance, including autonomy, transparency, accountability, and administrative capacities.) They find a positive and significant correlation between the three measures of existence, experience, and governance levels and sector performance.

Along the same lines as Andrés et al. 2008, Gutierrez (2003) estimates the impact of regulation on telecom outcomes in 22 Latin American and Caribbean countries. Gutierrez measures regulation through a regulatory governance index composed of different formal characteristics of regulatory agencies as well as patterns of the regulatory framework. Gutierrez finds a positive correlation in sector performance when associating the aggregated index or its separate components. Estache and Rossi (2008) find that the introduction of regulatory agencies in electricity distribution in developing countries is associated with more efficient firms and with higher social welfare.

The second approach could be defined as qualitative. It makes use of rather descriptive and normative types of analysis, focusing on certain attributes of independent regulatory agencies such as their autonomy, the transparency of their procedures, and their accountability to both institutional and noninstitutional actors. A common research design has been to construct different indexes to benchmark IRAs in infrastructure sectors. Gutierrez (2003) develops a Regulatory Framework Index (RFI) to assess the evolution of regulatory governance in the telecommunications sector during the period 1980–2001 in 25 LAC countries. The index, an aggregated measure of formal legal and institutional attributes of IRAs in telecommunications, ranks agencies in the region on their performance in each component.

Andrés et al. (2007) benchmark IRAs of LAC countries in electricity distribution. Through different indexes that combine formal and informal attributes of the governance of regulatory agencies, the study compares 19 national electricity regulators of the region. An aggregated index of regulatory governance (Electricity Regulatory Governance Index) and 16 indexes of formal and informal aspects of regulatory agencies related to their autonomy, transparency, and accountability are developed. The paper makes an interesting distinction between different dimensions of each of the variables. For instance, the variable autonomy is analyzed in terms of its political, regulatory, and managerial dimensions. Results show several shortcomings in the implementation of the independent regulatory model in electricity, with autonomy as the variable with the lowest value among all indexes that aim at measuring regulatory governance.

Correa et al. (2006) provide a detailed analysis of Brazilian regulatory agencies in different infrastructure sectors (six federal and 15 state regulatory agencies in electricity, natural gas, water and sanitation, ground transportation, petroleum, railroads, and telecommunications). Agencies' governance is measured through three indexes. The first index, Regulatory Governance Index, is the baseline indicator and represents the most comprehensive data of all the indexes. The second index, the Parsimonious Index, captures those variables of the survey that are less subjective. The third index, the Facto Index, is related to actual practices of regulatory agencies. The report finds that the independence and accountability attributes are more developed than regulatory means and instruments (particularly qualified personnel and regulatory tools) and decision-making procedures (particularly with respect to those mechanisms that can guarantee consistency of decisions and reduce arbitrariness). It also finds a clear partition between federal and state regulatory agencies, with the former achieving higher results in the autonomy, decision-making, and decision tools components of the Regulatory Governance Index.

Despite the significant developments in understanding the role of IRAs in the performance of utilities, the research on the political and governance aspects of regulation in the LAC region remains limited. The main gap in the existing literature is the low explanatory power. Few, if any, attempts have been made to address issues of causality, sequencing, and complex interaction effects that contribute to a better explanation of IRAs in policy making.

Methodology and Data Sources

This chapter combines both qualitative and quantitative techniques, with emphasis on the former. Qualitative comparative analysis is used to describe the design and practices of airport regulatory agencies. The framework of analysis focuses on four main aspects of the governance of airport regulators: the autonomy of the decision-making process, the transparency of the design, the accountability of the design, and the quality of the bureaucracy (table 4.1). The analysis includes both IRAs and non-IRAs.

Our analysis focuses on the institutional design of airport regulators, omitting indicators related to actual effectiveness. Thus, the reader should be aware that when, for instance, autonomy is measured, a degree of factual independence is not automatically attributed to the agency. Institutional design refers to the inputs or characteristics of IRAs and government departments that would allow them to be more autonomous and accountable. Nevertheless, even when the institutional design incorporates the best possible attributes, that does not guarantee either effective autonomy or accountability.

Table 4.1 Aspects of Governance of Airport Regulators

Aspects	Autonomy of decision making	Transparency	Accountability	Quality of bureaucracy
Components	- Regulatory powers (e.g., tariffs, quality of service) - Status of agency - Procedures to appoint/remove board members - Budget sources	- Civic engagement in rule making - Consultations - Publication of agency's decisions - E-government - Registry of board meetings and decisions - Publication of job vacancies	- Appeals of agency's decisions - Effects of consultations - Evaluation of agency's performance - Accountability instrument - Performance instrument	- Structure of staff positions within the agency - Educational levels of agency's staff - Publication of vacancies

Source: Author's elaboration.

A study that addresses effectiveness has to rely on in-depth case studies. At this stage, considering the gap in the literature on the subject, the analysis of this chapter is focused on identifying typologies and institutional design patterns at the regional level. The ultimate goal is then to compare regulators in terms of their institutional design. The hope is that the findings of this chapter will lead to further research aimed at establishing correlations between the performance of the sector and the design and practices of regulators.

Data were collected through a survey (a copy can be found in appendix B) submitted to 24 airport regulators in the LAC region. Both IRAs and non-IRAs were included. The survey was the result of a thorough consultation process and literature review; its framework builds on similar surveys carried out by Andrés et al. (2007). Final respondents include 13 regulators, four of them IRAs and nine nonindependent regulators. Questions cover each of the dimensions of governance summarized in table 4.1 as well as several questions on economic regulation.

Measures of autonomy, transparency, accountability, and bureaucratic quality in airport regulators were created by assigning values, between 0 (worse) and 1 (best), to different indicators. These measures are aimed only at providing the reader with a quantitative approximation of the governance structure of airport regulators; they are not indexes or tools of benchmarking. The methodology section of this chapter describes each indicator and the criteria used in assigning values. Table 4.2 maps each regulator, country, and legal configuration (IRA or non-IRA).

Regulatory Governance

Autonomy of Decision Making

The discussion around the autonomy of independent agencies has absorbed most of the space dedicated by policy analysts to the subject of regulatory authorities. Although this debate has been especially present in developing countries, it is also a current subject in developed governments (OECD 2002).

Independent commissions were the result of an agreement between President Franklin D. Roosevelt and both the judiciary and the Congress of the United States in 1930. The occurrence of the market crisis at that time convinced President Roosevelt of the need for stronger regulation in the economy. His response, creating public bodies in charge of establishing these standards, resulted in opposition from the other two branches of government, which were reticent to give the executive branch full

Table 4.2 Mapping of Regulator and Legal Configuration

Regulator	Country	IRA/Non-IRA
Organismo Regulador del Sistema Nacional de Aeropuertos	Argentina	IRA
Department of Civil Aviation	Bahamas, The	Non-IRA
Superintendencia de Transportes	Bolivia	IRA
Agência Nacional de Aviação Civil	Brazil	IRA
Dirección de Aeropuertos, Ministerio de Obras Públicas	Chile	Non-IRA
Unidad Administrativa Especial de Aeronáutica Civil	Colombia	Non-IRA
Dirección General de Aviación Civil	Costa Rica	Non-IRA
Comisión Aeroportuaria	Dominican Republic	Non-IRA
Dirección General de Aviación Civil	Ecuador	Non-IRA
Autoridad de Aviación Civil	El Salvador	Non-IRA
Dirección General de Aviación Civil	Guatemala	Non-IRA
Autoridad Aeronáutica Civil	Panama	Non-IRA
Organismo Supervisor de la Inversión en Infraestructura de Transporte de Uso Público	Peru	IRA

Source: Author's compilation.
Note: IRA = independent regulatory agency.

powers to intervene in the economy. The agreed–upon framework involved creating commissions, in which part of their public administration structure would be subject to the accountability of the Congress. Their main decision-making body would be a board of directors composed of members appointed by the president with the agreement of Congress. This was precisely the origin of the term *independent*, that is, commissions that would be independent from the executive branch and subject to the accountability of Congress.

These agencies were created to regulate intrastate trade, communications, energy, and transport. Nonetheless, in the 1980s under the Reagan administration, and in a different policy context, they were used to implement a vast economic deregulation process.

The independence and administrative configuration of these agencies have been discussed since their creation. Nowadays, the prevailing opinion is that independent commissions have an institutional design that is only explained historically but not functionally. Moreover, different specialists in the matter have suggested the transformation of IRAs into single decision-making bodies, with their members subject to the same stability of the board of directors and their adjudication powers assigned to a special tribunal within the same agency (Verkuil 1988). Moreover, in the United States, the introduction of the regulatory review process by the Office of Information and Regulatory Affairs has added one more reason to believe that the idea of absolute independence of IRAs is an illusion.

The discussion around the autonomy of regulatory agencies in Latin America has become abstract in some countries and increasingly relevant in others. It has become abstract in countries where regulatory agencies were affected by political discretion, having little influence in policy making. Yet it has become relevant in countries that have made significant progress in their regulatory institutions. In the latter, the emergence of professionalized and more influential agencies has generated policy debates around the equilibrium between policy formulators and regulatory agencies, the oversight of regulation, and the mechanisms to guarantee autonomy (that is, the discussions in Brazil around the accountability of regulatory agencies to sector ministries).

This study defines autonomy in terms of four main patterns of decision makers: (a) the composition and appointment of the authorities, (b) budget independence, (c) the procedure to appoint and remove the main decision makers, and (d) the reasons by which decision makers can be removed.

Our aggregate measure of autonomy finds IRAs in a better position than government departments. This is not an indication of actual levels of autonomy but of the inputs agencies would need to perform in an environment where decisions can be made with reasonable levels of transparency and independence. Figure 4.1 shows a clear advantage of IRAs versus non-IRAs in this regard. Nevertheless, the disaggregation of our measure of autonomy in different variables shows advantages and disadvantages for both IRAs and non-IRAs. While an independent regulator provides more guarantees in terms of the meritocracy with which authorities are appointed and removed, not yet clear are the advantages of IRAs vis-à-vis non-IRAs in terms of their regulatory powers and the stability of their decision-making authorities. IRAs have more independent budgetary sources than government departments, although non-IRAs have significant contributions from inspection taxes (a parallel form of the regulatory tax that IRAs charge to private operators).

Composition and appointment of decision-making authorities. A critical aspect of the autonomy of any government body, with or without independent status, is the way the top authorities are appointed. In fact, the creation of IRAs in LAC countries was intended to cut the cycle of

Figure 4.1 Decision-Making Autonomy

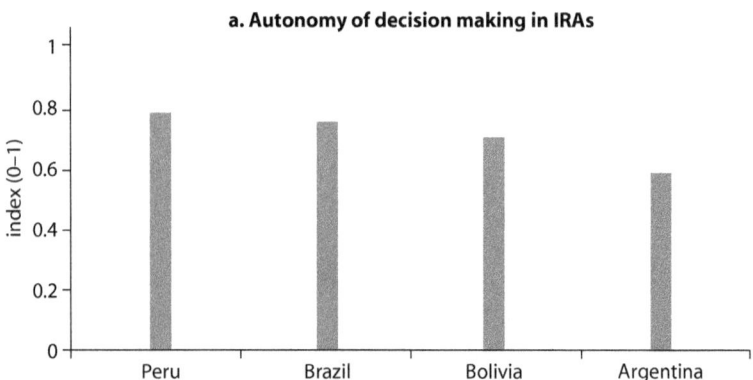

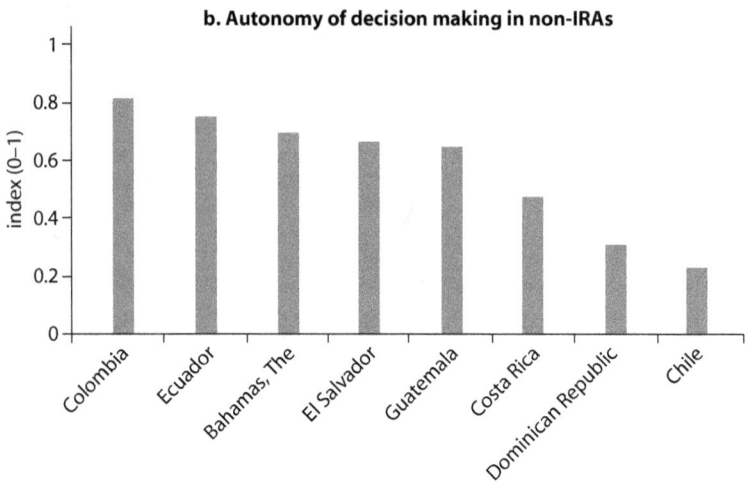

Source: Authors, based on responses to the Governance of Airport Regulators survey (see appendix B).

political appointees and discretional decision making in the infrastructure sectors. The initial configuration of independent regulators included the appointment of a board of directors with sufficient proficiency in economic regulation and a reasonable level of political independence. Unfortunately, this trend was reversed in the majority of the cases.

Independent regulators are in 50 percent of the cases appointed by the executive with different levels of intervention of the parliament. The involvement of the parliament is generally seen as positive, especially because it allows the participation of other stakeholders (especially the opposition parties) in the selection of directors to the board. The involvement of the executive (both through the president and the line minister) explains 70 percent of appointments in non-IRAs. Interestingly, in 30 percent of the cases, special agencies and trade associations linked to the airport sector also appoint representatives to the board. This last aspect of non-IRAs could be considered a positive development, considering the nontransparent norm of leaving the appointment of decision makers entirely to elected officials (figure 4.2).

Figure 4.2 Appointment Authorities

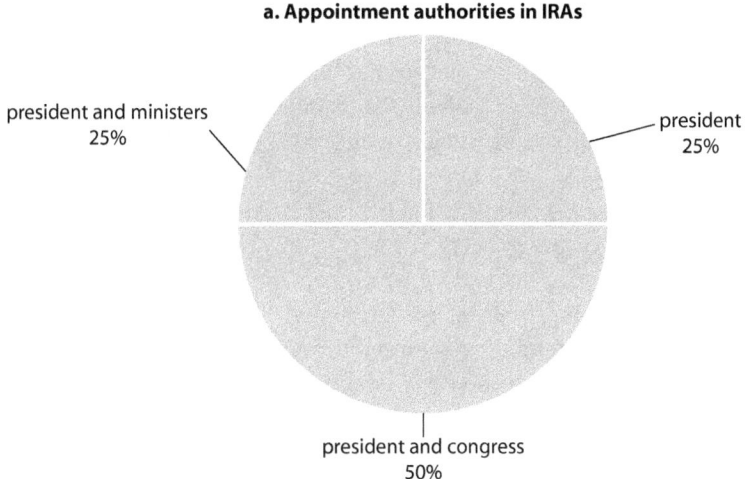

a. Appointment authorities in IRAs

- president and ministers 25%
- president 25%
- president and congress 50%

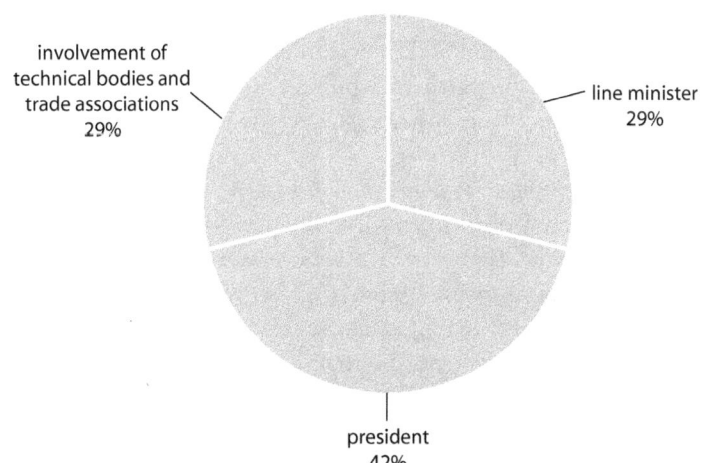

b. Appointment authorities in non-IRAs

- involvement of technical bodies and trade associations 29%
- line minister 29%
- president 42%

Source: Authors, based on responses to the Governance of Airport Regulators survey (see appendix B).

Budget independence. The composition of the budget is a critical aspect of the regulator's independence, perhaps its most salient characteristic (figure 4.3). Inspired by international best practices (Latifulhayat 2008), regulatory agencies of the region established a regulatory tax that would be charged to service providers. This source of funding would prevent the agency from being fully dependent on government support.

In the case of airport regulators, the majority of IRAs finance their budget with a tax or fee charged to service providers. The only exception is ANAC in Brazil, which receives 30 percent of funds from the central government. In accordance with the literature, we assume that agencies with budget autonomy have more freedom and flexibility to design programs and monitor operators. In fact, our measure of autonomy gives higher values to agencies whose budget is integrated with taxes or fees charged either to service providers (majority of IRAs) or passengers (some government departments).

Non-IRAs enjoy a combination of sources. Although in the majority of cases they receive government support, they also integrate their budgets with different taxes charged to passengers and airlines. Non-IRAs with autonomous funding present an alternative scheme to an institutional design of an independent regulator. So far, the literature in the LAC region has not yet addressed the benefits of these arrangements in the context of regulatory agencies.

Procedure to appoint and remove the main decision makers. Similar in relevance to the appointment of decision-making authorities is the way they can be removed from office (figure 4.4). In the case of IRAs, the legal statute requires a justified cause to proceed with the removal. In the cases of government departments, public servants may be removed under the sole discretion of the line minister or the president.

Reasons decision makers leave their positions. A complementary aspect related to the procedure to dismiss directors is the actual reasons they leave their positions (figure 4.5). Agencies were given four options: end of mandate, voluntary leave, external pressure, or retirement. Our measure of autonomy gives higher values to the first option. We would expect that a director that ends her or his mandate is the most desirable situation for the independence of regulators. We could also assume the same for a director that leaves the agency based on her or his own will. Nonetheless, voluntary leave may also reflect a disagreement with policy formulators (line minister or president) or undue pressures from the same actors.

Figure 4.3 Budget Composition

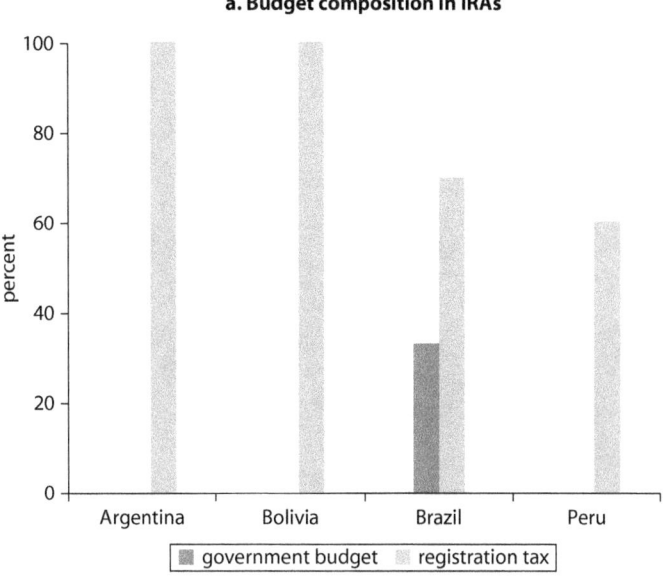

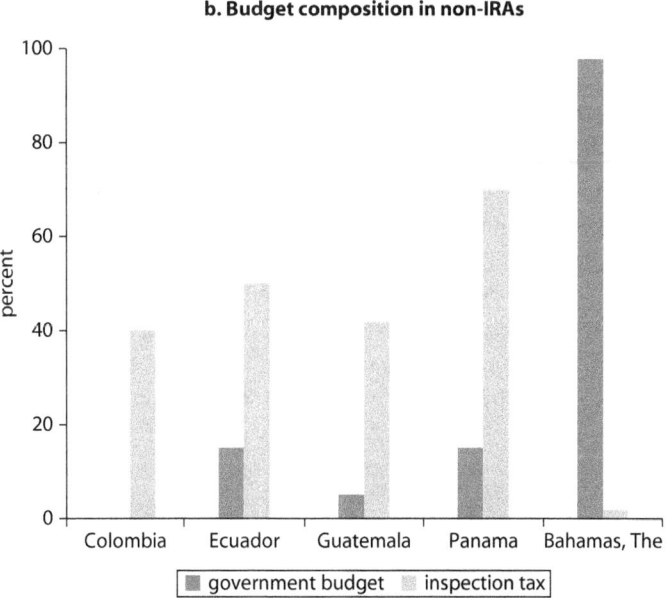

Source: Authors, based on responses to the Governance of Airport Regulators survey (see appendix B).

Figure 4.4 Procedure to Remove Decision Makers

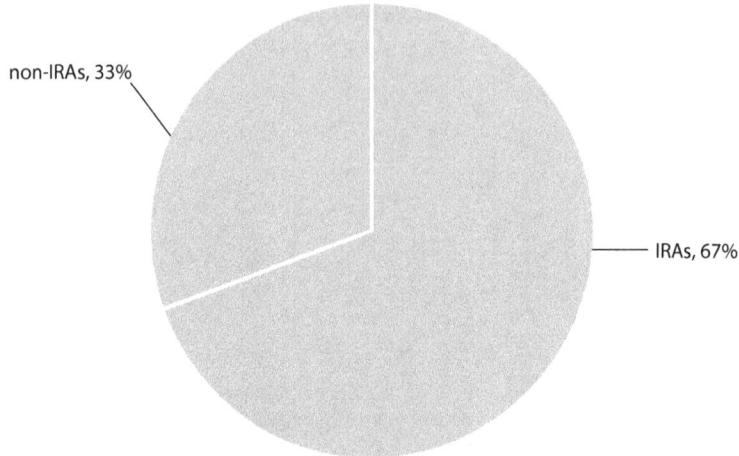

Source: Authors, based on responses to the Governance of Airport Regulators survey (see appendix B).
Note: Directors can only be removed under a bad performance cause.

End of mandate explains about 30 percent of the reasons why regulators leave both agencies and government departments. This percentage is higher in non-IRAs (35 percent) than in IRAs (29 percent).

The main difference between IRAs and non-IRAs with regard to why decision makers leave is seen in voluntary leave. Directors of IRAs leave office voluntarily in 57 percent of the cases, while in government departments this number is 29 percent. On the other hand, dismissal explains around 40 percent of the cases in government departments, while it is only 14 percent in the case of IRAs.

The previous numbers show contradictory results. The evidence shows that the likelihood of directors leaving voluntarily in a regulatory agency is higher than that for a civil servant in a government department. While this is consistent with the flexibility of a private law regime in regulatory agencies (they are hired under private law in most of the cases), it is not a positive sign for the stability of regulatory policies. It can even show that in practice, influence by the executive over directors is high, and they react by leaving the IRA.

Criteria to appoint authorities. In the context of highly volatile political environments and undue influence, meritocracy emerges as a critical factor in making regulatory decisions that are sound and transparent. The survey asked regulators to identify the criteria under which top decision makers are appointed.

Figure 4.5 Reasons Directors Leave Positions

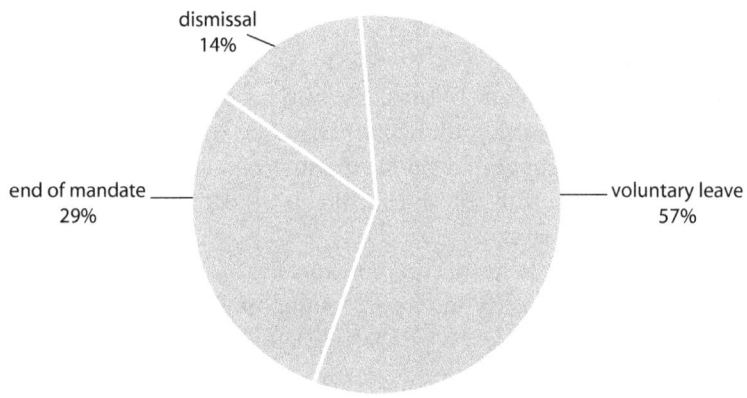

a. Reasons directors leave positions in IRAs

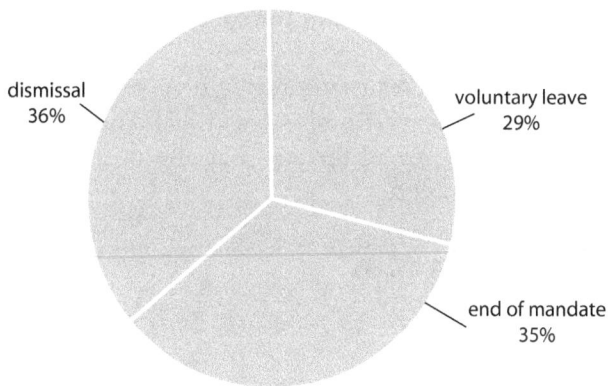

b. Reasons directors leave positions in non-IRAs

Source: Authors, based on responses to the Governance of Airport Regulators survey (see appendix B).

Our sample shows that in the cases of non-IRAs, requirements to be appointed as directors are soft. In the cases of IRAs, statutes require technical expertise in the appointment of decision-maker authorities. In only 25 percent of the cases, IRAs do not require any criteria for appointment. In the case of government departments, this number reaches 55 percent.

Regulatory autonomy. Another aspect included in the autonomy dimension of governance is the power of the agency vis-à-vis the government, the airport operator, and other institutions to set tariffs, quality of service standards, and other regulatory competencies. Surprisingly, results are similar for both IRAs and government departments in the LAC region's airport sector.

Quality of Bureaucracy

It is usually argued that one of the contributions of regulatory agencies to policy making is technical rationality (Thatcher 2007). An agency composed of directors appointed under meritocratic criteria and well-paid officials would constitute relevant factors to insulate it from politics and improve decision making.

In this section we focus on the bureaucracy of airport regulators. We define bureaucratic quality in airport regulators in terms of three main aspects: (a) educational levels of the regulator's staff, (b) the flexibility and powers of the agency to decide its own human resources policies, and (c) the publication of the agency's vacancies. Our definition of bureaucracy excludes directors to the board. Agency staff was defined in terms of three main categories: managers, technical workers, and administrative employees. In general, responses for educational levels were low compared to other questions.

In our measure of bureaucratic quality, IRAs present better scores than government departments (figures 4.6 and 4.7). This is reflected not only in the educational levels of the staff but also in the way vacancies are advertised and promoted.

Figure 4.6   Bureaucratic Quality

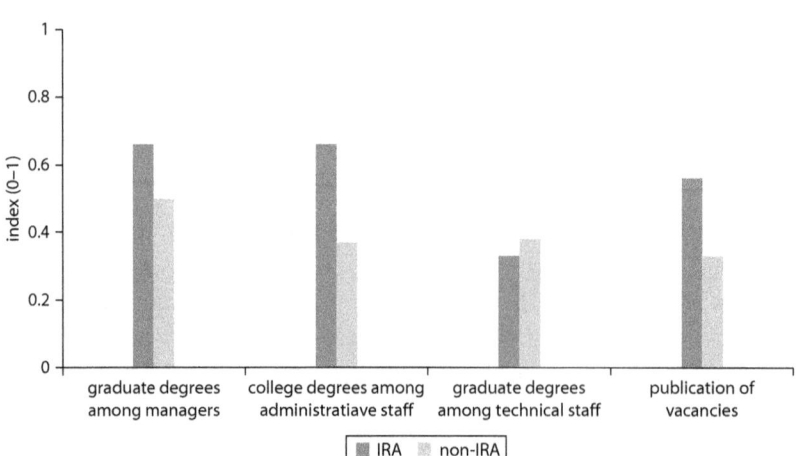

Source: Authors, based on responses to the Governance of Airport Regulators survey (see appendix B).

Figure 4.7 Bureaucratic Quality by Type

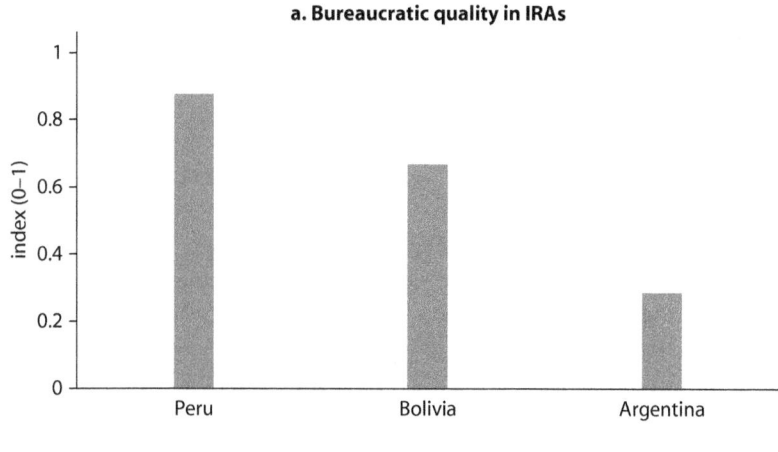

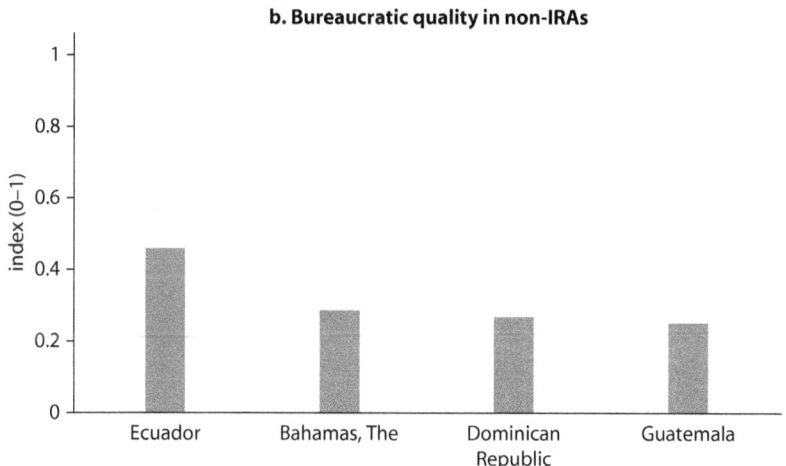

Source: Authors, based on responses to the Governance of Airport Regulators survey (see appendix B).

At the level of managers, IRAs present better results than government departments. On average, the majority of managers in IRAs have graduate degrees. Technical employees present a different landscape. Government departments show better results for graduate education than IRAs. Nevertheless, technical employees with college degrees have a higher incidence in IRAs than in government departments.

IRAs also present better results among administrative employees. When measured by those with a college degree, IRAs show, on average, a higher percentage of employees with this background.

Another important aspect of a high-quality bureaucracy is the way staff of the agency is selected. Regulators were given four options: (1) no publication, (2) publication on the agency's website, (3) publication in a newspaper, and (4) both options 2 and 3. We assigned higher values to those agencies that use both websites and newspapers to publish job vacancies. In this measure, IRAs also show, on average, more transparent human resource policies than government departments.

Transparency of Decision Making

The establishment of IRAs in the regulation of the infrastructure sector has been considered as a way of opening the regulatory process to affected parties. Attached to decision making in regulation was the development of different instances of consultations with both providers and consumers. Arrangements to promote and advocate consumers' rights include users' councils within the agency, consumer organizations, and consultations. The a priori expectation is that these tools are more likely to be used in the context of an IRA than in a government department.

In this section we compare practices of transparency in regulatory agencies and government departments. Our measure of transparency focuses on five main aspects: public consultations, legal effect of consultations, publication of the agency's decisions, publication of vacancies, and registration of board meetings.

Overall, IRAs offer a better framework for more transparent regulatory policies than government departments (figures 4.8 and 4.9).

On average, IRAs achieve better results than government departments in most of the dimensions. The regulatory agency model seems to provide a more suitable space for the involvement of consumers and other stakeholders in rule making and consultations. Consultations seem to have, according to the responses obtained, a larger influence in IRAs than in government departments.

ANAC in Brazil is the agency with the largest number of consultations. Since its establishment in 2006, the agency has conducted 12 consultation procedures that focused on tariffs, licenses, investment, safety, and consumers' rights. IRAs in Argentina and Peru, to a lesser extent, also perform consultations. In the case of Peru, consultations have focused mainly on tariff regulation.

Several IRAs of the region have established consultative committees as advisory bodies to the board of directors. OSITRAN, the transport

Figure 4.8 Transparency in Airport Regulators

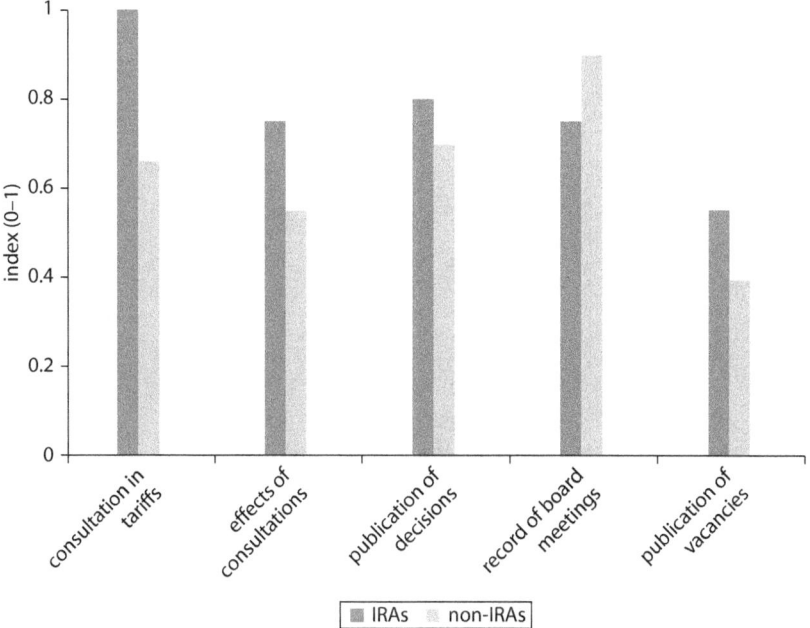

Source: Authors, based on responses to the Governance of Airport Regulators survey (see appendix B).

infrastructure investment regulator in Peru, created a consumer council to deal with demands from different sector stakeholders. ANAC in Brazil established a consultative committee that provides advice to the board of directors. A frequent criticism of these councils is the low levels of involvement of final consumers and the majority presence of service providers. For instance, there is only one association of passengers involved in the consumer council of OSITRAN, the majority of representation coming from airlines and other trade associations.

Accountability

The balance between independence and accountability is one of the most critical issues in the governance of independent agencies (OECD 2005). Politicians have traditionally questioned the independence of agencies headed by nonelected officials. From their perspective, regulatory agencies are part of the public administration and, as such, they should be held accountable to the government. Policy responses, in terms of the

Figure 4.9 Transparency by Type

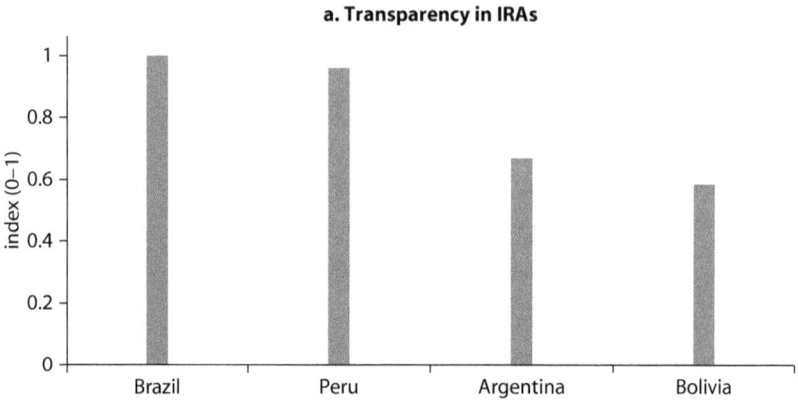

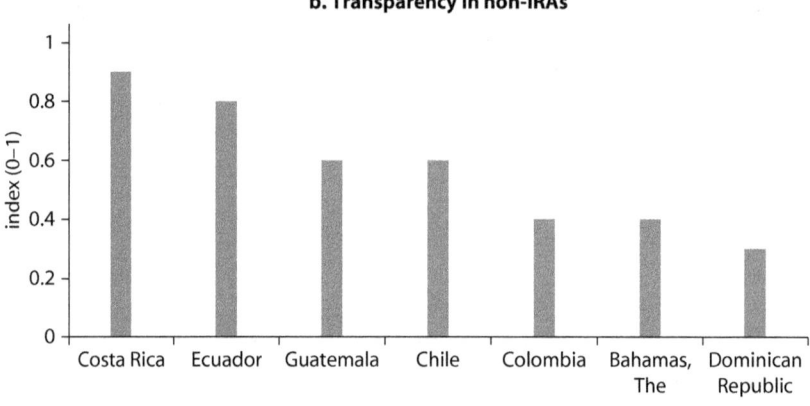

Source: Authors, based on responses to the Governance of Airport Regulators survey (see appendix B).

accountability of IRAs, range from those that prefer providing agencies with a significant playing field (Australia and the United Kingdom) to those imposing different controls and standards (New Zealand and the United States) (figures 4.10 and 4.11).

Our definition of accountability includes both its internal and external dimensions. Measures related to internal accountability are represented by the agency's staff evaluations. Measures of external accountability include public consultations and the instrument the agency uses to report its performance to external stakeholders. The definition also includes judicial accountability, or the review of the agency's decision by the courts.

Figure 4.10 Dimensions of Accountability in Airport Regulators

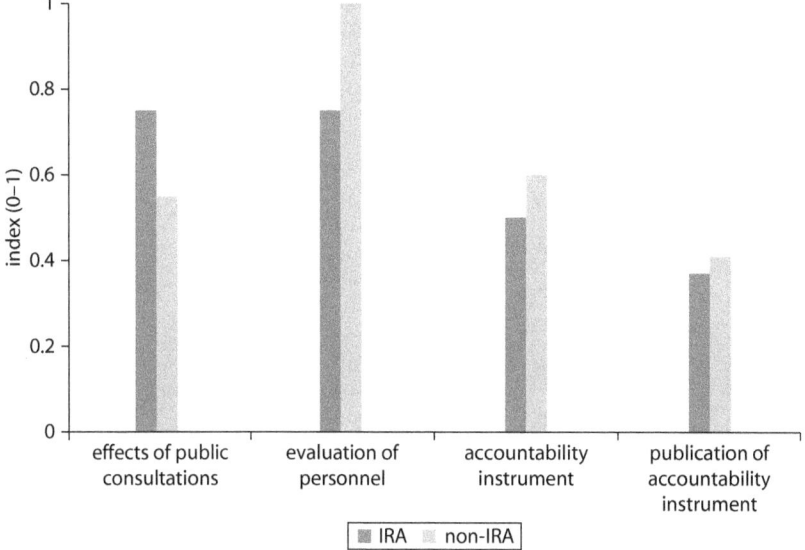

Source: Authors, based on responses to the Governance of Airport Regulators survey (see appendix B).

Our measure of accountability shows better results for non-IRAs than for independent regulators. Results may be consistent with the nature of government departments. Contrary to IRAs, government departments are subject to more public sector controls; hence, the monitoring of their decisions may have stronger accountability measures than regulatory agencies. In fact, as previously mentioned, the introduction of IRAs as completely independent entities has made governments question if independent commissions are the best institutional response to regulating infrastructure sectors.

With no exception, all IRAs and non-IRAs prepare an annual report of their performance. In some cases, such as Chile and Colombia, directors must give a presentation on sectoral issues before the congress when asked to do so. The agency's website is the preferred way to publish annual reports.

Economic Regulation

The main concern of all economic agents in the airport sector is how tariffs are set. Tariff regulation in airports should be concerned exclusively with those services that have characteristics of natural monopoly and thus

Figure 4.11 Dimensions of Accountability in IRAs and Non-IRAs

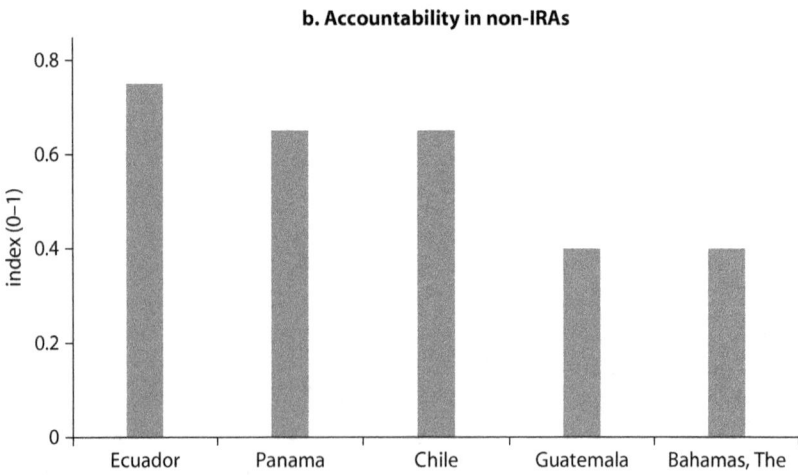

Source: Authors, based on responses to the Governance of Airport Regulators survey (see appendix B).

where price regulation is necessary. These services are usually referred to as aeronautical services and include runway use, aircraft parking, air traffic control, meteorological services, and passenger handling. There are different approaches to setting regulated tariffs, but they can be grouped under two main methodologies: single till and dual till. Under the first of these methodologies, regulated operational costs related to aeronautical services are recovered through revenues generated by aeronautical and nonaeronautical (that is, commercial) activities, with profits from commercial activities used to help maintain low levels of regulated aeronautical tariffs. On the other hand, under a dual till model, operational costs related to aeronautical services are exclusively recovered through revenues obtained from charging for the provision of aeronautical services (Starkie and Yarrow 2000). With the risk of oversimplifying the differences between the two approaches, the single till method allows the existence of cross-subsidies between airports' aeronautical and commercial activities.

Following the example set by the United Kingdom, most airports in Latin America rely (explicitly in a few cases and implicitly in most) on the single till approach. Table 4.3 shows that six countries reported setting tariffs following a single till model. However, the answers provided by regulatory agencies regarding this issue are contradictory. For instance in Argentina, Brazil, El Salvador, and Guatemala, regulatory agencies claim that their tariff-setting mechanism responds to the single till model. However, in a separate question, these four regulatory agencies claim that the costs associated with the provision of aeronautical services are fully recovered through aeronautical tariffs.

To be able to set tariffs, regulatory agencies should develop and maintain a comprehensive economic and financial model. If an agency does not have an economic and financial model, it will have only a partial understanding of the performance of the regulated airports. To feed an economic and financial model, regulators develop regulatory accounting manuals specifying the information that operators need to submit to regulatory agencies. Within our sample, only 8 of the 14 regulatory agencies that answered the questionnaire stated that they employ an economic and financial model. However, it is not easy to assess if the economic and financial models are being used in practice to regulate airport operators. Other responses indicate that of the eight agencies that rely on an economic and financial model, only four use a regulatory accounting manual.

The regulator needs to make sure that the operator reaches an economic and financial equilibrium. In other words, it needs to make sure the operator's internal rate of return (IRR) is equal to the weighted average cost of capital (WACC). If the WACC is higher than the IRR, the operator will exit the market. Only 5 of the agencies that responded to the questionnaire estimate the WACC faced by the operators (and only 3 of those 5 perform these estimations on a regular basis). Finally, only 5

Table 4.3 Answers to Selected Questions on Economic Regulation in the Airport Sector

Country	Does agency regulate private operators?	Was agency created before introduction of private management?	Single till, dual till, or hybrid?	Are aeronautical services' costs recovered through aeronautical tariffs?	Are commercial tariffs subject to any regulation?	Does agency use an economic and financial model?	Manual of regulatory accounting?	Does agency estimate cost of capital?	Does agency conduct economic and financial audits?
Argentina	Y	Y	Single till	Y	Y	Y	Y	N	Y
Bahamas, The	Y	Y	Single till	N	Y	Y	Y	Y	Y
Bolivia	Y	Y	Single till	N	N	N	N	Y	N
Brazil	Y	N	Single till	Y	N	Y	N	N	N
Chile	Y	Y	Dual till	Y	Y	N	N	Y	N
Colombia	Y	Y	Single till	N	N	Y	Y	N	Y
Costa Rica	Y	Y	Single till/hybrid	Y	Y	Y	N	N	Y
Dominican Republic	Y	Y	Dual till	Y	Y	Y	N	N	N
Ecuador	Y	Y	Hybrid	Y	N	N	N	n.a.	N
El Salvador	n.a.	n.a.	Single till	Y	N	n.a.	N	N	N
Guatemala	N	—	Single till	Y	Y	N	N	N	N
Panama	N	—	Dual till	Y	N	Y	N	Y	N
Peru	Y	Y	Dual Till/hybrid	Y	N	Y	Y	Y	Y

Source: Authors, based on responses to the Governance of Airport Regulators survey (see appendix B).

Note: n.a. = answers were missing, incomplete, or unclear.

a. Ecuador's regulatory agency estimates the cost of capital for only those airports that are still operated by the state (nonconcessioned airports).

out of the 14 agencies frequently conduct economic and financial audits of the airport operators they regulate.

Airport regulators are well aware of the trade-off between tariffs and quality of service. When tariffs are regulated (and in particular, when they are subject to a binding price cap), airport operators will naturally tend to lower the quality of service in order to reduce their costs and thus obtain higher profit margins. Against this backdrop, it becomes essential for regulators to introduce the right incentives for operators to increase the quality of the service they provide. Strikingly, only three agencies in our sample (Brazil, Costa Rica, and Peru) responded positively to the question of whether the regulatory framework includes tools to monitor the evolution of quality of service and to design proper economic incentives for improvement.

The results from our survey suggest that there are serious deficiencies regarding economic regulation in the airport sector in the LAC region. On the one hand, very few of the agencies in charge of enforcing regulations have in place the necessary information systems (regulatory accounting manuals, economic and financial models) necessary to perform their tasks correctly. Even when agencies declared that they have adequate information systems in place, they are not using them to estimate the WACC, which is an essential variable for a regulator. In addition, the regulatory frameworks do not seem to provide appropriate incentives for regulators to properly carry out frequent oversight of the quality of services provided by operators.

Conclusions

Regardless of the existence or nonexistence of a private sector provision, an institutional design identified with an independent regulatory agency appears to provide a better space for good regulatory governance than a government department. Both regional and international experiences show the importance of a government agency that is highly specialized and makes consumers the focus of their policies. Nonetheless, a regulatory agency is not capable, on its own, to introduce institutional quality into an airport system where policies are ill-designed. But it may, even in an adverse context, enable an adequate representation of stakeholders and a filter to discretional decisions.

The division of transparency into different dimensions allowed the identification of several advantages in IRAs versus government departments. Consultations are the most notable of these advantages. The consumer orientation of regulatory agencies versus government departments, whether in the context of state-owned companies or private providers, is a powerful factor to bring stakeholders' opinions into the decision-making process.

Technical expertise is another aspect where IRAs show advantages. Our measure of bureaucratic quality found, on average, higher bureaucratic quality levels in independent commissions than in government departments. These results are reflected not only in the educational levels of the staff but also in the way vacancies are posted and filled.

The most controversial aspect of the governance of IRAs is autonomy. Our measure of autonomy found, on average, more guarantees of autonomy in IRAs than in non-IRAs. Nevertheless, non-IRAs also show similar regulatory powers and lower turnover rates in their policy makers.

Regional experiences provide interesting findings in support of our arguments. The cases of Brazil and Peru are, perhaps, the most illustrative. The introduction of regulatory agencies has, in both countries, contributed to more transparent and accountable decision making. These cases are interesting as they present two situations of regulatory agencies in contexts of private sector (Peru) and state (Brazil) provision of the service.

A worrisome outcome of the surveys' analysis was the serious deficiency of economic regulation in the airport sector in the LAC region. On the one hand, very few of the agencies in charge of enforcing regulations have in place the information systems (regulatory accounting manuals, economic and financial models) necessary to perform their tasks correctly. On the other hand, even when agencies claim to have adequate information systems in place, the vast majority are not using them to estimate the weighted average cost of capital, which is an essential variable for a regulator. In addition, the regulatory frameworks do not seem to provide appropriate incentives for regulators to properly carry out frequent oversight of the quality of services provided by operators.

Despite the overall advantage of IRAs for good regulatory governance, conclusions should not be interpreted in a "one model fits all" approach. Rather, they should be used for the purpose of identifying those mechanisms that better guarantee open and sound decision making in the regulation of airport services. The comparison between IRAs and non-IRAs in airports allowed the disaggregation of governance in different dimensions and the selection of advantages and disadvantages in both models. It is up to policy makers to prioritize those aspects that better fit in their institutional and policy frameworks.

References

Andrés, L., J. L. Guasch, M. Diop, and A. S. Lopez. 2007. "Assessing the Governance of Electricity Regulatory Agencies in Latin America and the Caribbean: A Benchmarking Analysis." Policy Research Working Paper 4380, World Bank, Washington, DC.

Andrés, L. A., J. L. Guasch, T. Haven, and V. Foster. 2008. *The Impact of Private Sector Participation in Infrastructure: Lights, Shadows and the Road Ahead*. Washington, DC: World Bank.

Correa, P., C. Pereira, B. Mueller, and M. Melo. 2006. "Regulatory Governance in Infrastructure Industries: Assessment and Measurement of Brazilian Regulators." World Bank/Public-Private Infrastructure Advisory Facility (PPIAF), Washington, DC.

Estache, A., and M. Rossi. 2008. "Regulatory Agencies: Impact on Firm Performance and Social Welfare." Policy Research Working Paper 4509, World Bank, Washington, DC.

Gutierrez, L. H. 2003. "Regulatory Governance in the Latin American Telecommunications Sector." *Utilities Policies* 11 (4): 225–40.

Latifulhayat, A. 2008. "The Independent Regulatory Body: A New Regulatory Institution in the Privatised Telecommunications Industry." *International Journal of Technology Transfer and Commercialisation* 7 (1): 15–33. doi: 10.1504/IJTTC.2008.018800.

Levi-Faur, D., and J. Jordana. 2004. "The Rise of the Regulatory State in Latin America: A Study of the Diffusion of Regulatory Reforms Across Countries and Sectors." Centre on Regulation and Competition, Institute for Development Policy and Management, University of Manchester, U.K.

Lipovich, G. A. 2008. "The Privatization of Argentine Airports." *Journal of Air Transport Management* 14: 8–15.

OECD (Organisation for Economic Co-operation and Development). 2002. "Regulatory Policies in OECD Countries: From Interventionism to Regulatory Governance." OECD, Paris.

———. 2005. *Designing Independent and Accountable Regulatory Authorities for High Quality Regulation*. Proceedings of an Expert Meeting in London, United Kingdom, January 10–11.

Starkie, D., and G. Yarrow. 2000. "The Single Till Approach to the Price Regulation of Airports." Civil Aviation Authority, London, U.K. http://www.caa.co.uk/docs/5/ergdocs/starkieyarrow.pdf.

Thatcher, M. 2007. "Regulatory Agencies, the State and Markets: A Franco-British Comparison." Working Paper RSCAS 2007/17, European University Institute, Florence School of Regulation, Florence, Italy.

Verkuil, P. 1988. "The Purpose and Limits of Independent Agencies." Faculty Publications Paper 1029, College of William and Mary Law School, Williamsburg, VA.

CHAPTER 5

Benchmarking of Aeronautical Charges at Latin American Airports

Overview

A study of tariffs was not envisaged at the time this report was conceived. However, the study of performance indicators and the feedback received from airport regulators, airlines, and other stakeholders consulted during the preparation of this report prompted us to calculate the evolution of airport tariffs and generate a regional benchmark that constitutes the only one publicly available.

The tariff benchmarking exercise includes 26 airports within 20 Latin American and Caribbean (LAC) countries (see table 5.1) and for three years: 1995, 2003, and 2009. The selection of years responds to the dual objective of including ample data and measuring the changes in tariff structures and levels as a result of introducing private sector participation in airport infrastructure management. Since most airport concessions in the region took place before 2002, the year 2003 was selected to test the assumption that price increases took place after airports were concessioned to the private sector.[1] The year 2009 was included to present the latest available information on tariffs at the time this report was written, while 1995 was chosen because in that year no private sector participation policy discussions were held in LAC.

Table 5.1   Airport Sample Used for the Aeronautical Tariff Benchmarking Analysis

	Country	Airport name
1	Argentina	Buenos Aires – Ministro Pistarini International
2	Bahamas, The	Nassau – Lynden Pindling International Airport
3	Bolivia	La Paz – El Alto International
4		Santa Cruz – Viru Viru International
5	Brazil	Rio de Janeiro – Galeão International
6		São Paulo – Guarulhos International
7	Chile	Santiago – Comodoro Arturo Merino Benitez International
8	Colombia	Bogotá – El Dorado International
9		Cali – Alfonso Bonilla Aragón International
10	Costa Rica	San José – Juan Santamaría International
11	Dominican Republic	Santo Domingo – Las Américas International
12	Ecuador	Quito – Mariscal Sucre International
13	El Salvador	San Salvador – Camalapa International Airport
14	Guatemala	Guatemala City – La Aurora International
15	Honduras	Tegucigalpa – Toncontín International
16	Jamaica	Kingston – Norman Manley International
17	Mexico	Cancún International
18		Guadalajara – Miguel Hidalgo y Costilla International
19		Mexico City – Benito Juárez International
20		Monterrey – General Mariano Escobedo International
21	Nicaragua	Managua – Augusto C. Sandino International
22	Panama	Panama – Tocumen International
23	Paraguay	Asunción – Silvio Pettirossi International
24	Peru	Lima – Jorge Chávez International
25	Uruguay	Montevideo – Carrasco International
26	Venezuela, RB	Caracas – Simón Bolivar International
27	France	Paris – Charles de Gaulle International
28	Germany	Frankfurt – am Main International
29	Spain	Madrid – Barajas International
30	United Kingdom	London – Heathrow International
31	United States	Los Angeles – Los Angeles International
32		New York – John F. Kennedy Airport
33		Miami – Miami International

The preparatory work for this chapter included extensive research to obtain cross-country comparisons of tariffs, including an exploration of airports' and regulators' web pages and specialized publications, as well as consultations with airport and airline international organizations. Research showed that international benchmarking of aeronautical tariffs of LAC airports is not publicly available, but several sources contain limited information for a price. However, in most cases, these sources offer incomplete data for LAC airports, and there is limited tariff data prior to 2005 for a large sample of LAC airports. Even private consulting firms engaged in international benchmarking exercises have scarce information on LAC airports.

Surprisingly, regulators and ministerial departments reported during the preparatory work of this study that they do not carry out frequent benchmarking studies. This is particularly worrisome given that regional tariff benchmarking studies should be a basic instrument for regulators, especially when they need to make informed decisions about tariff changes as part of ordinary tariff review processes and when contract renegotiation with a private operator is required.

To provide an international reference to the benchmarking analysis, the following airports were included in the sample: New York (JFK), Los Angeles (LAX), Miami (MIA), Madrid (MAD), Paris (CDG), London (LHR), and Frankfurt (FRA). These European and North American airports concentrate most of their Latin American international flights outside of the LAC region.

The tariff benchmarking presented in this section focuses solely on the aircraft-passenger tariff dimension of the charges that aircrafts (airlines) and passengers pay according to established norms and regulations. No attempt is made to analyze the tariff structure between the components (landing fees, aircraft parking, and use of boarding bridges, among other tariffs) and the economic incentives embedded in them. This topic, however, merits further research as it is very relevant for economic regulation of airports and planning of infrastructure investments.

Methodology

The tariff benchmarking exercise includes an analysis of regulated tariffs that are part of the total turnaround costs established by airports on any given flight. The analysis covers the following regulated charges: landing fees (and night surcharge for lighting), aircraft parking, use of boarding bridges, and passenger charges (passenger facility charges, security, and federal taxes).

To make sure the benchmarking analysis is a true cross-comparison, specific assumptions were made regarding the type of aircraft, time spent on the ground, number of passengers on board (or percentage of aircraft seats occupied), and other variables.

The aircraft selected for comparison are consistent with the types of fleets most commonly found in the LAC region in 2009. The Airbus A320 is the most popular aircraft in LAC, serving short- and medium-haul routes. The Boeing 767-300 is the most widely used aircraft for medium- and long-haul destinations. The parameters and assumptions used are summarized in table 5.2. While charges were estimated and compared for both types of aircraft, detailed calculations of aeronautical tariffs are presented only for the Airbus A320 to avoid producing a very long and repetitive chapter. Summary graphs, including total turnaround costs, are presented for the Boeing 767-300.

Information to carry out the benchmarking exercise was obtained from two main sources: the International Air Transport Association's (IATA) *Airport and Air Navigation Charges Manual* and countries' Aeronautical Information Publications (AIP 1993, 2003, 2009). The former contains detailed information on regulated charges for about 300 airports worldwide, which is updated on a regular basis.[2] For this study, the information provided by IATA was crosschecked with tariffs published in the AIPs of the countries included in the sample. In cases of discrepancies between information provided by IATA and the AIPs, the data used correspond to the AIP data sets.

Tariffs are measured in real terms (in 2009 U.S. dollars). Nominal prices were converted to real prices according to the United States Consumer Price Index (CPI), as reported by the International Monetary Fund's (IMF) World Economic Outlook database. The U.S. CPI was selected instead of each country's CPI because the price adjustment clauses of airport privatization contracts in the region generally use the U.S. CPI as the benchmark.

One important assumption in the analysis was the type of flight: all flights considered for this analysis correspond to international flights. Some countries discriminate airport tariffs according to the origin and destination of flights. In some countries, domestic flights enjoy lower

Table 5.2 Key Parameters of the Aircraft Used in the Analysis

Parameter	Airbus A320	Boeing 767-300
Fuselage	Narrow-body	Wide-body
Range	Short, medium	Medium, long
Maximum take-off weight (MTOW)	77 tons	187 tons
Seating capacity	150 seats	269 seats
Assumed load factor	71%	71%

Source: Author's estimation with data from Airbus S.A.S. and Boeing Commercial Airplanes.

regulated charges despite the fact that the aircraft is the same and demands the same infrastructure service as a flight with an international destination. Thus, the "international" price was used at airports that set different rates for international and domestic operations.

Landing Charge and Lighting Surcharge

Landing fees at every airport in the sample are based on the aircraft maximum takeoff weight (MTOW), which is a standard manufacturer feature of the aircraft. In 2009, rates in LAC ranged from US$0.4 to US$13.30 per ton. However, calculation methods differ greatly from airport to airport. Some airports charge per ton of MTOW, some include a fixed-amount component, and some employ weight bands to establish the unit rate per ton. Given the variety of approaches and to ensure a true cross-comparison, landing fees were compared for the cost of landing an aircraft of the same characteristics (for an Airbus A320 and Boeing 767–300, with parameters listed in table 5.2). Using this method, the calculation of the landing fees included every aspect of the tariff structure, such as fixed amounts, minimums, and weight bands. In other words, it compares how much the same aircraft pays at each one of the different airports.

Some airports, especially those in Europe, levy a noise charge that varies according to the aircraft noise category (which is usually defined by the airport). Since these charges were created either to avoid (through the operation of quieter aircraft) or to penalize the generation of noise during landing and takeoff, they were included in the landing fees calculation.

Half the airports in the sample also feature a lighting surcharge (or night surcharge) for operations taking place during the night hours. The following graphs show the landing fees (total charge) for an Airbus A320 during day hours (figure 5.1) and during night hours (figure 5.2).

According to the sample, average landing charges for an Airbus A320 on a daylight operation is US$298 in LAC, and US$591 for the European and U.S. airports in our sample. Quito has the highest landing fees in LAC, at US$781, while Santo Domingo has the lowest, with total landing charges of US$54. For landing fees during night operations, Quito and Santo Domingo are also the most and least expensive airports in LAC, as landing fees total US$1,014 and US$54, respectively, for an Airbus A320. The average charge for an Airbus A320 on a night operation in LAC is US$330 and rises to US$663 in Europe and the United States.

Landing fees have decreased in real terms between 1995 and 2009 at most airports in Latin America and the Caribbean (figure 5.3).

Figure 5.1 Landing Fees for an Airbus A320, Daylight Operation

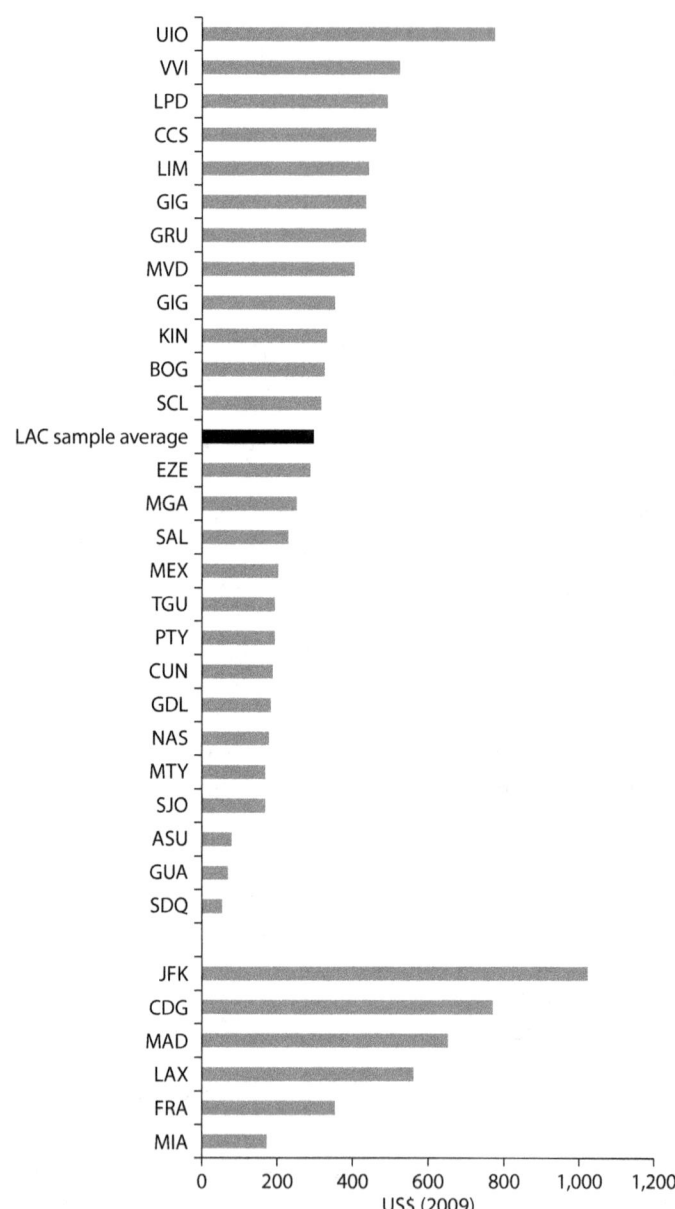

Source: Author's elaboration based on information from IATA (2009), Aeronautical Information Publication (AIP) Colombia, AIP Costa Rica, El Salvador Airport, AIP Nicaragua, Panama Civil Aviation Authority (CAA), Dirección Nacional de Aviación Civil e Infraestructura Aeronaútica (DINACIA) Uruguay.
Note: Buenos Aires assumes that payments are made on time; San Jose includes airside infrastructure charge; Santo Domingo assumes landing during off-peak hours; Guatemala includes ramp fees; Mexico assumes tariff A (off-peak); Los Angeles assumes the airline is a signatory carrier; New York assumes landing during off-peak hours. For a list of airport codes and the airports they represent, see page xxiii.

Figure 5.2 Landing Fees for an Airbus A320, Night Operation

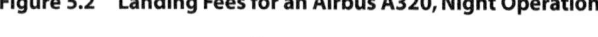

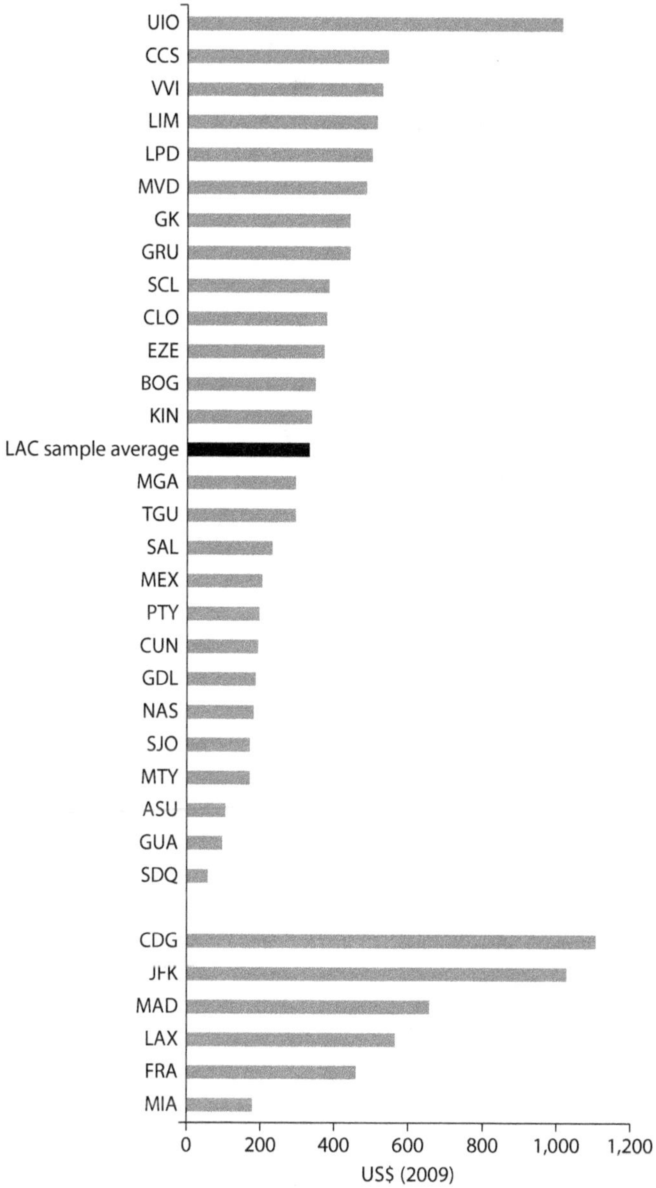

Source: Author's elaboration based on information from IATA (2009), AIP Colombia, AIP Costa Rica, El Salvador Airport, AIP Nicaragua, Panama CAA, DINACIA Uruguay.
Note: See note for figure 5.1.

Figure 5.3 Changes in Landing Fees for an Airbus A320, Daylight Operation

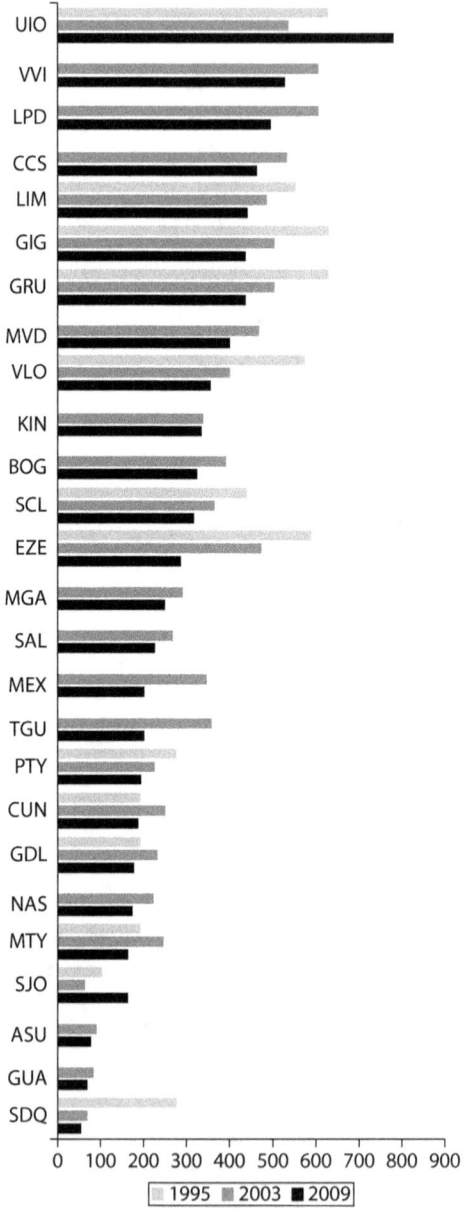

Source: Author's elaboration based on information from IATA (1995, 2003, and 2009), AIP Colombia, AIP Costa Rica, El Salvador Airport, AIP Nicaragua, Panama CAA, DINACIA Uruguay.
Note: For a list of airport codes and the airports they represent, see page xxiii.

In the sample, nominal landing fees increased on average by 4.7 percent between 1995[3] and 2003 and remained constant between 2003 and 2009. However, if the inflationary effect is incorporated, landing fees in real terms declined in the majority of airports in the region from 1995 to 2009. As seen in figure 5.3, landing fees measured in constant dollars decreased at 10 out of 13 airports between 1995 and 2003 and at 11 of those airports between 1995 and 2009. When only the 2003–09 period is considered, there was a reduction in real landing fees at 24 of the 26 airports in the sample (figure 5.4).

On average, landing fees fell by 14 percent in real terms between 1995 and 2003, and by 10 percent between 2003 and 2009. San José is clearly the airport with the most significant price escalation (167 percent between 2003 and 2009), although, as significant as the increase seems in relative terms, it did not have a dramatic impact in absolute terms, as San José features one of the cheapest landing fees in the region. If San José was excluded from the sample, landing fees on average would have fallen by 17 percent in real terms between 2003 and 2009 in the LAC region.

Aircraft Parking Charges

Parking fees are time and weight based and, as with landing fees, airports employ different methods of charging airlines, varying significantly from airport to airport. Most of the airports include a grace period (free time) after landing, which ranges from one hour to up to six hours from the moment of engine shutdown ("chocks-in").

Figure 5.5 compares parking charges for a two-hour period for an Airbus A320. Zero values indicate that the two-hour period is within the free time allowance included in the landing charge, and hence the airline is not levied with any additional charges for parking.

Only nine airports in LAC charge parking for two-hour periods. Fees for an Airbus A320 range from US$373 in Cancún to US$15 in Managua, with an average of US$145. In Europe and the United States, four out of seven airports included in our sample charge for parking for two-hour periods, and the average price is US$72.

Parking fees have declined in real terms between 1995 and 2009, as seen in the figure 5.6. Airports where parking fees were raised in real terms between 1995 and 2003 experienced reductions between 2003 and 2009. The net effect is that at five of the six airports where prices for 1995 were available, 2009 parking fees were lower in real terms than those of 1995.

Figure 5.4 Landing Fees Percentage Change for an Airbus A320, Daylight Operation

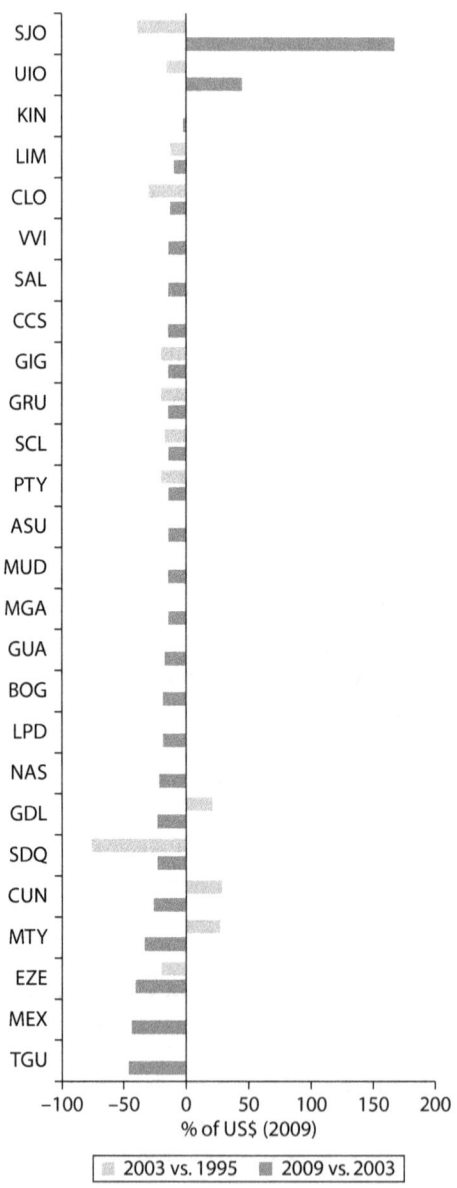

Source: Author's elaboration based on information from IATA (1995, 2003, and 2009), AIP Colombia, AIP Costa Rica, El Salvador Airport, AIP Nicaragua, Panama CAA, DINACIA Uruguay.
Note: For a list of airport codes and the airports they represent, see page xxiii.

Figure 5.5 Parking Charge for an Airbus A320, for 2 Hours

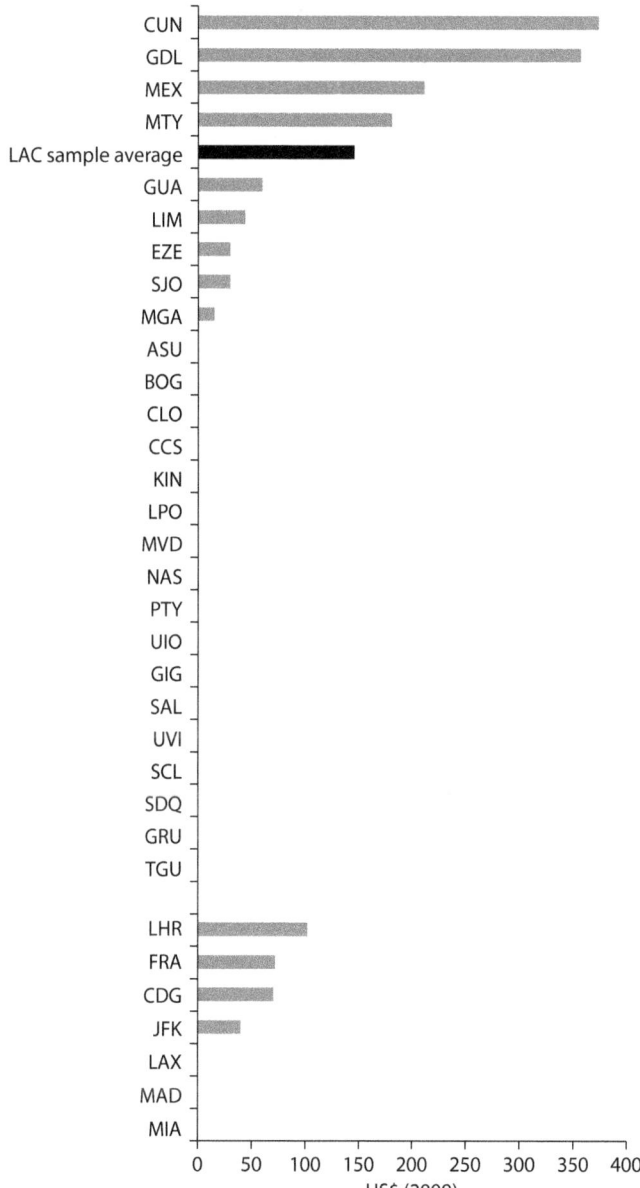

Source: Author's elaboration based on information from IATA (2009), AIP Colombia, AIP Costa Rica, El Salvador Airport, AIP Nicaragua, Panama CAA, DINACIA Uruguay.
Note: Buenos Aires assumes parking in operating apron; São Paulo and Rio de Janeiro assume parking in operating apron; Mexico assumes tariff A (off-peak); London assumes off-peak period. For a list of airport codes and the airports they represent, see page xxiii.

Figure 5.6 Changes in Parking Charges for an Airbus A320, for 2 Hours

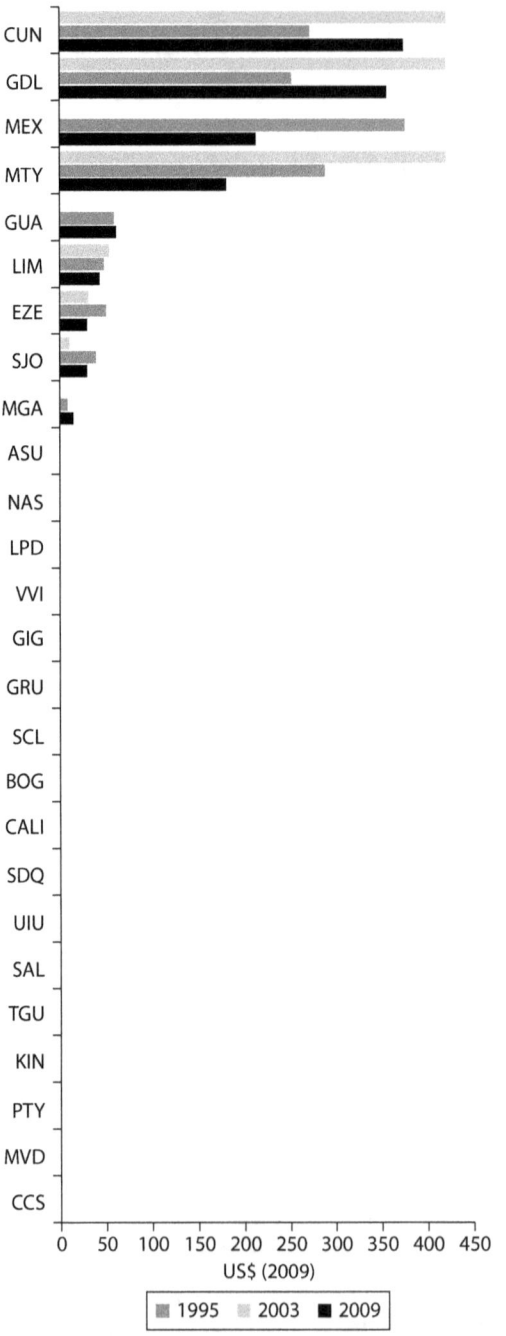

Source: Author's elaboration based on information from IATA (1995, 2003, and 2009), AIP Colombia, AIP Costa Rica, El Salvador Airport, AIP Nicaragua, Panama CAA, DINACIA Uruguay.
Note: For a list of airport codes and the airports they represent, see page xxiii.

Landing and Parking Charges

Less than half of the 26 airports in this sample separate landing from parking charges. In the rest, the fee paid for landing includes limited free time on the ground. Therefore, in order to make an accurate comparison of landing fees, fees have to be aggregated with the cost for parking. Figure 5.7 shows the consolidated cost of landing and parking for the same sample of airports.

Figure 5.7 illustrates that when aggregating landing and parking fees into one measurement, the ranking of airports changes significantly. For example, Quito is now the most expensive airport in the sample, followed by Cancún, although Cancún was among the least expensive when the comparison considered only landing fees costs. It should be highlighted that airports in Central America and the Caribbean tended to congregate at the lower end of the graph, indicating that they generally are among the cheapest in the LAC sample when landing and parking fees are analyzed jointly. More generally, under this scenario, landing and parking charges declined in real terms between 1995 and 2009 (figure 5.8).

For the airports where 1995 prices were available, average landing and parking fees dropped from US$511 in 1995 to US$408 in 2003 and US$386 in 2009. If all the airports in the sample are considered, the average charge in real terms decreased from US$398 in 2003 to US$348 in 2009.

Boarding Bridge Charges

The charge for the use of a boarding bridge also differs among airports in the sample: some charge a fixed amount per usage (connection fee), while others consider the aircraft's MTOW and the time it stays connected to the gate. Figure 5.9 presents the calculation of boarding bridge charges for an Airbus A320, relying on the assumptions outlined in table 5.2.

As seen in figure 5.9, there is less variation for boarding bridge charges than for landing fees, as charges in the majority of the airports consider only the time the aircraft is connected with the gate. Airports like San José, Santo Domingo, Asunción, Montevideo, and Quito are exceptions, as they contemplate the type of aircraft when charging for the use of a boarding bridge.

An Airbus A320 is charged for a two-hour boarding bridge usage between US$200 in Buenos Aires and US$25 in Santo Domingo, with an average of US$89 in the 22 LAC airports that charge for this service.[4] There is a significant variance in this charge among the European and U.S. airports included in our sample. Some airports, such as London

Figure 5.7 Landing Fees and Parking Charge for an Airbus A320, for 2 Hours, 2009

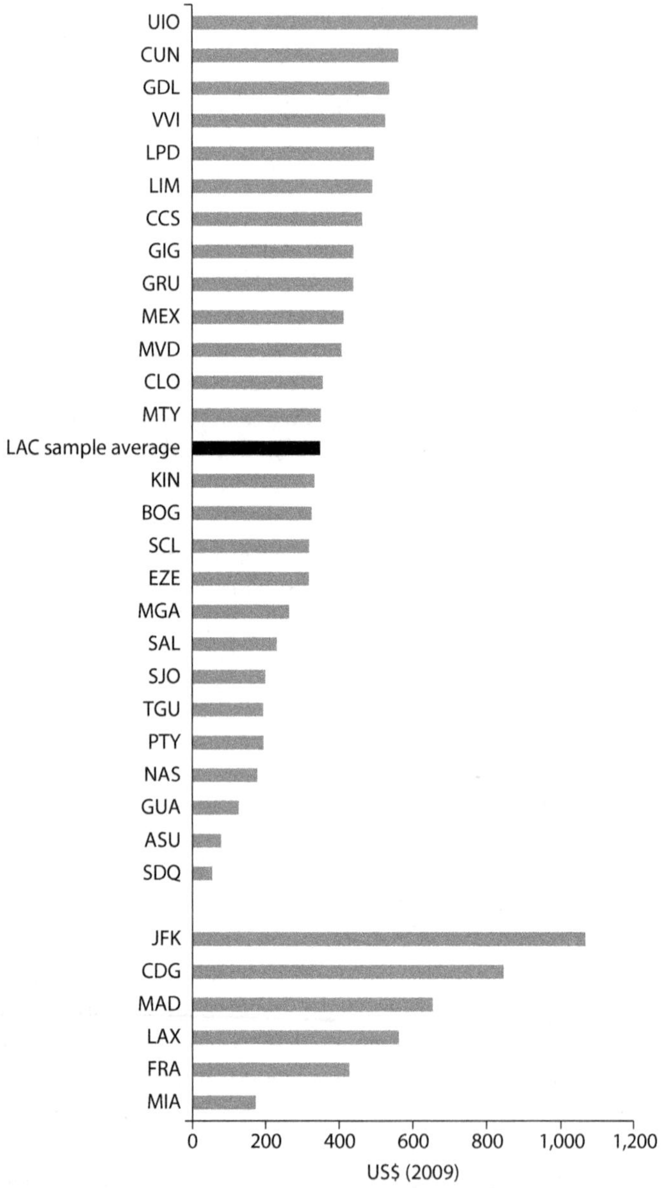

Source: Author's elaboration based on information from IATA (2009), AIP Colombia, AIP Costa Rica, El Salvador Airport, AIP Nicaragua, Panama CAA, DINACIA Uruguay.
Note: Buenos Aires assumes on-time payments and parking in operating apron; São Paulo and Rio de Janeiro assume parking in operating apron; San José includes airside infrastructure charge; Santo Domingo assumes landing during off-peak hours; Guatemala includes ramp fees; Mexico assumes tariff A (off-peak); Los Angeles assumes the airline is a signatory carrier; New York assumes landing during off-peak hours. For a list of airport codes and the airports they represent, see page xxiii.

Figure 5.8 Landing Fees and Parking Charge for an Airbus A320, for 2 Hours, 1995–2009

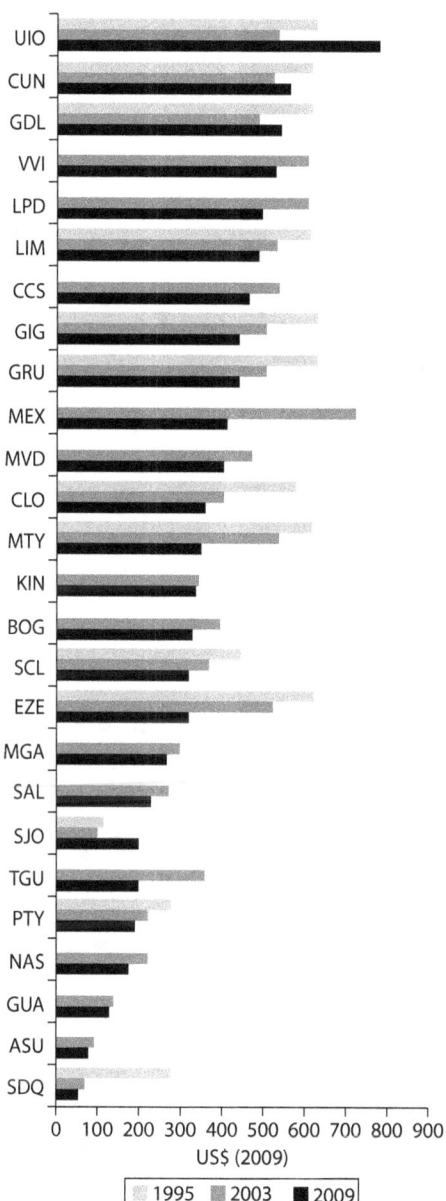

Source: Author's elaboration based on information from IATA (2009), AIP Colombia, AIP Costa Rica, El Salvador Airport, AIP Nicaragua, Panama CAA, DINACIA Uruguay.
Note: For a list of airport codes and the airports they represent, see page xxiii.

Figure 5.9   Boarding Bridge Charges for an Airbus A320, for 2 Hours, 2009

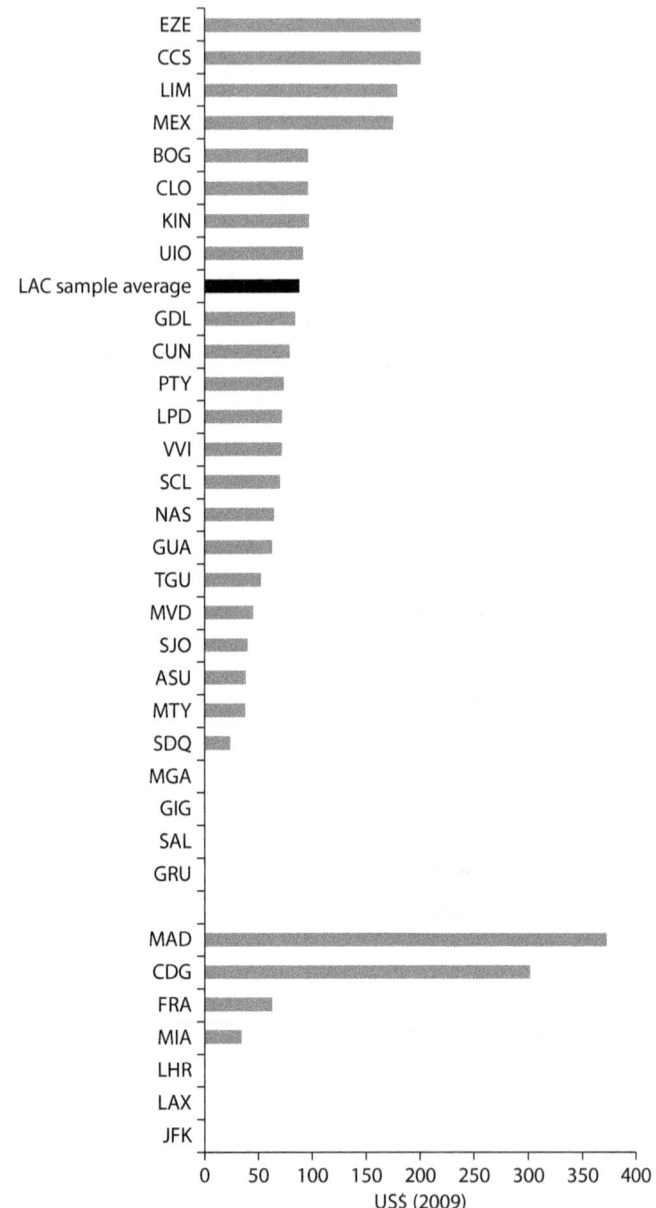

Source: Author's elaboration based on information from IATA (2009), AIP Colombia, AIP Costa Rica, Aerodom, Dominican Republic, El Salvador Airport, AIP Guatemala, AIP Honduras, AIP Nicaragua, Panama CAA, Direccion Nacional de Aviación Civil (DINAC) Paraguay, Montevideo Airport.
Note: Mexico assumes tariff A (off-peak); Madrid assumes normal tariff. For a list of airport codes and the airports they represent, see page xxiii.

LHR, Los Angeles, and New York's JFK, do not charge for the use of a boarding bridge, while others, such as Madrid and Paris CDG, charge more than US$300.

It is difficult to draw a general conclusion regarding the evolution of boarding bridge charges given the lack of information for 1995 prices at many airports (figure 5.10). Considering all the airports in the sample where prices were available in 2003 and 2009, the average boarding bridge charge in LAC increased by less than 10 percent, from US$80 in 2003 to US$86 in 2009 (there were increases in real terms at 8 airports, and reductions at 10).

Passenger Charges

Charges levied on passengers—regardless of whether they are collected directly from passengers or through airline tickets—are referred to as "passenger charges" for the purpose of this analysis. Passenger charges include the passenger facility charge (also commonly referred to as the "boarding fee"), security fees, and other taxes. Some passenger charges are imposed by the national government (such as tourist taxes), and the airport may not collect nor receive those funds. They could be included by the airlines in the ticket price or collected from passengers upon check-in at airport counters or through commercial banks located at the airport. Although these country-specific taxes levied on passengers are not part of the airfare, they do represent an integrated cost of the journey for the passenger. Consequently, depending on the price elasticity of demand, taxes could have a substantial impact on the decision to travel.

Two different evaluations were carried out. The first (figure 5.11) includes only those charges that are levied by the airport, while the second (figure 5.12) contains all charges and taxes levied on the passengers, including airport-related services and federal taxes.[5] All passenger charges presented in this section of the study pertain to departing international passengers. For airports charging separately for arriving and departing passengers, both charges were considered as if collected from departing passengers. Charges other than the passenger facility charge and security fees were labeled as federal taxes, since ultimately they serve the same purpose. The federal taxes concept is summarized in table 5.3 and can include tourist taxes, taxes levied within tickets, customs and immigration fees, among others.

The passenger facility charge ranges from US$44.10 in Nassau to US$7.60 in Kingston, with a LAC sample average of US$27.70. Including

Figure 5.10 Boarding Bridge Charges for an Airbus A320, for 2 Hours, 1995–2009

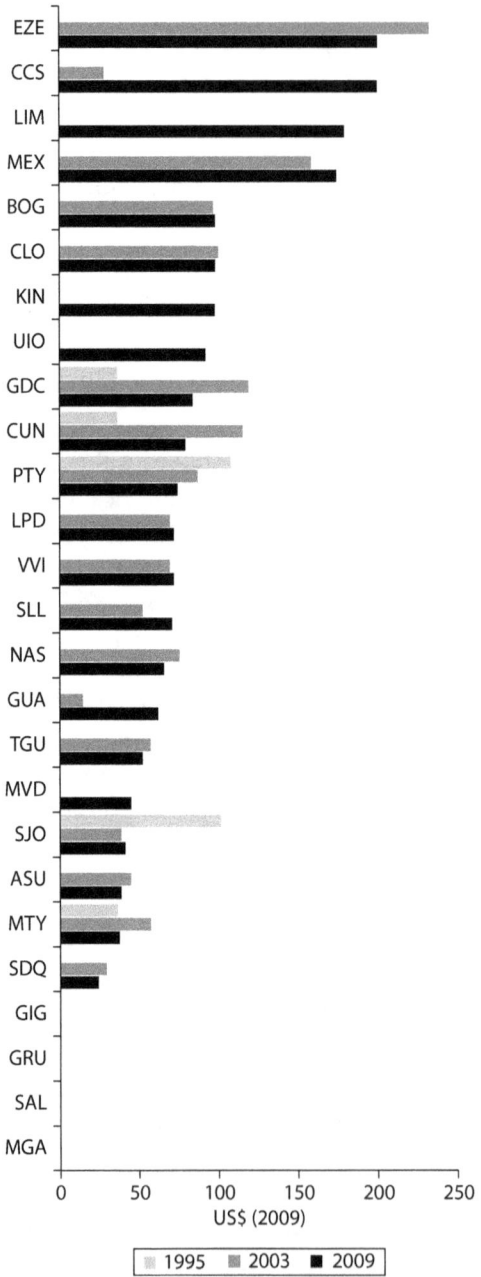

Source: Author's elaboration based on information from IATA (2009), AIP Colombia, AIP Costa Rica, Aerodom, Dominican Republic, El Salvador Airport, AIP Guatemala, AIP Honduras, AIP Nicaragua, Panama CAA, Direccion Nacional de Aviación Civil (DINAC) Paraguay, Montevideo Airport.
Note: Mexico assumes tariff A (off-peak); Madrid assumes normal tariff. For a list of airport codes and the airports they represent, see page xxiii.

Figure 5.11 Passenger Charges per Passenger (Charges Levied by the Airport)

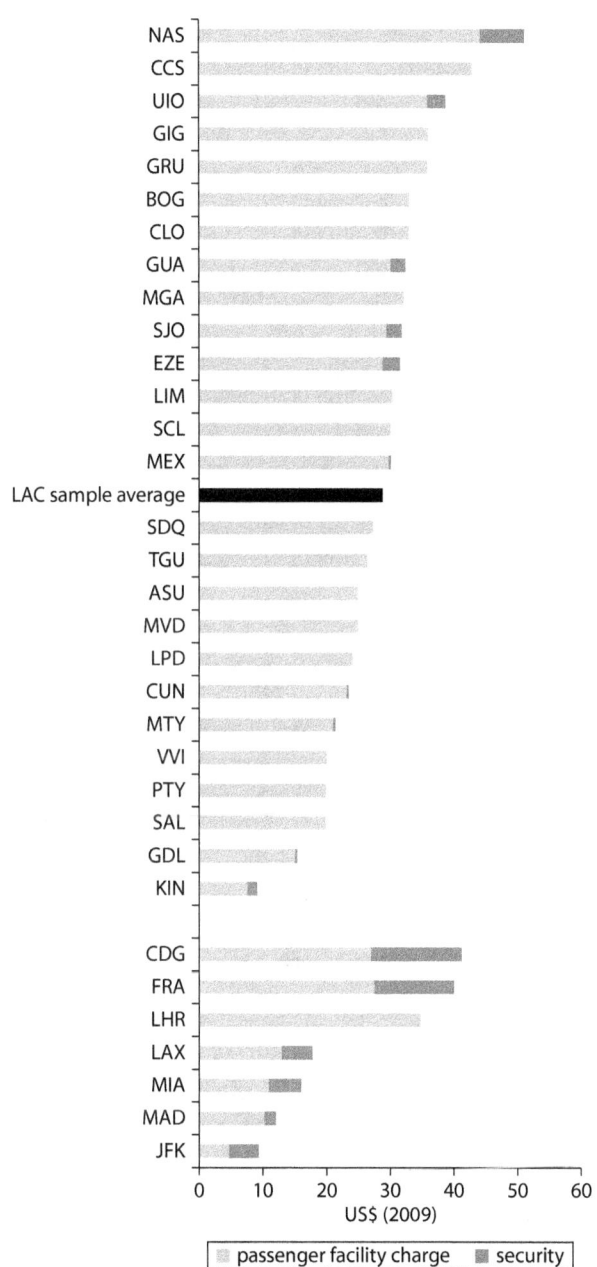

Source: Author's elaboration based on information from IATA (2009), AIP Colombia, AIP El Salvador, AIP Honduras, AIP Nicaragua, Panama CAA, DINACIA Uruguay.
Note: Mexico assumes tariff A (off-peak); Madrid assumes normal tariff. For a list of airport codes and the airports they represent, see page xxiii.

Figure 5.12 Charges and Taxes Levied on Passengers, per Passenger

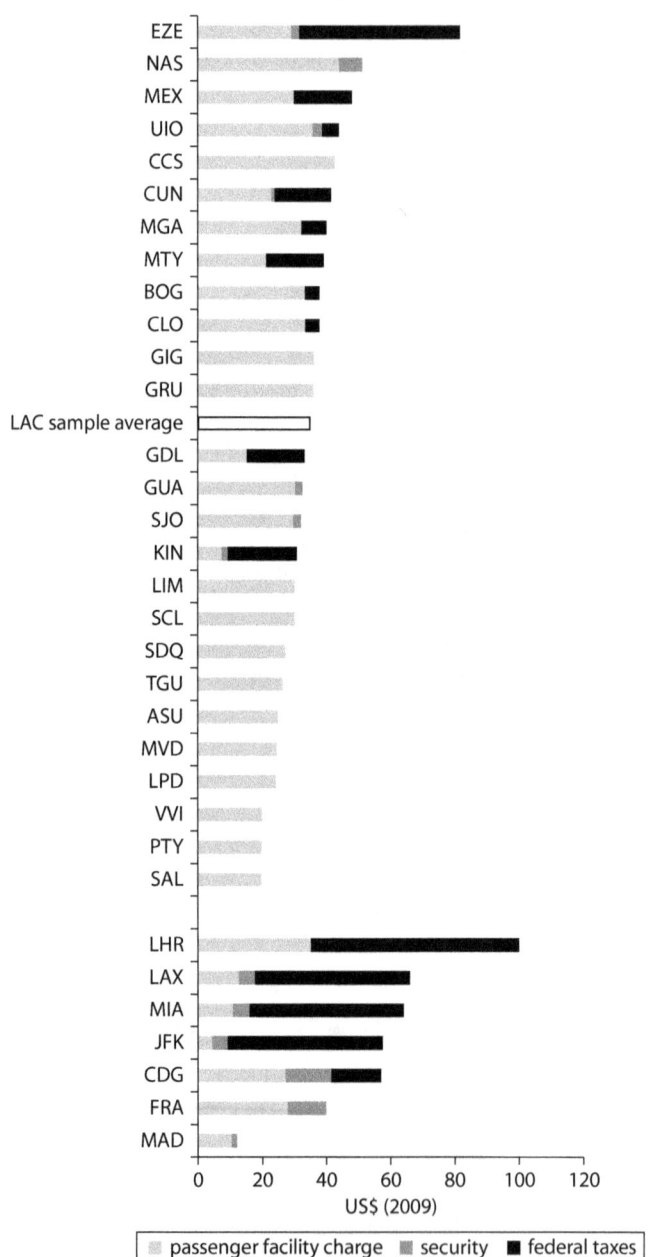

Source: Author's elaboration based on information from International Air Transport Association (IATA) *Airport and Air Navigation Charges Manual* (2009), Aeronautical Information Publication (AIP) Colombia, AIP El Salvador, AIP Honduras, AIP Nicaragua, Panama Civil Aviation Authority (CAA), Dirección Nacional de Aviación Civil e Infraestructura Aeronaútica (DINACIA) Uruguay.
Note: Mexico assumes tariff A (off-peak); Madrid assumes normal tariff. For a list of airport codes and the airports they represent, see page xxiii.

Table 5.3 Passenger Charges and Taxes per Departing Passenger
U.S. dollars

Airport	Passenger facility charge	Security fee	Federal taxes Charge	Remarks
Buenos Aires EZE	29.0	2.5	10.0 + 40.0	Customs and immigration + ticket tax (5% of fare, assumes US$800)
Nassau	44.1	7.0	n.a.	
La Paz	24.0	n.a.	n.a.	
Santa Cruz	20.0	n.a.	n.a.	
Rio de Janeiro	36.0	n.a.	n.a.	
São Paulo	36.0	n.a.	n.a.	
Santiago	30.0	n.a.	n.a.	
Bogotá	33.0	n.a.	5.0	Tourist tax
Cali	33.0	n.a.	5.0	Tourist tax
San José	29.3	2.4	n.a.	
Santo Domingo	27.5	n.a.	n.a.	
Quito	35.8	3.0	5.0	Tourist tax
San Salvador	19.9	n.a.	n.a.	
Guatemala	30.0	2.5	n.a.	
Tegucigalpa	26.4	n.a.	n.a.	
Kingston	7.6	1.4	11.6 + 10.0	Air passenger tax + tourist tax
Cancún	23.2	0.2	18.1	Tourist tax
Guadalajara	15.0	0.2	18.1	Tourist tax
Mexico City	29.6	0.2	18.1	Tourist tax
Monterrey	21.1	0.2	18.1	Tourist tax
Managua	32.0	n.a.	8.0	Tourist tax
Panama	20.0	n.a.	n.a.	
Asunción	25.0	n.a.	n.a.	
Lima	30.3	n.a.	n.a.	
Montevideo	25.0	n.a.	n.a.	
Caracas	42.9	n.a.	n.a.	
Paris CDG	26.9	14.6	9.9 + 5.6	Civil aviation tax + solidarity tax
Frankfurt	27.7	12.3	n.a.	
Madrid	10.2	2.0	n.a.	
London LHR	34.7	n.a.	65.5	Air transportation tax
Los Angeles	12.9	5.0	17.5 + 30.8	Immigration, customs + air transport tax
Miami	10.9	5.0	17.5 + 30.8	Immigration, customs + air transport tax
New York JFK	4.5	5.0	17.5 + 30.8	Immigration, customs + air transport tax

Source: Author's elaboration based on information from International Air Transport Association (IATA) *Airport and Air Navigation Charges Manual* (2009), Aeronautical Information Publication (AIP) Colombia, AIP El Salvador, AIP Honduras, AIP Nicaragua, Panama Civil Aviation Authority (CAA), Dirección Nacional de Aviación Civil e Infraestructura Aeronaútica (DINACIA) Uruguay.
Note: n.a. = not applicable.

security charges, which are levied at 10 LAC airports (in some countries the service is provided by the government and paid for with general taxes), total passenger charges levied by the airport vary from US$51.10 to US$9.00 in the LAC region. In the European and U.S. airports included as benchmarks, the passenger charge average is US$24.40, and the maximum and minimum charges are US$41.50 in Paris CDG and US$9.50 in New York JFK, respectively.

When considering all charges and taxes levied on passengers (figure 5.12), Buenos Aires is the most expensive airport to depart from, with US$81.50 per passenger.[6] Travel taxes can also become a significant part of the ticket price in Europe and the United States, as is the case, in our sample, of London, Los Angeles, Miami, and New York. Table 5.3 details all passenger charges and taxes.

When measured in real terms, passenger charges have clearly increased since 1995, as seen in figure 5.13.

Out of 14 airports for which 1995 information was available, 11 raised passenger charges in real terms. The average passenger facility and security charge at those 14 airports rose from US$20 in 1995 to US$29 in 2009.

Total Turnaround Cost

As some charges are levied on the aircraft and others on the passengers, the appropriate method to compare aeronautical charges as a whole (and their evolution in time) is by calculating the cost of a turnaround.[7] The cost of a turnaround is an agglomeration of all the above-mentioned charges levied by the airport, including landing fees, parking fees, boarding bridge charges, passenger facility charge (or boarding fees), and security charges.

Charges levied by other entities, such as tourist and travel taxes, are excluded from the analysis, as they are subject to great variation between countries.

The calculation was performed for an Airbus A320 and for a Boeing 767-300 with a 71 percent load factor, for a two-hour turnaround.[8] Figure 5.14 presents turnaround costs for an Airbus A320.

Total aeronautical charges (paid by airlines and passengers) for a two-hour turnaround for an Airbus A320 range from US$5,603 in Nassau to US$1,378 in Kingston. In the sample, average aeronautical charges in LAC for an Airbus A320 with a 71 percent load factor on a two-hour turnaround is US$3,433, whereas for the selected airports in Europe and the United States the average charge is US$3,233.

Figure 5.13 Changes in Passenger Charges per Passenger (Charges Levied by the Airport)

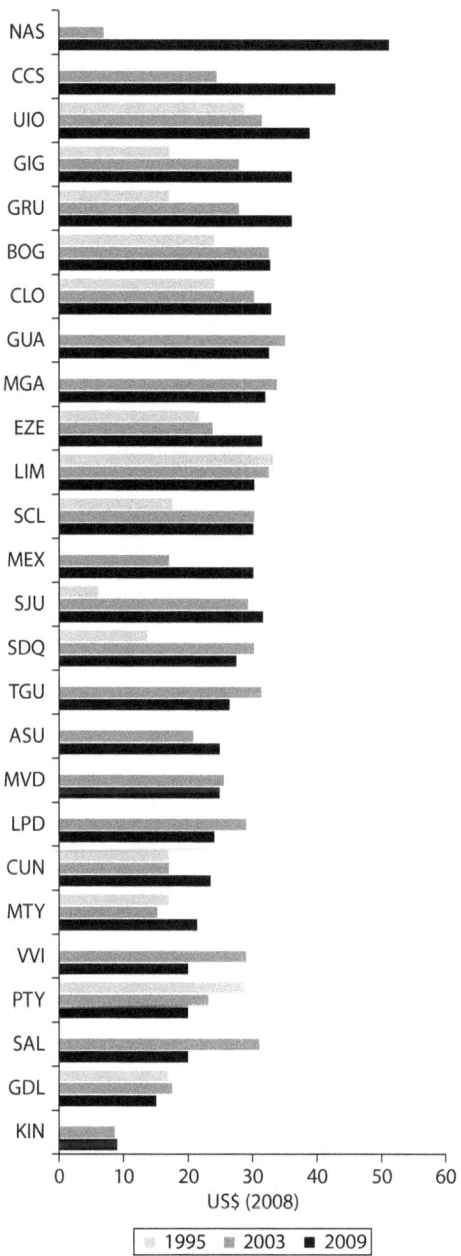

Source: Author's elaboration based on information from International Air Transport Association (IATA) *Airport and Air Navigation Charges Manual* (2009), Aeronautical Information Publication (AIP) Colombia, AIP El Salvador, AIP Honduras, AIP Nicaragua, Panama Civil Aviation Authority (CAA), Dirección Nacional de Aviación Civil e Infraestructura Aeronaútica (DINACIA) Uruguay.
Note: Mexico assumes tariff A (off-peak); Madrid assumes normal tariff. For a list of airport codes and the airports they represent, see page xxiii.

Figure 5.14   Turnaround Costs for an Airbus A320 (2 Hours, Daylight Operation)

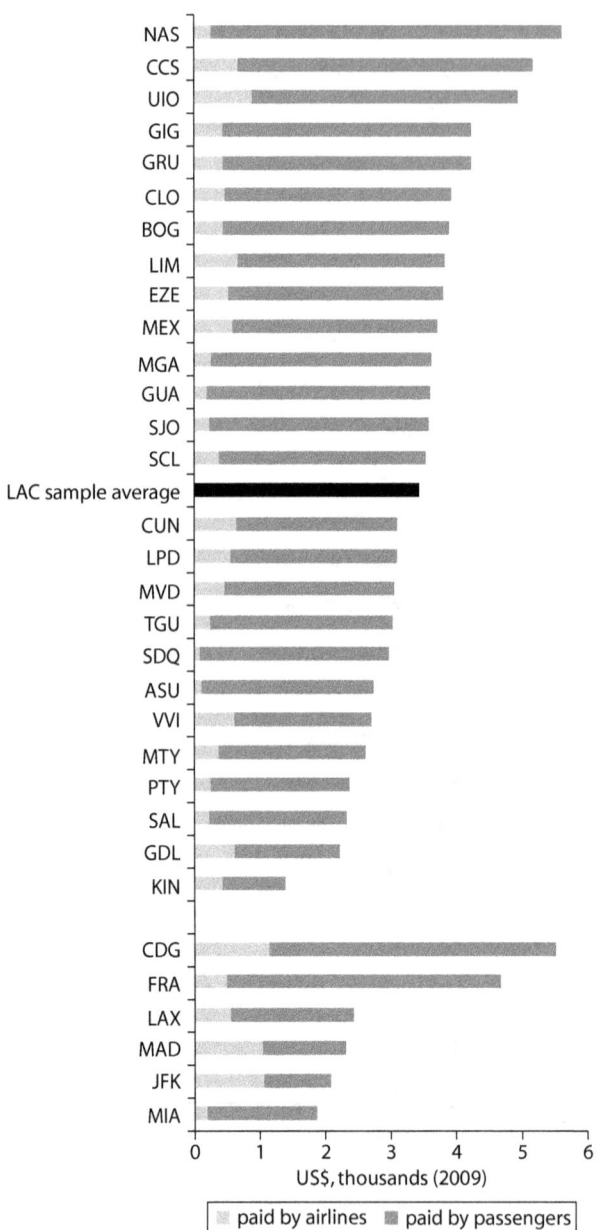

Source: Author's elaboration based on information from International Air Transport Association (IATA) *Airport and Air Navigation Charges Manual* (2009), Aeronautical Information Publication (AIP) Colombia, AIP El Salvador, AIP Honduras, AIP Nicaragua, Panama Civil Aviation Authority (CAA), Dirección Nacional de Aviación Civil e Infraestructura Aeronaútica (DINACIA) Uruguay.
Note: Includes landing, parking, boarding bridge, passenger facility charge, and security. Assumes a 71 percent load factor. For a list of airport codes and the airports they represent, see page xxiii.

Total aeronautical charges, as defined in this report, increased in real terms at most airports between 1995 and 2009, as seen in figure 5.15. Considering the 14 airports for which 1995 information was available, the average total turnaround cost increased in real terms from US$2,617 in 1995 to US$3,241 in 2003, and then to US$3,516 in 2009. This represents a 20 percent increase between 1995 and 2003, an 8 percent increase between 2003 and 2009, and a 26 percent increase between 1995 and 2009. Considering all the airports in the sample, the average turnaround cost increased 9.8 percent between 2003 and 2009.

The ranking of airport turnaround costs is virtually unchanged when the analysis is done for a Boeing 767-300 (figure 5.16 and figure 5.17). The evolution of turnaround costs between 1995 and 2009 for a Boeing 767-300 is the same as for the A320. The only significant difference in total turnaround costs is the absolute magnitude of costs. Turnaround costs are, as expected, much higher for a Boeing 767-300, as it carries many more passengers and the fee structure relies more heavily on charges to passengers. Furthermore, in cases where charges are defined by MTOW, Boeing 767-300 aeronautical charges are naturally higher.

Although total charges for both types of aircraft increased in real terms from 1995 to 2009, it is important to note that the structure of charges changed during this period. Fees paid by airlines decreased between 1995 and 2009, while fees levied on passengers increased. This result is independent of the type of aircraft. Figure 5.18 and figure 5.19 show charges levied on airlines for the Airbus A320 and the Boeing 767-300. Figure 5.18 shows that charges paid by airlines for an A320 have decreased in real terms at most airports. For the airports where 1995 charges were available, the average aeronautical charges paid by airlines decreased from US$535 in 1995 to US$472 in 2003 and to US$462 in 2009. When considering all the airports in the sample, average charges dropped from US$454 in 2003 to US$424 in 2009. The reductions in charges measured in real terms are mainly caused by the effects of inflation, as nominal prices either remained constant or grew slightly. In 2009, charges levied on passengers account for, on average, over 85 percent of the total aeronautical charges.

Considering only those airports where 1995 prices were available, average aeronautical charges paid by airlines for a Boeing 767-300 declined from US$1,353 in 1995 to US$1,129 in 2003 and to US$1,089 in 2009. If the 26 airports in the sample are included, charges in real terms decreased from US$1,028 in 2003 to US$935 in 2009.

Figure 5.15 Changes in Turnaround Costs for an Airbus A320 (2 Hours, Daylight Operation)

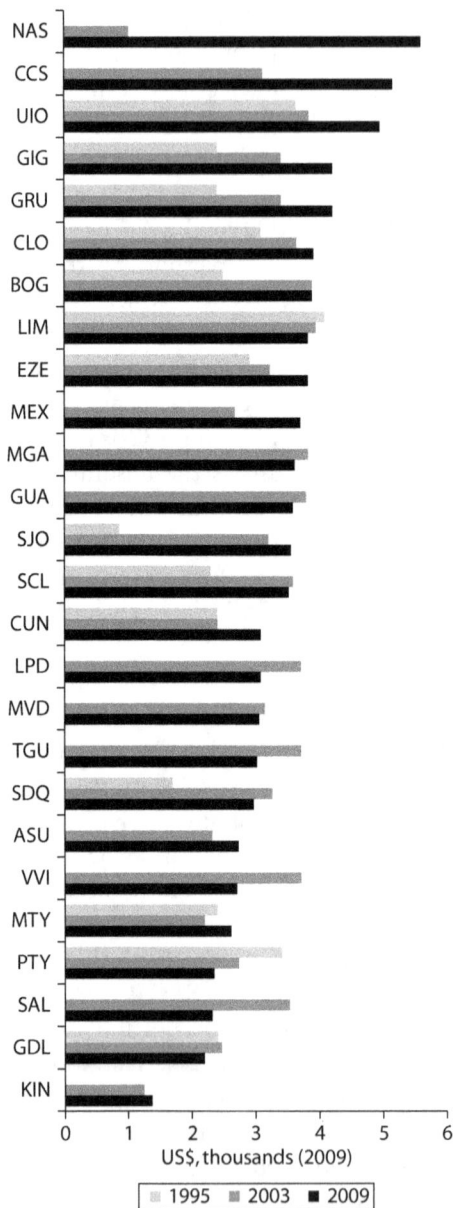

Source: Author's elaboration based on information from International Air Transport Association (IATA) *Airport and Air Navigation Charges Manual* (2009), Aeronautical Information Publication (AIP) Colombia, AIP El Salvador, AIP Honduras, AIP Nicaragua, Panama Civil Aviation Authority (CAA), Dirección Nacional de Aviación Civil e Infraestructura Aeronaútica (DINACIA) Uruguay.
Note: Includes landing, parking, boarding bridge, passenger facility charge, and security. Assumes a 71 percent load factor. For a list of airport codes and the airports they represent, see page xxiii.

Figure 5.16 Turnaround Costs for a Boeing 767-300 (2 Hours, Daylight Operation)

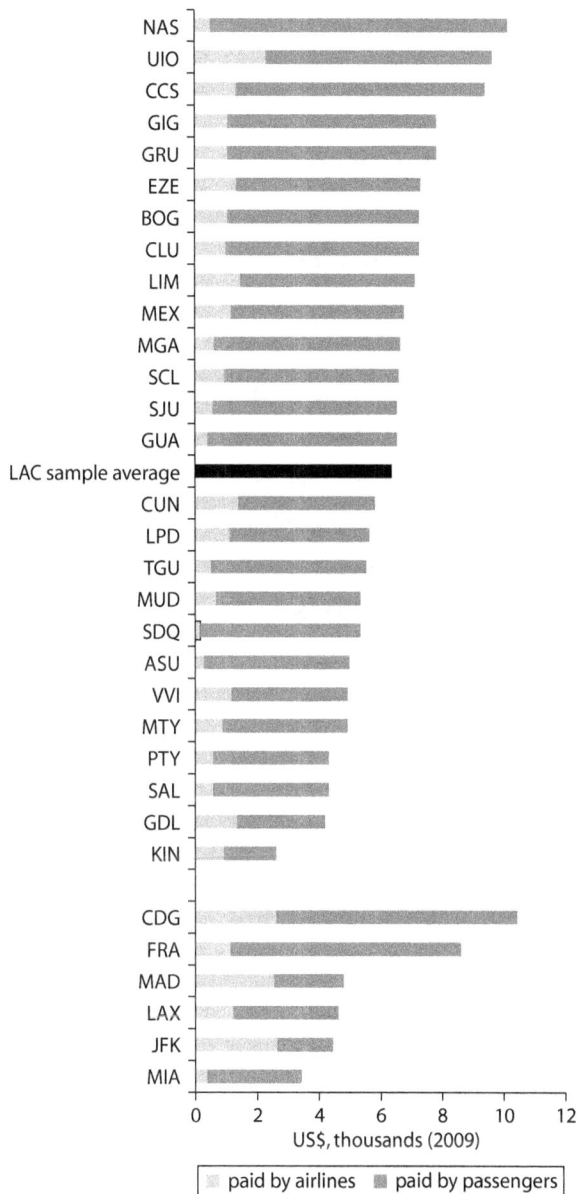

Source: Author's elaboration based on information from International Air Transport Association (IATA) *Airport and Air Navigation Charges Manual* (2009), Aeronautical Information Publication (AIP) Colombia, AIP El Salvador, AIP Honduras, AIP Nicaragua, Panama Civil Aviation Authority (CAA), Dirección Nacional de Aviación Civil e Infraestructura Aeronaútica (DINACIA) Uruguay.
Note: Includes landing, parking, boarding bridge, passenger facility charge, and security. Assumes a 71 percent load factor. For a list of airport codes and the airports they represent, see page xxiii.

Figure 5.17 Changes in Turnaround Costs for a Boeing 767-300 (2 Hours, Daylight Operation)

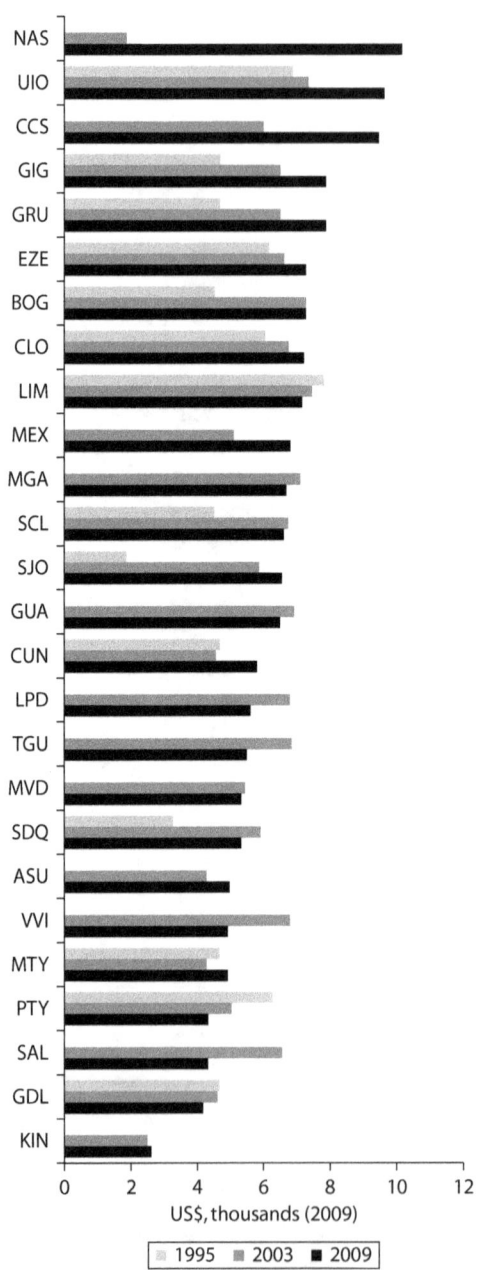

Source: Author's elaboration based on information from International Air Transport Association (IATA) *Airport and Air Navigation Charges Manual* (2009), Aeronautical Information Publication (AIP) Colombia, AIP El Salvador, AIP Honduras, AIP Nicaragua, Panama Civil Aviation Authority (CAA), Dirección Nacional de Aviación Civil e Infraestructura Aeronáutica (DINACIA) Uruguay.
Note: Includes landing, parking, boarding bridge, passenger facility charge, and security. Assumes a 71 percent load factor. For a list of airport codes and the airports they represent, see page xxiii.

Figure 5.18 Turnaround Costs Levied on Airlines for an Airbus A320 (2 Hours, Daylight Operation)

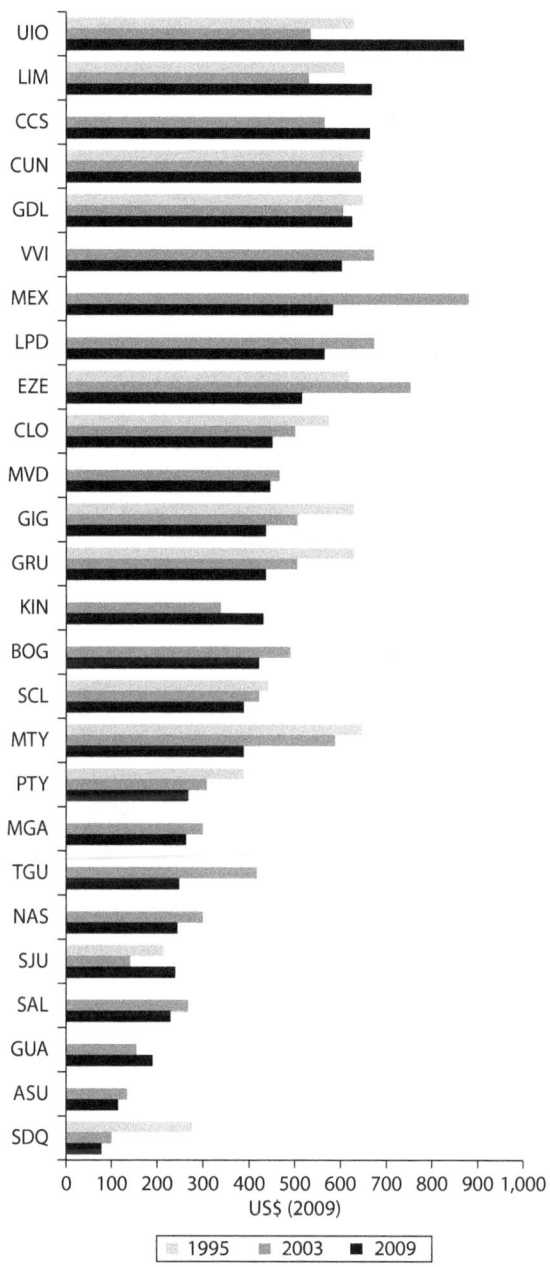

Source: Author's elaboration based on information from International Air Transport Association (IATA) *Airport and Air Navigation Charges Manual* (2009), Aeronautical Information Publication (AIP) Colombia, AIP El Salvador, AIP Honduras, AIP Nicaragua, Panama Civil Aviation Authority (CAA), Dirección Nacional de Aviación Civil e Infraestructura Aeronaútica (DINACIA) Uruguay.
Note: Includes landing, parking, and boarding bridges. For a list of airport codes and the airports they represent, see page xxiii.

Figure 5.19 Changes in Turnaround Costs Levied on Airlines for a Boeing 767–300 (2 Hours, Daylight Operation)

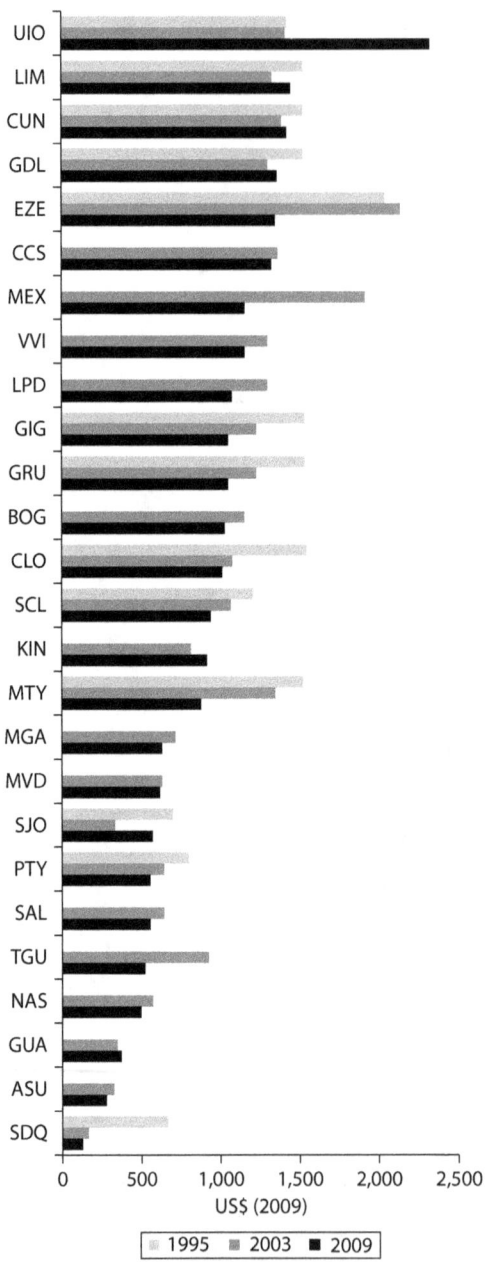

Source: Author's elaboration based on information from International Air Transport Association (IATA) *Airport and Air Navigation Charges Manual* (2009), Aeronautical Information Publication (AIP) Colombia, AIP El Salvador, AIP Honduras, AIP Nicaragua, Panama Civil Aviation Authority (CAA), Dirección Nacional de Aviación Civil e Infraestructura Aeronaútica (DINACIA) Uruguay.
Note: Includes landing, parking, and boarding bridges. For a list of airport codes and the airports they represent, see page xxiii.

With respect to charges levied on passengers, on the other hand, these have been raised in real terms at more than half of the airports in the sample. Average charges levied on passengers increased from US$2,120 in 1995 to US$2,767 in 2003 and US$3,057 in 2009 for those airports where 1995 information was available. If the 26 airports in the sample are considered, average charges grew from US$2,672 in 2003 to US$3,010 in 2009 (figure 5.20).

Conclusion

According to the sample of airports gathered for this report, total aeronautical charges in LAC increased between 1995 and 2009 (34 percent for those with 1995 data and 9.8 percent between 2003 and 2009 for all airports). The tariff benchmarking analysis does not permit us to reach a conclusion about the relationship between changes in aeronautical charges and the introduction of private sector participation. A simple visual analysis indicates that the increase in aeronautical charges observed between 1995 and 2009 is shared by both publicly and privately operated airports. Further research through a case-specific approach should be conducted to assess whether the introduction of private sector participation has led to an increase in aeronautical charges and to link changes in aeronautical charges to the changes in the level and quality of airport services.

An important conclusion regarding aeronautical charges is that for both types of aircrafts, the Airbus A320 and the Boeing 767-300, total turnaround costs in LAC in 2009 are, on average, at a comparable or higher level than those in European and U.S. airports that are most frequently served by Latin American airlines. Several questions, which merit further research, need to be answered in order to fully understand why this is the case. For example, are aeronautical tariffs set on a cost-recovery basis? Do aeronautical tariffs reflect an adequate due diligence process? How are they modified through time? Do aeronautical tariffs provide the right incentives for infrastructure investments?

Finally, the results indicate that the structure of aeronautical charges has changed in the last decade. The importance of charges applied to passengers is increasing relative to those levied on airlines. Passenger charges currently account for over 85 percent of total aeronautical charges. On the other hand, charges levied on airlines (such as landing fees, aircraft parking, and boarding bridges) either remained constant in nominal terms or grew at a slower pace than inflation, demonstrating that charges in real

Figure 5.20 Turnaround Costs Levied on Passengers, for an Airbus A320

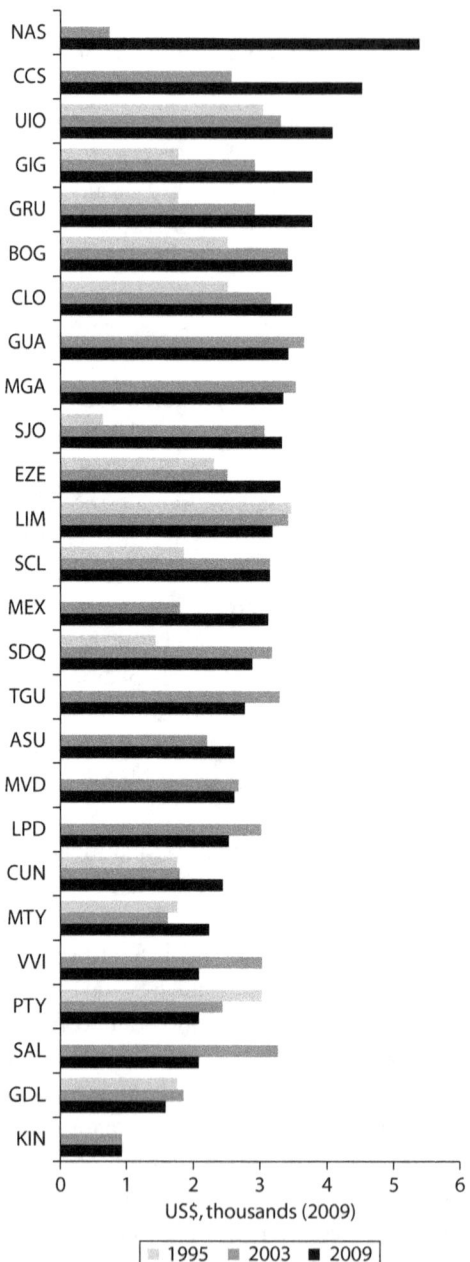

Source: Author's elaboration based on information from International Air Transport Association (IATA) *Airport and Air Navigation Charges Manual* (2009), Aeronautical Information Publication (AIP) Colombia, AIP El Salvador, AIP Honduras, AIP Nicaragua, Panama Civil Aviation Authority (CAA), Dirección Nacional de Aviación Civil e Infraestructura Aeronaútica (DINACIA) Uruguay.
Note: Includes passenger facility charge and security. Assumes a 71 percent load factor. For a list of airport codes and the airports they represent, see page xxiii.

terms are lower today than they were in 1995. The current tariff structure in LAC airports is similar to that prevailing in the sample of European and U.S. airports, with a slightly higher percentage of the share of passenger charges versus airline charges in LAC.

Two main explanations can be provided to account for the changes in the tariff structure. The first, based on a political economy argument, is that airlines as a group have a higher negotiating power through their trade associations, such as IATA or the Latin American Airline Association (ALTA), whereas individual travelers have neither the resources nor the organization to fight tariff increases. This is not to say that airlines show resistance only toward price increases in aircraft-based charges and not toward charges paid by passengers. Clearly, it is in the airlines' best interest to ensure that passengers assume the lowest possible travel cost. As ticket prices increase, in turn, demand is reduced, affecting the airlines' bottom lines. Another potential explanation is that the current tariff structure better reflects relative demand elasticities. If this is the case, then relative charges were modified by regulatory agencies because passengers have lower demand elasticity (for the use of a given airport) than airlines.

While further research needs to be conducted in order to provide a more in-depth analysis of the evolution of tariffs, the present work represents an important first step in fostering dialogue on these issues and in laying down the basis for a more robust tariff benchmarking exercise.

Notes

1. This assumption has significant weaknesses. Concessions took place in different years throughout LAC. To correctly test the hypothesis that tariffs increase after the introduction of the private sector, a detailed study of the evolution of tariffs in each airport in each country should be conducted. We opted to include, arbitrarily, the year 2003, as it is the year with the most comprehensive information on tariffs available.
2. The frequency depends on the type of airport, but for the major airports, information on charges is collected on a semiannual basis.
3. Aeronautical charges for 1995 could be obtained for only a set of 13 airports.
4. It is interesting to note that INFRAERO, the Brazilian company operating the airports in Brazil, does not have a separate charge for boarding bridges. The use of the bridges is included in the parking charge, which is the same for remote stands as for contact positions. According to collected information, the reason for pricing both services equally is that although boarding bridges are generally more expensive to purchase (cost of capital) and operate (increased

level of service following a principle of the airline's "willingness to pay") than remote positions, the latter have to cover the extra cost of shuttle services for passengers (following a principle of operating cost recovery).
5. Visa costs are not considered for the purpose of this study.
6. Airfares for international travel in Buenos Aires (EZE) are charged with a tourist tax calculated as 5 percent of the airfare (called "DNT" or Dirección Nacional de Turismo). For the purpose of this analysis, an assumption of a US$800 airfare was employed; aggregated fees, taxes, and duties total US$40 on top of the ticket cost.
7. *Turnaround* refers to all activities involved in handling an aircraft between its arrival and its departure (typically known as "from chocks-in to chocks-out"). In this chapter, turnaround costs do not include any operational costs for the airline other than airport charges.
8. Average load factor for Latin America in 2009 was reported to be 71 percent, according to Air Transport World, June 2009.

References

Air Transport World Media Group. 2009. *Air Transport World*. June. http://atwonline.com.

IATA (International Air Transport Association). 1995. *Airport and Air Navigation Charges Manual*. Montreal, Quebec: IATA.

———. 2003. *Airport and Air Navigation Charges Manual*. Montreal, Quebec: IATA.

———. 2009. *Airport and Air Navigation Charges Manual*. Montreal, Quebec: IATA.

APPENDIX A

Survey of Airport Performance for Operators

QUESTIONNAIRE ON AIRPORT SECTOR PERFORMANCE
IN LATIN AMERICA AND THE CARIBBEAN

Please fill in the questions to the best of your knowledge. We realize that it may not be possible for you to find all the information we are asking for. For those years for which data are available, we would appreciate it if you could provide as many details as possible. Finally, please indicate if there is any specific information that you would prefer for us to keep confidential.

Airport Information and Point of Contact:

Country:
Airport name:
Code (IATA):
Name of the point of contact:
Phone number:

Fax:
E-mail:

General Information:
1. What is the airport's form of ownership (Public/Management Contract/Concession/Private)?
2. If a concession, management contract, or privatization, what year did the transition take place?
3. If a concession or management contract, what is its duration?
4. What is the name of the airport's operator?
5. Please list the names of the major shareholders/companies that operate the airport. Specify the percentage of shares and voting rights of each.
6. What is the airport's fiscal year? (e.g., April to March)

If your data do not relate to a calendar year, please include data in the box for which the year ends, e.g., data for April 1998 to March 1999 would correspond to the 1999 box.

OUTPUT VARIABLES

1. Passenger Data:

1.1–1.5 How many passengers of each type were handled by the airport? (Numbers in thousands)

	1995	1996	1997	1998	1999	2000	2001	2002	2003	2004	2005	2006	2007
1.1 International passengers													
1.2 Domestic passengers													
1.3 Scheduled passengers													
1.4 Non-scheduled passengers (i.e., charter passengers)													
1.5 Transfer passengers													

1.6 What was the total number of passengers handled by the airport? (Numbers in thousands)

	1995	1996	1997	1998	1999	2000	2001	2002	2003	2004	2005	2006	2007
1.6 Total passengers													

2. Cargo Data:

2.1–2.3 What were the total tons of cargo (freight and mail) handled by the airport? (Thousand metric tons)

	1995	1996	1997	1998	1999	2000	2001	2002	2003	2004	2005	2006	2007
2.1 Total cargo handled (loaded and unloaded) INTERNATIONAL													
2.2 Total cargo handled (loaded and unloaded) DOMESTIC													
2.3 Total cargo handled (loaded and unloaded)													

3. Intermediate Output Data:

3.1–3.5 What were the total aircraft movements registered by the airport (ATMs)? (Numbers in thousands)

	1995	1996	1997	1998	1999	2000	2001	2002	2003	2004	2005	2006	2007
3.1 Passenger aircraft INTERNATIONAL													
3.2 Passenger aircraft DOMESTIC													
3.3 Total passenger aircraft													
3.4 Cargo-only aircraft													
3.5 General aviation and other aircraft													

3.6 (3.6.1–3.6.6) What was the aircraft mix? (Percentage of total aircraft movements related to each of the following type of aircrafts)

	1995	1996	1997	1998	1999	2000	2001	2002	2003	2004	2005	2006	2007
3.6.1 Largest wide-body aircraft (e.g., 747/777/A340/A330)													
3.6.2 Other large wide-body aircraft (e.g., DC10/DC11/L1011)													
3.6.3 Medium wide-body aircraft (e.g., 757/767/A300/A310)													
3.6.4 Narrow-body aircraft (e.g., 727/737/A320/DC9/MD80/MD90)													
3.6.5 Commuter/Turboprops													
3.6.6 Other/General aviation													

4. Traffic Peaking:

4.1 What were total passenger numbers in the busiest month of the year?

	1995	1996	1997	1998	1999	2000	2001	2002	2003	2004	2005	2006	2007
4.1 Peak month passenger traffic													

4.2 What were total passenger numbers during the busiest hour of the year?

	1995	1996	1997	1998	1999	2000	2001	2002	2003	2004	2005	2006	2007
4.2 Peak hour passenger traffic													

4.3 What were total ATMs (air traffic movements) during the busiest hour of the year?

	1995	1996	1997	1998	1999	2000	2001	2002	2003	2004	2005	2006	2007
4.3 Peak hour ATMs													

4.4 During the busiest month or hour of passenger numbers, where can the capacity restriction be found? In the arrival or departure of passengers?

Arrival ☐   Departure ☐

5. Financial Data: Costs and Revenues

In all cases, we are specifically interested in data referring to the airport indicated on page 1 only. If, however, your airport is part of a larger group and there are no airport-level data available, please provide any corporate figures at the group level. In addition, please provide details on any assumptions that have been made to allocate costs across airports when answering the questions.

Currency used for financial data in this section:

Units used for financial data in this section (e.g., thousands or millions):

Assumptions: (Please make any clarification you deem appropriate. Indicate the types of services that are accounted for in the costs and revenues.)

COSTS:

5.1 What were total operating costs? (Local nominal currency)

	1995	1996	1997	1998	1999	2000	2001	2002	2003	2004	2005	2006	2007
5.1. Total operating costs													

Please provide any additional information with respect to the definition of operating costs:

5.2 Are there any corporate costs associated with your airport that are not included in the total operating costs provided in 5.1 above?

Yes ☐   No ☐

If yes, what is the estimated level of corporate costs associated with your airport that are not included in the total operating costs given in 5.1 above?

	1995	1996	1997	1998	1999	2000	2001	2002	2003	2004	2005	2006	2007
5.2 Corporate costs (not included in operating costs)													

Please provide details with respect to the estimation method used or any further details on these corporate costs:

5.3 What was the total capital expenditure? (Local nominal currency)

	1995	1996	1997	1998	1999	2000	2001	2002	2003	2004	2005	2006	2007
5.3 Total capital expenditure													

5.4 What were the total depreciation costs? (Local nominal currency)

	1995	1996	1997	1998	1999	2000	2001	2002	2003	2004	2005	2006	2007
5.4 Total depreciation costs													

5.5 What was the total operation and capital expenditure? (Local nominal currency)

	1995	1996	1997	1998	1999	2000	2001	2002	2003	2004	2005	2006	2007
5.5 Total operation and capital expenditure													

REVENUES:

5.6 What was the aeronautical revenue? (Local nominal currency)

	1995	1996	1997	1998	1999	2000	2001	2002	2003	2004	2005	2006	2007
5.6 Aeronautical revenue													

5.7 What was the nonaeronautical revenue? (Local nominal currency)

	1995	1996	1997	1998	1999	2000	2001	2002	2003	2004	2005	2006	2007
5.7 Nonaeronautical revenue													

5.8 Was there any other kind of revenue? (Local nominal currency)

	1995	1996	1997	1998	1999	2000	2001	2002	2003	2004	2005	2006	2007
5.8 Other revenue													

Please specify what kind of revenue the data refer to:

5.9 Has the airport received any operational subsidy? (Local nominal currency)

	1995	1996	1997	1998	1999	2000	2001	2002	2003	2004	2005	2006	2007
5.9 Operational subsidy													

Please specify types of subsidies and sources (local, federal governments):

5.10 What was the airport's total revenue? (Local nominal currency)

	1995	1996	1997	1998	1999	2000	2001	2002	2003	2004	2005	2006	2007
5.10 Total revenue													

5.11 What were the airport's earnings before interest, taxes, depreciation, and amortization (EBITDA)? (Local nominal currency)

	1995	1996	1997	1998	1999	2000	2001	2002	2003	2004	2005	2006	2007
5.11 EBITDA													

5.12–5.16 Please provide the following information regarding assets and liabilities of your airport:

	1995	1996	1997	1998	1999	2000	2001	2002	2003	2004	2005	2006	2007
5.12 Fixed assets													
5.13 Current assets													
5.14 Capital + reserves													
5.15 Current liabilities													
5.16 Long-term liabilities													

6. Capital Assets and Capacity Utilization:

6.1–6.11 What were the total:

	1995	1996	1997	1998	1999	2000	2001	2002	2003	2004	2005	2006	2007
6.1 Number of runways (number)													
6.2 Runway capacity (movements per hour)													

(continued next page)

6.1–6.11 What were the total: *(continued)*

	1995	1996	1997	1998	1999	2000	2001	2002	2003	2004	2005	2006	2007
6.3 Passenger terminal capacity (passengers per hour)													
6.4 Terminal size (square meters)													
6.5 Terminal space used for retail activities (square meters)													
6.6 Number of contact gates (boarding bridges) (number)													
6.7 Aircraft parking stands (remote + bridges) (number)													
6.8 Cargo terminal capacity (square meters)													
6.9 Number of check-in desks (number)													
6.10 Number of baggage claim units (number)													
6.11 Number of seats provided by airport defined by airside seating after security check (number)													

7. Quality Data:

7.1–7.3 What were the following?

	1995	1996	1997	1998	1999	2000	2001	2002	2003	2004	2005	2006	2007
7.1 Average baggage delivery time (minutes)													
7.2 Average check-in waiting time (minutes)													
7.3 Average security waiting time (minutes)													

Please provide any clarification or explanation with respect to the measurement of the data contained in boxes 7.1 to 7.3:

8. Employee Composition:

8.1 How many employees were contracted directly by the airport management company?

	1995	1996	1997	1998	1999	2000	2001	2002	2003	2004	2005	2006	2007
8.1 Employees contracted directly by the airport management company (number)													

8.2 How many employees worked in the airport? (total, includes those who are contracted directly by the operator plus those employed in services outsourced)

	1995	1996	1997	1998	1999	2000	2001	2002	2003	2004	2005	2006	2007
8.2 Total employees in airport (number)													

9. Total Aeronautical Fees for an Airbus A320 Aircraft:

Characteristics of an Airbus A320 Aircraft:
Aircraft type: A320-200
Maximum takeoff weight: 73.5 metric tons

208 Airport Economics in Latin America and the Caribbean

Passengers: 120 (load factor: 73.8%, typical seating: 162)
Type of flight: Regular, international (LAC country/LAC country)
Turnaround time: 2 hours (at peak hour)

Please do not include discounts (i.e., transfer passenger discounts) when reporting data.

9.1–9.9 What were the fees for each of the following? (Local nominal currency)

	1995	1996	1997	1998	1999	2000	2001	2002	2003	2004	2005	2006	2007
9.1 Landing													
9.2 Passengers													
9.3 Security													
9.4 Parking													
9.5 Contact gate (aerobridge)													
9.6 Terminal navigation													
9.7 Noise/pollution													
9.8 Other (please specify below)													
9.9 Total													

9.9 Please specify what other aeronautical fees, if any, are charged to the operation of an Airbus A320 aircraft:

EXTRA VARIABLES

10. Fee Structure:

Please describe the fee structure for each of the following. Of particular importance is the change of each fee structure over time. For landing, please specify if the tariff changes by weight of aircraft, time of day, or other variables. For passenger, please differentiate between domestic and international tariffs.

APPENDIX B

Governance of Airport Regulators Survey

QUESTIONNAIRE ON THE GOVERNANCE OF REGULATORY AGENCIES IN THE AIRPORT SECTOR IN LATIN AMERICA AND THE CARIBBEAN

Regulatory agency
Country
Name of the person in charge of answering the questionnaire
Position in the agency
Telephone number
E-mail

The present questionnaire is divided into three main sections. The first section is composed of general questions related to the regulation of the airport sector in your country. The second contains questions that intend to identify different aspects related to the governance of regulatory agencies in the airport sector. Finally, the third section contains questions that ask your opinion on the institutional scheme adopted to regulate airports in your country. The questionnaire contains a glossary of those terms that could lead to confusion.

In the present questionnaire, the word **agency** is used indistinctly to refer to both independent regulatory bodies and civil aviation administrations (without independent regulator characteristics).

In accordance with the objectives of this research project led by the World Bank, it is very important that you answer the present questionnaire based on your experience and objectives as regulatory agency of the sector. A better understanding of this subject will allow us to conduct a more comprehensive analysis of the airport sector in Latin America and the Caribbean.

When answering the questionnaire, you will note that in several cases, the questions are not numbered consecutively. The reason for this kind of nontraditional numbering is explained by the need to facilitate the comparison of the answers received by agencies in the airport sector to those received by other infrastructure sectors that are answering similar questionnaires.

I. General Questions:

1. List the major airport operators in your country:

OPERATOR	MANAGED AIRPORTS	MAJOR SHAREHOLDERS

2. Who has decision-making competencies over the following aspects?

	Agency	Government operator	Airport	Other	Not applicable
Tariff structure (aeronautical)	☐	☐	☐	☐	☐
Tariffs (commercial services)	☐	☐	☐	☐	☐
Tariff modifications (aeronautical)	☐	☐	☐	☐	☐

(continued next page)

	Agency	Government operator	Airport	Other	Not applicable
Tariff modifications (commercial)	☐	☐	☐	☐	☐
Quality of service	☐	☐	☐	☐	☐
User complaints	☐	☐	☐	☐	☐
Investment plans (ex ante approval)	☐	☐	☐	☐	☐
Investment plans (ex post, fulfillment)	☐	☐	☐	☐	☐
Slot allocation	☐	☐	☐	☐	☐
Anticompetitive practices	☐	☐	☐	☐	☐
Merger and acquisition reviews	☐	☐	☐	☐	☐
Authorization of ground handling providers	☐	☐	☐	☐	☐
Technical/security standards	☐	☐	☐	☐	☐

3. Since 1995 until today, have there been significant changes in the management and regulation of airports (concessions, legislative changes, changes in airport operators, among others)? Please describe briefly.

4. When did the agency begin to operate?
   Month/Year:

5. Describe the main functions that the agency performs according to the specified mandate within the legal instrument that created it.

6. Is the agency sectoral or multisectoral? If it is multisectoral, specify the sectors that are regulated by the agency.

7. If your agency regulates private airport operators, was the agency created before the introduction of private management?
   Yes ☐
   No ☐

If the answer is yes, what was your agency's role in the process through which private management was introduced? (mark all that apply):

The agency:

Issued nonbinding opinions	☐
Was actively involved in the design of the concession	☐
Developed the economic-financial model	☐
Developed the technical specifications	☐
Defined the concession's initial aeronautical tariffs	☐
Participated in the selection of the concessionaire	☐

If you wish to explain the agency's role in the process of introduction of private sector management in the airport sector in more detail, please do so below:

8. Tariff regulation:

a) What is the option that better describes the regime or modality of changes in the aeronautical tariffs of the airports under your jurisdiction?

	Mark (only one)
The tariffs are freely set by the airports without any intervention from a state entity.	☐
The tariffs are freely set by the airports, but the state reserves the right to revise them when necessary.	☐
The level and change in tariffs is negotiated between the operator and the agency without a process that has been established in norms or manuals.	☐
Tariffs are modified through a formal petition from the operator, following a formal administrative process that requires approval from your agency or from a ministry.	☐
Tariffs are fixed for a predetermined period of time (for example, every five years) and are revised through a formal process that has been established in a concession contract or in the regulatory agency's procedures.	☐
Other mechanisms.	☐

Please explain the methodology and procedure of tariff setting and review in your country. Please specify authorities involved, timeline, and mechanisms.

9. Describe the current tariff structure in the airports under your jurisdiction (for example, specify if different tariffs apply to international passengers, if landing tariffs vary by hour or day and weight of the aircraft, etc):

    Passengers:
    Landing:
    Security:
    Others:

10. Have there been significant modifications since 1995 in the tariff structure mentioned in question 9?

11. Are the tariffs corresponding to nonaeronautical (commercial) services subject to any kind of regulation?

    Yes ☐   No ☐

    If yes, please describe the tariff structure and the modification mechanisms of these tariffs.

12. Are the costs associated with the provision of aeronautical services recovered through the aeronautical tariffs?

    Yes ☐   No ☐

13. The current mechanisms for tariff setting respond better to:

	Mark (only one)
Single till (The operational costs related to aeronautical services are recovered through revenues generated by the charging of aeronautical services and through revenues obtained from non-aeronautical [commercial] activities.)	☐
Dual till (The operational costs related to aeronautical services are exclusively recovered through revenues generated by the charging of aeronautical services.)	☐
Hybrid	☐

If hybrid, please explain:

14. Does the agency use an economic-financial model as a basis to calculate changes in tariffs?

    Yes ☐   No ☐

    If yes, describe if this model was developed by the agency or by consultants.

15. Does the agency rely on a manual of regulatory accounting developed for the airport sector in your country to request information from the operator(s) (e.g., detailed information on costs differentiated by type of services)?

    Yes ☐   No ☐

    If yes, describe if this model was developed by the agency or by consultants.

16. Does the agency estimate the capital costs incurred by the operators in the airport sector? How often is this estimation performed? Is it performed by internal staff or by external consultants?

    Explain

17. Does the regulatory framework allow operators to grant airport tariff discounts to airlines (e.g., by amount of flights or types of airplanes)?

    Yes ☐   No ☐

    Explain

18. Does the regulatory framework establish minimum levels of service quality in the airports?

    Yes ☐   No ☐

    If yes, who sets the service quality levels?

19. What economic incentives do airport operators have to increase the quality of their services?

19B. Does the legal framework allow the airport operator to charge different aeronautical tariffs as a function of the quality of service provided (e.g., if a low-cost airline wants to receive a lower quality of service, can the airport operator charge lower tariffs)?

    Yes ☐   No ☐

    Explain:

19C. Does the agency conduct economic-financial audits of the airport operators? If so, with what frequency?

    Yes ☐   No ☐
    Frequency:

19D. Is the ground-handling service liberalized in your country?

Yes ☐   No ☐

Is there any regulation for this type of service?

If there is a limit to the number of ground-handling service providers, please indicate the total number allowed, the current number, and their names (and shareholders if the information is available).

19E. Slots allocation policies in your country:

What entity grants slots?

In what airports are slots allocated?

Do airlines have to pay for them? Can they buy them and sell them?

19F. What is the agency's role in mergers and acquisitions and in antitrust cases?

	Mark (only one)
Final decision made by the aviation agency	☐
Final decision made by another agency with previous mandatory consultation with the aviation regulatory agency.	☐
Final decision made by another agency. The final decision maker is not obliged either to request or to consider the authority's opinion.	☐
Other	☐

If other, please explain:

19G. Does your agency regulate the provision of services related to terminal (air side) navigation?

Yes ☐   No ☐

Explain how this service is financed.

19H. Does your agency regulate the provision of services related to airport security?

Yes ☐   No ☐

Explain how this service is financed.

19I. Does your country have a master plan for airport investments?

Yes ☐ No ☐

Please indicate who has the authority to develop this investment plan and what airports are included in it.

19J. Specify, contingent upon data availability, the capital investments (runways, terminals, airport systems, among others) that the airport system has undergone since 1997 (in local nominal currency or U.S. dollars. Please specify currency used).

	1997	1998	1999	2000	2001	2002	2003	2004	2005	2006
Investments										
Airports that received investments										

19K. If the airports that your agency regulates are concessioned:

Does the agency approve investment plans? Yes ☐ No ☐
Does the agency determine, before authorizing the investment, if it corresponds to capital or maintenance? Yes ☐ No ☐

19L. Conflict resolution: describe if the regulator performs a mediating role in conflicts between users (airlines) and the airport operator.

19M. Did the airport system in your country run a surplus in 2006?

Yes ☐
No ☐

19N. Considering the 10 airports with the highest annual passenger volumes, indicate which have run surpluses or deficits.

Names of the airports with surpluses:
Name of the airports with deficits:

How are losses from deficitary airports covered?

Contributions from the Treasury or Ministry ☐

Cross-subsidies from airports with financial surplus ☐

Debt issued by airport ☐

Other ☐

If other, please specify

II. Agency's Governance Variables:

1. Autonomy:

20. Through what legal instrument was the agency created? Please indicate the norm's number and year.

    Law ☐
    Number/Year

    Decree ☐
    Number/Year

    Ministerial Resolution ☐
    Number/Year

    Other (please indicate)

21. What is the agency's legal status?

    It is a separate and autonomous entity from the sectoral minister. ☐

    It is a separate, but non-autonomous entity from the sectoral minister. ☐

    There is no agency as regulation is conducted by a ministry. ☐

    Other (please indicate) ☐

22. Can the agency be intervened? If so, please indicate what authority has the power to intervene. SEE DEFINITION IN GLOSSARY

    Yes ☐

    Authority

    No ☐

23. Has the agency ever been intervened?

    Yes ☐   No ☐

    Number of interventions and dates:

25. What institution is competent in the economic regulation of the airports in your country?

    Agency only ☐

    Agency and another independent agency ☐

    Agency and Parliament ☐

    Agency and government ☐

    Agency has only consultative competencies ☐

28. Is the agency's independence explicitly established? If so, please indicate what legal instrument establishes this independence.

    Yes ☐   No ☐

    Law/decree where the agency's independence is established:

    Clause/article of the law/decree where this independence is established (provide its text):

29. Have there been any major changes during the past five years in the responsibilities of the regulatory agency?

    Yes ☐   No ☐

    Yes, responsibilities have decreased   ☐

    Please specify

    Yes, responsibilities have increased   ☐

    Please specify

30. What are the agency's competencies? (Mark all that apply)

    Consultative/advisory ☐

    Oversight ☐

    Contract/license approval ☐

    Tariff approval ☐

    Normative creation ☐

    Other ☐

    If other, please indicate

32. How do you evaluate the degree of interference by the sectoral minister (e.g., Transport or Public Works) in the decisions adopted by the agency?

    Very high   ☐
    High   ☐
    Low   ☐
    Very low   ☐

33. If there is conflict over the application/interpretation of a norm, what is the administrative authority in charge of making the final decision?

    Explain

34. What is the mechanism for the selection of the agency's directors?

    The minister appoints the members of the board/director ☐

    The president appoints the members of the board/director ☐

    The president appoints the members of the board/director with authorization from Congress ☐

    Other (please specify)

35. Assign a value between 1 (WORST) and 5 (BEST) to the following aspects of the board member's selection process:

    Transparency

    Merit-based

    Insulation from political influence

36. What are the necessary requirements to be designated as a director?

    College degree   ☐
    Experience in airport regulation   ☐
    Political independence   ☐
    There are no requirements   ☐
    Other (please specify)

36A. What are the previous positions and educational levels of the agency's current directors?

  Director 1
  Public sector ☐   Private sector ☐
  Previous position and organization
  Education
  Director 2
  Public sector ☐   Private sector ☐
  Previous position and organization
  Education
  Director 3
  Public sector ☐   Private sector ☐
  Previous position and organization
  Education
  Director 4
  Public sector ☐   Private sector ☐
  Previous position and organization
  Education
  Director 5
  Public sector ☐   Private sector ☐
  Previous position and organization
  Education

37. What is the duration of a director's mandate?

  Fixed mandate   ☐   Number of years ☐
  Undefined mandate   ☐

38. Is it renewable? For how long?

  No   ☐
  Yes, for an additional period   ☐
  Yes, for more than one period   ☐

39. If mandate is fixed, how many directors have not completed their mandates?

  Less than five   ☐
  Please indicate the number of directors.

More than five ☐
Please indicate the number of directors.

39A. What authority is responsible for removing the agency's directors?

Parliament (or Congress) ☐

President ☐

Minister ☐

Other ☐

Please describe the dismissal procedure.

39B. Should the removal of the agency's director be carried out according to specific causes?

Yes ☐   No ☐

If justification is necessary, please specify the required causes for dismissal.

40. Has the mechanism for the dismissal of directors ever been used?

Yes ☐

If so, how many times?

No ☐

There are no mechanisms for the dismissal of directors ☐

41. Select the reasons for which directors leave their positions:

	Yes	No
Removal	☐	☐
External pressure	☐	☐
Retirement	☐	☐
Voluntary leave	☐	☐
End of mandate	☐	☐
Other	☐	

If others, please specify

42. Does the agency have the power to establish its administrative/organizational structure (e.g., creation of new departments/units/divisions in the organizational framework, management assessment mechanisms, appointments, etc.)?

    Yes ☐

    No ☐

    If no, please specify who is the responsible authority.

43. Identify the labor regime that regulates the following situations:

	Private law	Civil service law
Directors of the board	☐	☐
Managers	☐	☐
Technical employees	☐	☐
Rest of the staff	☐	☐
Other(s)		

45. Is the agency free to make its own personnel decisions (e.g., hire, promote, discipline)?

    Yes ☐   No ☐

    If no, please identify the authority with the power to make those decisions.

46. What are the sources of the agency's budget? Identify the percentage of each.

	Percentage
Government budget	%
Fines	%
Donations	%
Tariffs	%
Specify type of tariff and percentage	%

Tariff   %
Tariff   %
Tariff   %
Other(s)   %

47. Does the agency have financial autonomy to determine its own expenses?

    Yes ☐   No ☐

    If no, please identify the authority with the power to assume this role.

48. What has been the evolution of the agency's budget over the past three years? (Local nominal currency or U.S. dollars. Please specify currency.)

    2005
    2006
    2007

2. Accountability:

51. To whom is the agency accountable? SEE DEFINITION IN GLOSSARY.

    Congress   ☐
    Government   ☐
    Both   ☐

51A. Is the agency's performance evaluated? SEE DEFINITION IN GLOSSARY.

    Yes ☐   No ☐

51B. What are the main areas examined in the agency's performance evaluation and who performs this evaluation?

    Administrative Efficiency (delays in addressing a complaint, transparency in appointments, other institutional quality measures)   ☐
    Evaluating Authority

Economic Efficiency (impact of the agency's decisions on the market) ☐
Evaluating Authority

Budgetary Performance ☐
Evaluating Authority

Please describe the areas that are evaluated in further detail

54. Can the regulating agency's decisions be appealed?

Yes ☐   No ☐

55. By whom are the appeals considered? Please identify the court/tribunal.

General law courts (excluding the Supreme Court of Justice/
Supreme Tribunal) ☐
Name of the tribunal

Tribunals established specially to treat regulatory aspects ☐
Name of the tribunal

Ministry/government ☐
Name of the tribunal

Special administrative tribunal to deal with regulatory
matters ☐
Name of the tribunal

Combination of the above ☐
Name of the tribunal

Other(s) (please specify) ☐

3. Transparency:

59. Does the agency publish the methodology/data and other tools used in the application of it regulatory decisions in economic matters (e.g., the calculation of price caps)?

Yes ☐   No ☐

If yes, please specify how the data is published (i.e. through the agency's web site, bulletins, etc.).

60. How are the agency's procedures for the elaboration of rules and the due process regulated?

   The agency has its own procedures ☐

   The agency is subject to the same administrative procedures as those of the rest of the public sector ☐

   There are no procedures for the elaboration of rules ☐

   Please describe the procedures.

61. Does the airport sector legislation establish the participation of the main economic agents and of civil society (businesses, users, etc.) in the agency's rule-making process?

   Yes ☐   No ☐

   Please describe the procedure/mechanism through which the various actors participate in the agency's rule-making process.

63. Does the agency perform public consultations when changes in tariffs are undertaken? SEE DEFINITION IN GLOSSARY.

   Yes ☐   No ☐

   Who is invited to participate in the consultations?

   Airlines   Yes ☐   No ☐
   Passengers   Yes ☐   No ☐
   Nongovernmental organizations (NGOs)   Yes ☐   No ☐
   Others_____

64. If yes, how are the public consultations regulated?

   Informally   ☐
   Formally   ☐

   If formally, please specify what legal instrument regulates the public consultations.

65. What are the matters that need to be consulted with the economic agents (airlines)?

   Changes in tariffs   ☐
   Approvals of investment plans   ☐
   Variables that affect the quality of service   ☐
   Others   ☐

65A. What is the legal effect of the agency's consultations?

    The consultation's outcome is binding for the agency ☐

    The consultation's outcome is NOT binding for the agency ☐

    The outcome does not bind the agency, but the agency must justify why it made a different decision ☐

66. How frequently and how many consultations are performed by the agency?

    Every two months ☐

    Every six months ☐

    Annually ☐

    Other ☐

    How many public consultations?

66A. Please list and describe the main public consultations/hearings performed to date. Please list them in order of importance.

Hearing/Consultation (name)	Date	Outcome	Other comments
1.			
2.			
3.			
4.			
5.			
Other hearings/consultations:			

67. Is the agency obliged to publish its decisions?

    Yes ☐   No ☐

    Please specify how the agency's decisions are published.

70. Does the agency have a collective or individual decision-making structure?

    Collective ☐   Individual ☐

71. Are there quarantine rules for the directors? SEE DEFINITION IN GLOSSARY.

    Yes ☐   No ☐

72. If so, for how long?

4. Regulatory, Management, and Institutional Tools:
74. Is benchmarking used by the agency?

    Yes ☐   No ☐

75. If the agency uses benchmarking, what is the methodology used?

Partial indicators	☐
Total factor productivity	☐
Data evolving analysis	☐
Statistical techniques	☐
Process comparison	☐
Customer service comparison	☐
Model engineer corporation	☐
Combination of these	☐

    If a combination, please specify what methods are included.

77. How would you rank the agency's effectiveness in the enforcement of its decisions in matters of economic regulation?

Very high	☐
High	☐
Medium	☐
Low	☐
Very low	☐

    Comments

78. Has the agency developed its own structure of posts and salaries?

    Yes ☐   No ☐

    Please, briefly describe the agency's staff grades and salary scales.

79. How many employees does the agency have? Please specify the number of technical and administrative staff under each range.

Technical staff   Administrative staff
(Area of economic regulation)

Less than 20

Between 21 and 50

Between 51 and 100

More than 100

79A. Please specify, using percentages, the current educational levels in the agency (elementary, middle school, high school, college, graduate level).

	Elementary	Middle School	High School	College	Graduate School
Managers	☐	☐	☐	☐	☐
Percentages	%	%	%	%	%
Technical staff	☐	☐	☐	☐	☐
Percentages	%	%	%	%	%
Administrative staff	☐	☐	☐	☐	☐
Percentages	%	%	%	%	%

79AA. Does the agency hire external consultants to carry studies/work on economic regulation?

Yes ☐   No ☐

Please specify how many individual consultants and firms were contracted between 2005 and 2007 and the tasks they performed.

79B. How does the agency evaluate its staff? SEE DEFINITION IN GLOSSARY.

There is a periodic evaluation according to preestablished assessment mechanisms (e.g., performance indicators)   ☐

There is an ad hoc, discretionary evaluation, in a nonsystematic or regular way   ☐

The agency does not evaluate staff performance ☐

Please describe the evaluation mechanisms.

80. **Does the agency publish its job openings and if so, where?**

    Yes ☐   No ☐

    Newspaper   ☐

    Agency's website   ☐

    Both   ☐

    Other(s)

81. **Does the agency use performance-based payments for its employees?**

    Yes ☐   No ☐

    If so, briefly describe the payment system.

82. **From the positions listed below, please select those whose hiring requires public examinations.**

    Director[1]   ☐

    Manager   ☐

    Technical staff   ☐

    Administrative assistants   ☐

    Rest of the staff   ☐

    Public examinations are not required   ☐

82A. **How would you describe the salary levels in the agency?**

    Similar to those of businesses in the sector ☐

    Below the market level in the sector but
    above the public sector level   ☐

    Similar to those of the public sector   ☐

83. **How would you rate the training the agency's employees receive?**

    Excellent   ☐

    Very good   ☐

Good ☐
Bad ☐
Very bad ☐
There is no training available ☐

83A. In what areas does the agency provide training to its employees?

Leadership ☐
Briefly describe the kind of training.

Sector regulation ☐
(tariff regime, investment evaluation, regulatory law, regulatory accounting, etc.)
Briefly describe the kind of training.

Financial and auditing ☐
Briefly describe the kind of training.

83B. What is the budget share that is annually devoted to employees' training and development?

%

84. What is the agency's reporting instrument? SEE DEFINITION IN GLOSSARY.

Annual report ☐
Agency governing authorities' hearings before the Parliament ☐
Both ☐
There are no reporting instruments ☐
Other

85. Are consumers' rights and obligations legislated in regulatory or nonregulatory legal instruments?

Regulatory instruments ☐
Nonregulatory instruments ☐
There is no regulation ☐

Please identify the legal instruments that regulate consumers' rights and obligations.

86. Does the agency evaluate customers' (i.e., users) satisfaction with the quality of the service provided?

    Yes ☐   No ☐

    Please describe the evaluation procedure.

87. Does the agency prepare an annual report? SEE DEFINITION IN GLOSSARY.

    Yes ☐   No ☐

88. If yes, is the report published?

    Yes ☐   No ☐

    Please specify through which medium (website, printed publication, etc.).

91. Does the agency have a website?

    Yes ☐   No ☐

91A. What type of information does the website contain?

Airport legislation	☐
Content (periods and conditions) of concession and/or service provision contracts	☐
Public releases of the agency's decisions/resolutions	☐
Annual performance report/accountability report	☐
Addressing of customers' complaints	☐
Name and résumé of the board's directors	☐
Sector indicators Please specify	☐
Other Please specify	☐

92. Please answer the following questions related to users' claims:

A. Number of complaints received (per year)

Year	2000	2001	2002	2003	2004	2005	2006	2007	2008
Passengers									
Airlines									

B. Reasons for complaints (percentage)

Quality of service	Increases in taxes/tariffs	Airport installations	Others (specify)
%	%	%	%

C. What is the average time to resolve a user complaint?

D. What are the legal steps to solve a complaint?
   1. The airports' regulatory agency has final decision authority ☐
   2. Although the airports' agency intervenes in the process, the final decision is made by another administrative authority ☐
   3. The affected party can go to the courts without the need for a final administrative decision ☐
   4. The affected party can only go to the courts after a final administrative decision is made ☐

93. Does the agency apply regulatory quality standards to its regulations (i.e., cost-benefit analysis, alternatives to regulation, administrative simplification, regulatory impact analysis)?

   Yes ☐   No ☐

   If so, please identify these standards and describe each of them:

   Cost-benefit analysis of regulations ☐
   Description:

   Alternatives to regulation ☐
   Description:

   Regulatory impact analysis ☐
   Description:

Administrative simplification ☐
Description:

User participation in the development of regulations ☐
Description:

94. **Are the Board's meetings recorded?**

    Yes ☐   No ☐

95. **Does the agency publish its audited accounts?**

    Yes   ☐

    No   ☐

    The agency's accounts are not audited   ☐

    If yes, identify the media through which the audited accounts are published (website, print publications, etc.).

96. **Does the agency have norms of ethics?**

    Yes, it has its own norms/codes of ethics   ☐

    Yes, it applies the norms/codes of ethics of
    the public administration   ☐

    No   ☐

97. **Have these norms been used during the past five years?**

    Yes, it resulted in the dismissal of one of the
    agency's officials/employees   ☐

    Yes, it resulted in a minor punishment of
    one of the agency's officials/employees   ☐

    No   ☐

    If yes, please specify the employee's position and the type of sanction applied.

III. **AGENCY'S POINT OF VIEW: In this section, please answer the following questions according to your opinion and point of view. Please feel free to expand upon each question as you may deem necessary.**

A) Do you agree with the institutional framework that has been established to regulate the airport sector in your country? What changes, if any, would you make? We would appreciate if you could refer to the entity in charge of regulation, the regulatory framework (tariff regulation, private sector participation, granting of licenses, permits, etc.), the role of operators, the government, as well as any other reference that you consider relevant.

B) Are you satisfied with your agency's performance? We would appreciate if you could frame your answer in the context of the four themes of our analysis: autonomy; transparency; accountability; regulatory, management/institutional tools and capacities.

C) *Autonomy:*

   Transparency:

   Accountability:

   Tools and capacities:

D) Please include any other thoughts you consider relevant for a better understanding of the dynamics and functioning of the institutional framework of the airport activity in your country.

GLOSSARY OF DEFINITIONS:

Question 22. Agency intervention: By "agency intervention," we mean the ability to suspend the agency's authorities by the Executive branch or the Legislature, to overcome an extraordinary situation affecting the normal functioning of the body. In these cases, the intervening institution designates a power controller to act on their behalf during the transitory period.

Question 51. Agency accountability: In this question we try to identify the authority before which the agency must be accountable by complying with their duties. Generally, the authority is the same that created the body. In the Common Law, the independent administrative agencies are accountable for their performance to the Parliament. Accountability is understood here in a broad sense, not being limited exclusively to the budget.

Question 51A. Evaluation of the agency management: This question is complementing the previous one and inquires to the agency about the existence of procedures to assess the management area. In other words, we are interested in identifying mechanisms by which the entity's performance or management is assessed. We differentiate the assessment of the agency's management in three main areas: administrative efficiency, economic efficiency, and budget performance.

Both questions 51 and 51A are related, but do not necessarily address the same issue. While it may be the case that the same authority to which the agency is accountable can also be in charge of evaluating the performance, it can also be the case that the agency is assessed by a completely different body. It could be the case, for example, that the agency is subjected, and accountable, to the Parliament (because this institution determines the budget and appointments) and the evaluation of their performance (taking into account the previously identified issues) is done by an entity other than the Parliament.

Question 63. Public consultations: Procedure by which the agency makes available to the public at large particular issues for discussion and consideration. Unlike the decision-making procedures, in this kind of public consultation (e.g., a public hearing), the agency publicly releases a rule or decision that has already been drafted or that is in its final request of definition.

It is worth clarifying that each system has its regulatory and institutional peculiarities and that this difference (between participation in the development of standards and public hearings) may not be as clear, in some cases being confusing. In such cases, please make the clarifications that you may consider applicable to the case.

Question 71. Quarantine rules: Prohibitions by which the directors of the entity cannot serve in a private provider within the same sector after the end of their mandate at the agency. This ban is for a fixed term. It tries to prevent the perpetration of acts of collusion and abuse of influence in the industry during their mandate as directors.

Question 79B. Assessment of the agency staff: In this question we are interested in identifying the mechanisms used by the agency to evaluate the performance of their employees and officials. The options are three. The first one is related to the evaluation of the staff of the company on a regular basis and according to preestablished performance indicators. The second option refers to the evaluation of the staff of the company in a sporadic and incidental way, not obeying a constant and regular practice of the company. The third option is the absence of any personnel evaluation.

Question 84. Agency's reporting mechanism: In this question, we would like to know how the agency is made accountable (question 51). As we stated in the question 51A, this question can also be linked with the assessment of the management of the agency. The options can be a report or annual management report, the appearance of the agency directors before the Parliament, or any other mechanism you may have established for accountability purposes.

Question 87. Annual report by management: Report or reports containing, in detail, the actions that took place during the year. This document is of the utmost importance as it is, in some cases, the unique instrument of accountability of the agency for the users and the rest of society. Ideally, this report should contain the goals and objectives that were proposed at the beginning of the year and the rate of success fulfilling them. Also, it should contain an account of the obstacles and challenges faced by the agency in the implementation of its policies and regulatory decisions

Note

1. In this question, the term *director* refers to chiefs of units/departments/divisions and excludes the agency's governing authorities (Board Members/Directors).

APPENDIX C

Technical Efficiency Calculation

Table C.1 Results for the Technical Efficiency Scores for All Airports Other Than Latin American Airports

Airport	IATA code	CRS	VRS	Scale efficiency
Auckland, New Zealand	AKL	0.648	0.879	0.737
Bangkok, Thailand	BKK	0.935	0.951	0.983
Brisbane, Australia	BNE	0.655	0.718	0.912
Guangzhou, China	CAN	0.651	0.665	0.979
Jakarta, Indonesia	CGK	0.854	0.867	0.985
Christchurch, New Zealand	CHC	0.357	0.371	0.964
Chiang Mai, Thailand	CNX	0.245	0.329	0.745
Haikou, China	HAK	0.366	0.421	0.870
Hat Yai, Thailand	HDY	0.134	0.208	0.645
Hong Kong SAR, China	HKG	1.000	1.000	1.000
Phuket, Thailand	HKT	0.393	0.528	0.743
Seoul, Republic of Korea	ICN	0.962	0.962	1.000
Osaka, Japan	KIX	0.743	1.000	0.743
Kuala Lumpur, Malaysia	KUL	0.652	0.657	0.992
Macao SAR, China	MFM	0.465	0.844	0.555
Tokyo, Japan	NRT	0.860	0.876	0.982
Penang, Malaysia	PEN	0.386	0.898	0.430
Shanghai, China	PVG	0.909	0.931	0.976

(continued next page)

Table C.1 *(continued)*

Airport	IATA code	CRS	VRS	Scale efficiency
Seoul, Republic of Korea	SEL	0.618	0.619	0.999
Changi, Singapore	SIN	0.927	0.934	0.993
Sydney, Australia	SYD	0.828	0.837	0.991
Shenzhen, China	SZX	0.721	0.949	0.760
Xiamen, China	XMN	1.000	1.000	1.000
Amsterdam, Netherlands	AMS	0.637	0.856	0.745
Stockholm, Sweden	ARN	0.410	0.453	0.905
Athens, Greece	ATH	0.464	0.471	0.987
Barcelona, Spain	BCN	0.731	0.763	0.959
Birmingham, United Kingdom	BHX	0.365	0.367	0.994
Brussels, Belgium	BRU	0.370	0.419	0.881
Bratislava, Slovak Republic	BTS	0.102	0.105	0.971
Budapest, Hungary	BUD	0.331	0.332	0.996
Paris, France	CDG	0.826	0.922	0.896
Cologne, Germany	CGN	0.299	0.388	0.771
Rome, Italy	CIA	0.488	0.612	0.797
Copenhagen, Denmark	CPH	0.369	0.385	0.960
Dublin, Ireland	DUB	0.457	0.468	0.976
Düsseldorf, Germany	DUS	0.324	0.341	0.951
Edinburgh, Scotland	EDI	0.693	0.799	0.868
Rome, Italy	FCO	0.517	0.585	0.885
Frankfurt, Germany	FRA	0.759	0.846	0.897
Geneva, Switzerland	GVA	0.418	0.443	0.953
Hamburg, Germany	HAM	0.384	0.386	0.993
Helsinki, Finland	HEL	0.326	0.409	0.796
Istanbul, Turkey	IST	0.611	0.716	0.853
London, United Kingdom	LGW	0.995	1.000	0.995
London, United Kingdom	LHR	0.998	0.999	0.999
Lisbon, Portugal	LIS	0.527	0.538	0.980
Ljubljana, Slovenia	LJU	0.198	0.207	0.958
Madrid, Spain	MAD	0.969	0.995	0.974
Manchester, United Kingdom	MAN	0.488	0.498	0.981
Valletta, Malta	MLA	0.144	0.144	1.000
Munich, Germany	MUC	0.678	0.743	0.913
Paris, France	ORY	0.556	0.570	0.974
Oslo, Norway	OSL	0.526	0.539	0.975
Prague, Czech Republic	PRG	0.319	0.397	0.807
Riga, Latvia	RIX	0.206	0.227	0.909
Sofia, Bulgaria	SOF	0.186	0.205	0.910
London, United Kingdom	STN	0.911	0.970	0.940
Tallinn, Estonia	TLL	0.163	0.180	0.902
Berlin, Germany	TXL	0.372	0.377	0.986

(continued next page)

Table C.1 *(continued)*

Airport	IATA code	CRS	VRS	Scale efficiency
Vienna, Austria	VIE	0.507	0.508	0.997
Warsaw, Poland	WAW	0.349	0.355	0.986
Zurich, Switzerland	ZRH	0.434	0.497	0.874
Albuquerque, United States	ABQ	0.351	0.420	0.851
Albany, United States	ALB	0.195	0.243	0.827
Atlanta, United States	ATL	1.000	1.000	1.000
Austin, United States	AUS	0.381	0.453	0.867
Nashville, United States	BNA	0.344	0.362	0.958
Boston, United States	BOS	0.401	0.572	0.703
Baltimore, United States	BWI	0.402	0.484	0.835
Cleveland, United States	CLE	0.318	0.397	0.800
Charlotte, United States	CLT	0.793	0.835	0.949
Cincinnati, United States	CVG	0.550	0.626	0.877
Washington, D.C., United States	DCA	0.495	0.617	0.803
Denver, United States	DEN	0.599	0.898	0.667
Dallas, United States	DFW	0.596	0.840	0.711
Detroit, United States	DTW	0.419	0.572	0.736
Newark, United States	EWR	0.892	0.939	0.951
Ft. Lauderdale, United States	FLL	0.559	0.584	0.956
Honolulu, United States	HNL	0.458	0.653	0.702
Washington, D.C., United States	IAD	0.510	0.553	0.935
Houston, United States	IAH	0.575	0.702	0.814
Indianapolis, United States	IND	0.581	0.705	0.823
Jacksonville, United States	JAX	0.291	0.306	0.953
New York, United States	JFK	0.973	0.973	1.000
Las Vegas, United States	LAS	0.721	0.855	0.845
Los Angeles, United States	LAX	0.956	1.000	0.956
New York, United States	LGA	1.000	1.000	1.000
Kansas City, United States	MCI	0.255	0.298	0.855
Orlando, United States	MCO	0.574	0.651	0.881
Chicago, United States	MDW	0.690	0.697	0.990
Memphis, United States	MEM	0.996	0.999	0.998
Miami, United States	MIA	0.505	0.675	0.747
Milwaukee, United States	MKE	0.560	0.562	0.998
Minneapolis, United States	MSP	0.556	0.617	0.906
New Orleans, United States	MSY	0.245	0.247	0.993
Oakland, United States	OAK	0.839	0.849	0.988
Ontario, United States	ONT	0.442	0.464	0.956
Chicago, United States	ORD	0.768	1.000	0.768
West Palm Beach, United States	PBI	0.468	0.485	0.964
Portland, United States	PDX	0.457	0.520	0.881
Philadelphia, United States	PHL	0.510	0.678	0.751

(continued next page)

Table C.1 *(continued)*

Airport	IATA code	CRS	VRS	Scale efficiency
Phoenix, United States	PHX	0.698	0.718	0.973
Pittsburgh, United States	PIT	0.262	0.437	0.606
Raleigh, United States	RDU	0.425	0.481	0.892
Richmond, United States	RIC	0.306	0.314	0.978
Reno, United States	RNO	0.257	0.299	0.886
San Diego, United States	SAN	0.826	1.000	0.826
San Antonio, United States	SAT	0.376	0.492	0.814
Louisville, United States	SDF	0.970	0.971	0.999
Seattle, United States	SEA	0.743	0.768	0.967
San Francisco, United States	SFO	0.585	0.677	0.865
San Jose, United States	SJC	0.433	0.459	0.945
Salt Lake City, United States	SLC	0.439	0.677	0.649
Sacramento, United States	SMF	0.402	0.441	0.912
Costa Mesa, United States	SNA	0.893	1.000	0.893
St. Louis, United States	STL	0.288	0.435	0.662
Tampa, United States	TPA	0.451	0.506	0.893
Edmonton, Canada	YEG	0.332	0.335	0.990
Halifax, Canada	YHZ	0.289	0.303	0.955
Ottawa, Canada	YOW	0.297	0.317	0.935
Montréal, Canada	YUL	0.311	0.418	0.743
Vancouver, Canada	YVR	0.510	0.634	0.804
Winnipeg, Canada	YWG	0.502	0.518	0.970
Calgary, Canada	YYC	0.732	0.745	0.983
Toronto, Canada	YYZ	0.371	0.484	0.765

Source: Author's estimation.

Table C.2 LAC Airports Total Factor Productivity Change
annual %

Year	Argentina			Brazil						Chile	Colombia		Costa Rica
	AEP	EZE	FTE	BSB	CGH	GIG	GRU	MAO	VCP	SCL	BAQ	CLO	SJO
1995–1996	–	–	–	9.9	8.4	4.1	11.7	–21.5	–4.4	–	–	–	–
1996–1997	–	–	–	23.6	20.3	9.3	5.3	–3.0	9.0	–	–	–	–
1997–1998	–	–	–	9.6	17.7	8.8	0.2	15.2	8.5	–	–32.1	–	–
1998–1999	–	–	–	–1.5	9.1	–22.7	–2.5	4.0	–8.4	–	–12.7	–	–
1999–2000	–	–	–	8.2	12.9	5.6	1.2	5.9	20.0	11.8	9.2	–	–
2000–2001	–40.1	–24.8	–	–1.5	13.1	–1.6	–5.7	–7.6	–1.7	**–9.7**	–27.8	–	–
2001–2002	–15.8	–41.9	–	10.0	3.7	–8.2	–1.4	6.2	–22.7	–10.4	–0.9	–23.7	57.0
2002–2003	2.8	22.2	–	**–4.4**	–16.3	–16.5	2.3	–2.5	–20.0	3.7	**–9.7**	15.3	–5.0
2003–2004	5.9	20.0	60.3	12.1	**–84.2**	6.5	2.6	9.6	0.6	2.8	–2.8	–17.2	1.2
2004–2005	–2.5	–9.0	14.6	**–39.0**	9.0	43.7	9.4	2.0	–6.6	5.7	3.0	–5.2	–0.6
2005–2006	–9.3	5.2	3.9	–11.0	–15.4	2.3	–6.7	3.0	–18.6	–2.2	4.5	–2.6	–4.1
2006–2007	–5.5	1.9	19.7	9.2	**–26.5**	16.9	6.0	12.8	26.5	**–15.2**	1.3	5.9	3.6

(continued next page)

Table C.2 *(continued)*

Year	Ecuador GYE	El Salvador SAL	CUN	Mexico GDL	MEX	MTY	Panama PTY	Peru LIM	Dominican Republic SDQ
1995–1996	–	–	–	–	–	–	–	–	–
1996–1997	–	–	–	–	–	–	–	–	–
1997–1998	–	–	–	–	–	–	–	–	–
1998–1999	–	–	–	–	–	–	–	–	–
1999–2000	–	–	18.5	–	0.8	–1.2	–	–	–
2000–2001	–	–	–3.3	–	**–9.9**	–5.9	–	–	–
2001–2002	–	7.4	1.9	–	0.4	18.0	–	–	–
2002–2003	–	–1.8	10.4	–6.1	2.2	14.1	–	–	–
2003–2004	–	12.4	10.2	5.1	6.0	1.7	9.0	–	–
2004–2005	–	–0.6	–8.2	**–13.9**	3.3	3.8	6.8	–	–9.1
2005–2006	**–28.2**	–0.9	–2.1	12.3	5.5	–0.5	**–20.3**	9.6	**–10.5**
2006–2007	8.1	–4.7	–1.7	11.3	–6.9	14.2	6.3	9.8	2.0

Source: Author's estimation.
Note: Values in bold indicate the year of changes in capital stock, either in the number of runways or in the number of boarding bridges.

Table C.3 Average Technical Efficiency Scores and Scale Efficiency by Region (2005–06 average)

World region	Technical efficiency			Returns to scale diagnosis (% of observations)		
	CRS	VRS	Scale	IRS	CRS	DRS
Model with 3 outputs and 3 inputs (runways, staff, and boarding bridges)						
Latin America	0.532	0.690	0.801	70.5	9.1	20.5
Asia	0.670	0.771	0.869	84.6	12.8	2.6
Europe	0.490	0.530	0.927	43.9	6.1	50.0
Canada and United States	0.540	0.616	0.875	23.2	8.0	68.8
All	0.545	0.629	0.875	44.5	8.4	47.1
Model with 3 outputs and 2 inputs (runways and staff)						
Latin America	0.283	0.399	0.796	63.6	6.8	29.5
Asia	0.477	0.528	0.901	38.5	2.6	59.0
Europe	0.454	0.512	0.886	47.0	7.6	45.5
Canada and United States	0.443	0.491	0.911	36.8	5.6	57.6
All	0.425	0.487	0.885	43.8	5.8	50.4

Source: Author's estimation.

APPENDIX D

Data Sources

Air Transport Research Society (ATRS)

The Air Transport Research Society is a nonprofit organization that gathers individuals from various sources to exchange research ideas and results on issues of air transportation. Specific sources include air transport researchers from established institutions all over the world, senior policy makers from various government organizations and think tanks, and experts from the aviation industry, ranging from airports, airlines, aerospace manufacturers, and aviation consulting services.

One of ATRS's most important outputs is its Annual Global Airport Benchmarking Report, which comprehensively assesses airport performance based on productivity, efficiency, and unit cost competitiveness data. It provides over 30 performance measures identifying effects of the operating environment of the airport, business diversification efforts, outsourcing, and service quality. Airports are benchmarked among peer airports within geographical boundaries, which currently span three regions: North America, Europe, and Asia Pacific and Oceania.

For this particular report, we used ATRS's 2007 *Airport Benchmarking Report*, which uses 2005 data for its analysis. The results from the benchmarking report provided a basis of comparison for the performance of the Latin American and Caribbean (LAC) airports included in our sample.

Comparisons were made using 2005 data as reported by the airport operators surveyed for our study.

Website: http://www.atrsworld.org

Airports Council International (ACI)

ACI is an international association of the world's commercial service airports, which represents the interests of airport operators at international forums; develops standards and recommended practices in the areas of safety, security, and environmental initiatives; and fosters cooperation with partners throughout the air transport industry. It includes 597 members operating over 1,679 airports in 177 countries and territories. Regular members represent over 96 percent of the world's passenger traffic and are owners or operators, other than airlines, of one or more civil airports with commercial air services.

An important part of ACI's mission is to provide members with industry knowledge, advice, and assistance. In achieving this, it produces a wide range of publications that address global airport policies, standards and guidelines, industry statistics, operational surveys, analytical reports, briefs, and position papers. For this particular report, we made use of ACI's 2007 *World Airport Traffic Report*, which provides airport- and country-specific passenger and cargo traffic results, in addition to aircraft movement statistics.

Website: http://www.airports.org

Private Participation in Infrastructure Database (PPI)

The Private Participation in Infrastructure Database is a joint product of the World Bank's Infrastructure Economics and Finance Department and the Public-Private Infrastructure Advisory Facility (PPIAF). It provides information on private participation in infrastructure projects in low- and middle-income countries and regions as classified by the World Bank. The projects are grouped into four sectors with some monopoly or oligopoly characteristics: energy, telecommunications, transport, and water–sewerage. More competitive sectors, such as airlines and gas production, are not included.

Currently, the database contains data on more than 4,100 infrastructure projects dating from 1984 to 2007. Projects must meet the following three criteria: (a) Private parties must have at least a 25 percent participation in the project contract, except for divestitures, which are included with at least 5 percent of equity owned by private parties. (b) Projects must directly or indirectly serve the public; captive facilities (such as cogeneration power plants and private telecommunications networks) are excluded unless a significant share of output (20 percent) is sold to serve the public under a contract with a utility. (c) Projects must have reached financial closure after 1983 (database coverage currently extends to 2007). With over 30 fields per project record, the database details the project's country, financial closure year, infrastructure services provided, type of private participation, technology, capacity, project location, contract duration, private sponsors, investment commitments (in the form of physical assets and payments to government), and development bank support.

For purposes of this report, the PPI database was used to produce an overview of investment levels in the airport sector of developing countries at both the global and LAC-specific levels. It should be noted that the analysis derived from the use of this database presents only a partial picture of investments in the airport sector for three reasons: First, given that the database is compiled through publicly available information, some projects, particularly those involving local and small-scale operators, tend to be omitted because they are usually not reported by major news sources, databases, government websites, or other sources used by the PPI projects database. Second, the database does not record important public projects such as the network of Brazilian airports operated by the state-owned company, INFRAERO. Third, with few exceptions, the investment amounts in the database represent the total investment commitments entered into by the project entity at the beginning of the project (at contract signature or financial closure), not the planned or executed annual investments.

In addition to contributing to the overview of investment flows in the airport sector, the PPI database also proved useful in providing a general picture of the degree of private participation in the airport sectors in specific LAC countries. The latter was included within each of the case studies prepared for this benchmarking project.

Website: http://ppi.worldbank.org/

Dealogic ProjectWare Database

Dealogic ProjectWare is a database containing information on project and trade finance transactions since 1994 in both developing and developed nations. Collected directly from the banks and organizations involved in the deals, the data include financial and nonfinancial information that covers projects from preapproval to signing.

For this study, we made use of the Dealogic ProjectWare database to complement the overview of investment levels in the region produced through the use of the PPI database. Different from the PPI database, which records total investment commitments entered into by the project entity at the beginning of the project at contract signature or financial closure, ProjectWare presents total project amounts and their breakdown by financing sources, including shares in loans, bonds, and equity. Project amounts in the ProjectWare database reflect investments in infrastructure in the form of the construction, expansion, and refurbishment of physical assets as well as in the financing of acquisitions and the refinancing of existing debt. Any given project can consist of one or a combination of any of the above. Given that ProjectWare presents details on projects in five categories—preapproval, in tender, in finance, signed, and cancelled projects—it is important to mention that with the purpose of making the PPI and the ProjectWare data as comparable as possible, our analysis uses only those projects that have achieved financial closure and whose status was reported as "signed."

Website: http://www.dealogic.com

Asociación Latinoamericana de Transporte Aéreo (ALTA)

ALTA is a private, nonprofit organization composed of Latin American commercial airlines whose objective is to combine and coordinate its members' efforts to facilitate the development of air transport in the Latin American and Caribbean region.

As part of its objective to establish appropriate systems of information to be used by its members in order to promote safe and efficient air transport services in the LAC region, ALTA produces a yearly capacity analysis that is a comprehensive compendium of air transport statistics. More precisely, the ALTA analysis contains valuable information, including a ranking of the most important airports and city pairs in the region in terms of volume and growth. The 2008 analysis, more specifically, includes information on 496 airports and 1,918 city pairs throughout LAC and compares April 2008 figures with April 2007, as well as the average annual growth rates between 2000 and 2008. It identifies the top and fastest-growing airports (in terms of international, domestic, and total flights) and city pairs (in terms of available seats) across the region.

For the case studies produced for this report, the 2008 LAC Capacity Analysis data served as a tool to generate a picture of flight composition and growth at the regional and country level as well as at selected airports.

Website: http://www.alta.aero

Airport Charges

The Airport Charges database is a source of published airport charges worldwide. It contains over 2,000 charges documents covering airports on every continent and allows for comparison between regions, countries, and airports. Information contained within the database includes up-to-date fuel prices for every airport and historic evolution of charges dating back to 2005.

Website: http://www.airportcharges.com

www.ingramcontent.com/pod-product-compliance
Lightning Source LLC
Chambersburg PA
CBHW070939230426
43666CB00011B/2491